TRANSFO
HISPANIC-SERVING
INSTITUTIONS
FOR EQUITY
AND JUSTICE

TRANSFORMING
HISPANIC-SERVING
INSTITUTIONS
FOR EQUITY
AND JUSTICE

GINA ANN GARCIA

JOHNS HOPKINS UNIVERSITY PRESS | *Baltimore*

© 2023 Johns Hopkins University Press
All rights reserved. Published 2023
Printed in the United States of America on acid-free paper

2 4 6 8 9 7 5 3 1

Johns Hopkins University Press
2715 North Charles Street
Baltimore, Maryland 21218
www.press.jhu.edu

Library of Congress Cataloging-in-Publication Data

Names: Garcia, Gina Ann, 1978– author.
Title: Transforming Hispanic-serving institutions
for equity and justice / Gina Ann Garcia.
Description: Baltimore : Johns Hopkins University Press, 2023. |
Includes bibliographical references and index.
Identifiers: LCCN 2022021487 | ISBN 9781421445908 (paperback) |
ISBN 9781421445915 (ebook)
Subjects: LCSH: Hispanic Americans—Education (Higher) |
Hispanic American college students. | Universities and colleges—
United States—Administration. | Educational equalization—United States.
Classification: LCC LC2670.6 .G354 2023 | DDC 378.1/98268073—dc23/eng/20220707
LC record available at https://lccn.loc.gov/2022021487

A catalog record for this book is available from the British Library.

Proceeds from the sale of this book will support the development of a scholarship
fund for students attending Hispanic-Serving Institutions and will be administered
by the Alliance for Hispanic Serving Institution Educators (AHSIE).

*Special discounts are available for bulk purchases of this book. For more information,
please contact Special Sales at specialsales@jh.edu.*

To the students, families, communities, educators, and decision makers working with and for Hispanic-Serving Institutions

CONTENTS

TRANSFORMING
HISPANIC-SERVING
INSTITUTIONS
FOR EQUITY
AND JUSTICE

A Unique Approach to Organizing Hispanic-Serving Institutions

HISPANIC-SERVING INSTITUTIONS (HSIs) are defined in federal legislation as institutions of higher education with full-time equivalent enrollment of at least 25% Hispanic undergraduate students and a significant number receiving need-based assistance. As enrollment-driven institutions, the growth in the number of HSIs is correlated with the increase in enrollment of Hispanic and Latinx undergraduate students, with 2.1 million Latinx students enrolled in HSIs in 2020, up from 490,000 in 1995 (*Excelencia* in Education, 2020). HSIs were first acknowledged in the Higher Education Act in 1992 after Latinx political advocacy groups such as the Hispanic Higher Education Coalition testified to the US Congress about the need for increased funding for colleges and universities enrolling a high percentage of Latinx students (Valdez, 2015). HSIs have received funding from various federal agencies since 1995 (Garcia & Koren, 2020).

In the 25 years since becoming legitimized through federal legislation, the number of HSIs has increased 185%, from 189 in 1994–95 to 539 in 2018–19 (*Excelencia* in Education, 2020). There were also 362 institutions flagged as "emerging" HSIs in 2019–20, a term coined by *Excelencia* in Education to indicate colleges and universities that enroll 15%–24% Hispanic or Latinx students and are likely to become HSIs (*Excelencia* in Education, 2021a). These trends suggest that more colleges and universities will become HSIs. They are properly situated to have a significant influence on the postsecondary educational experiences of Latinx students as well as other students of color (Black, Indigenous, Asian American, Pacific Islander, Mixed Race) who also enroll in HSIs in high numbers. But are they ready?

As a public intellectual, scholar, and consultant who travels the country talking to HSIs about servingness,* I can say with much confidence that the answer is "No." If designated and eligible HSIs and emerging HSIs do not figure out how to conceptualize and enact servingness in practice, they will ultimately fail their Latinx and low-income students. To continue to enroll and serve students of color and low-income students the way that predominantly white colleges and universities have historically done will be detrimental to the students that HSIs and the federal government claim to serve. In the original legislation that established HSIs as a legitimate and distinct institutional type, there was no mention of racial equity, social justice, collective liberation, or community healing. There was no call to provide students with an antiracist, socially just, humanizing, empowering, liberatory, abolitionist educational experience. The more I write and talk about these things, the more I realize this is *my* freedom dream. The idea of freedom dreaming comes from Black radical traditions and is grounded in political and intellectual engagement, self-determination, and social movements (Kelley, 2002). Freedom dreaming is about imagining a better future for minoritized people, even if you can't see that future (Kelley, 2002). I dream about HSIs as spaces of justice and liberation. I dream about HSIs as something distinct and unique. This book is part of that freedom dream.

---

* The term "servingness" was coined by Garcia et al. (2019) and has since become common nomenclature among HSI educators, leaders, and researchers; it elevates the "S" in HSIs.

The Need for Transformation

In this book I present a framework called "Transforming Hispanic-Serving Institutions," which provides educators, decision makers, and leaders at HSIs a blueprint for organizing for racial equity, social justice, and collective liberation. Let me acknowledge that it is difficult to enact servingness in practice (I tried it once as a Title V coordinator and decided to get a PhD instead because that seemed easier). It's even harder to transform HSIs and enact a liberatory and empowering, socially just educational experience. The HSI federal designation is a political construct (Santiago, 2012); the designation came about through political advocacy and with the support of Latinx interest groups, lobbyists, and senators who knew that a collective effort to support colleges and universities enrolling the largest percentage of Latinx students was the best approach for advancing servingness (Valdez, 2015). As a political construct, HSIs are defined by federal legislation, based strictly on enrollment of Latinxs, and with the goal of addressing a national interest in increasing the college going and educational attainment of Latinxs. The policy further defines HSIs as underresourced and enrolling a high concentration of low-income students (Santiago et al., 2016). As written, the policy mostly defines HSIs by descriptors of students (i.e., Hispanic, low-income) and institutions (underresourced). Beyond the policy there is little federal guidance and accountability for transforming an entire college or university into one that actually serves and centers students of color who may also be low income, housing insecure, immigrants, undocumented, Deferred Action for Childhood Arrivals (DACA; DACAmented), from mixed-status families, Muslim, Jewish, neurodivergent, gender nonbinary, Trans*, former foster youth, parenting students, and/or formerly incarcerated students (among many other identities). Instead, the federal government has left it to the institutions themselves to define servingness.

This has led to a process of defining this political construct through a cycle of grant seeking and implementing. From my perspective, this is how HSI grant seeking and implementing works:

1. A person or group of people at an eligible HSI (who are still grappling with what it means to be an HSI) develop and submit a proposal for an HSI grant.
2. The sponsoring federal agency sends the proposal out to three or four external reviewers (who are probably still grappling with what it means to be an HSI).
3. The grant gets funded based on the proposal's alignment with normative measures that the field of higher education values (i.e., persistence; 150% graduation rate; science, technology, engineering, and mathematics [STEM] completion).
4. The grant implementers pay an external reviewer (who might not know what it means to actually be an HSI) to review the campus's grant activities.
5. The sponsoring federal agency requires the grant implementers to submit an annual report (that may be developed by people who are still grappling with what it means to be an HSI).

Perhaps I'm overgeneralizing and being humorous in my own sarcastic way, but I was a Title V grant implementer, so I know this process from my own experience. It was frustrating to figure out what it meant to be an HSI without knowing what an HSI was.

The most commonly funded grant proposals provide an idea of what the federal agencies value. Boland (2018) examined the abstracts of funded Minority-Serving Institution (MSI) projects and found that, unsurprisingly, a majority of MSI grant seekers proposed to increase retention and persistence (often used interchangeably), as well as graduation and degree attainment (again, used interchangeably). More specific to two-year institutions, course completion rates were also stated as goals and, to a lesser degree, MSIs wanted to increase successful transfer to four-year institutions (Boland, 2018). Boland (2018) found that very few MSI grant abstracts laid out nonacademic outcomes, or what I call "liberatory outcomes" (e.g., racial-ethnic-Indigenous identity development, academic self-concept, critical consciousness, social agency; Garcia, 2020b, 2021). What these abstracts suggest is that HSI grant seekers and implementers are largely implementing grants based on the white normative measures, meaning the measures are grounded in white histories and white knowledge and normalized among white populations with primarily white students (Garcia, 2019). Research shows that federal grants are awarded to HSIs with higher percentages of white students enrolled (Vargas, 2018), while HSI grant abstracts reveal race- and identity-neutral approaches to serving students (Vargas & Villa-Palomino, 2018), and grant seekers are race-evasive in their efforts to secure HSI funding (Aguilar-Smith, 2021). I call on HSIs to reconsider the approach to everything they (we) do; we cannot define and enact servingness in practice through grant activities that are grounded in white normativity and disconnected from the identities and lived experiences of Latinx students within HSIs.

Now don't get me wrong: I think that all colleges and universities, especially HSIs, should strive to increase graduation and retention of Latinx students and all students of color, especially those with the most inequitable outcomes. Yet the desire to increase academic outcomes should be done within the context of the historical oppression and discrimination of the students that enroll in HSIs (Garcia, 2018). Let us acknowledge that students who attend HSIs may have struggled through various educational pathways, not because they are incapable of succeeding but because there is an inequitable distribution of resources in primary and secondary schools (Acevedo-Gil, 2017). Let us acknowledge that in high school, students may have lacked access to Advanced Placement courses and information about financial aid (Means et al., 2019). Let us acknowledge that the students who attend HSIs may have had their spirits murdered in schools due to their race, ethnicity, indigeneity, gender, class, religion, ability, nationality, citizenship, and their queerness, among others (Love, 2019). Let us acknowledge that oppression of any kind is traumatic (Love, 2019). And, importantly, as I write this book during the COVID-19 pandemic, let us acknowledge that our students experienced new forms of trauma as a result of the global pandemic that shut down colleges and universities across the world. Not only did inequities in access and educational experiences become pronounced, but the

COVID-19 era also brought increased levels of housing insecurities, food insecurities, and health care disparities. Let us also acknowledge that institutions of higher education have not fulfilled their promise of ensuring economic mobility for all that have entered (Stein, 2021). To try to serve students without acknowledging their realities is harmful.

The HSI context and diversity of institutions that identify as HSIs must also be considered as we call on HSIs to enact servingness. The diversity among HSIs makes it nearly impossible to transform HSIs with one approach. In 2019–20, 44% of all HSIs were two-year and 56% were four-year (*Excelencia* in Education, 2021b). By their very nature, two-year and four-year institutions have different missions and purposes, making it difficult to transform HSIs across these types. In 2019–20, 67% of HSIs were public and 33% were private (*Excelencia* in Education, 2021b). Public and private institutions are also different, particularly when it comes to their ability to fund initiatives, programs, and financial aid packages for students.

There were 569 HSIs in 30 states in 2019–20, from California to Connecticut and including Puerto Rico (*Excelencia* in Education, 2021b). Yet colleges and universities are constrained in some ways by the state context. For example, in 2019 only 18 states offered in-state tuition for undocumented students, which could affect some HSIs' ability to serve undocumented students (if they so desire). Moreover, for HSIs that are also land-grant institutions, or comprehensive institutions with a strong commitment to state development, being an HSI may include serving and enhancing the state. HSIs also range in size, urbanicity, and mission (Núñez et al., 2016), affecting their ability to serve students. A small institution may be able to offer more hands-on experiences than a larger one, while a rural HSI must consider the specific needs of rural students. Expenditures for instruction, academic support, and student services also range tremendously across institutions (Núñez et al., 2016), which affects their ability to serve students. There is also huge variation in the number of associate's and bachelor's degree programs offered (Núñez & Elizondo,

2012), and less than half of all HSIs offer graduate programs (Garcia & Guzman-Alvarez, 2021).

Demanding change in academic outcomes without adequate context will not produce equitable outcomes, no matter how many policy mandates there are. I provide HSIs here with a framework for moving their institutions from "Hispanic-enrolling HSIs" to "transformed HSIs," which are those that advance racial equity, social, justice, and collective liberation. This will require an acknowledgment of the identities, experiences, and sociohistoric context of students, families, communities, and the institutions themselves. It will also require an elevated focus on achieving racial equity in academic, economic, and postgraduation outcomes as well as outcomes that advance social justice and collective liberation.

Need for a Unique Approach to Organizing

In this book I draw on theories about organizations and intentionally draw on critical theories, acknowledging that the HSI designation is a racialized one, meaning it is connected to and evolves from the racialized ethnic identities of the students within HSIs (Garcia, 2019; Garcia & Dwyer, 2018). By "racialized ethnic identities," I mean that the term "Hispanic" is not a race but instead a panethnic term created, promoted, and reinforced by the government, political activists, and the media between the 1960s and 1980s (Mora, 2014). As a social construct, the term has been "made racial through social interaction, positioning, and discourse" (Nasir, 2012, p. 5) with meaning being attached to it in ways that essentialize what it means to be a member of this group. As part of the racialization process, the panethnic "Hispanic" and "Latinx" umbrella terms inaccurately and inappropriately reify a demographically diverse group of people from various racial backgrounds (ranging from white to Black), with different histories of colonization and enslavement, and various connections to US imperialism. Hispanics/Latinxs have ethnic, cultural, and historic roots in many parts of the world, including the Caribbean,

South and Central America, Mexico, and the United States. Hispanics/Latinxs speak hundreds of Indigenous languages, Spanish, English, Portuguese, French, and others. Each of these distinctions has contributed to the racialization process with a hierarchy created *within* the group based on race, class, language, and documentation status. As a group we don't even agree on the umbrella term to be used (Hispanic, Latina, Latine, Latino, Latinx,* Afro-Latinx; the options go on and on), so how can institutions serve, educate, and empower such a broad racial-ethnic-Indigenous group?

I draw on theories about race and racialization to talk about serving students in HSIs because research shows that while Mexican Americans/Chicanxs are the largest ethnic group in HSIs, they also enroll Puerto Ricans, multiethnic Latinxs, and those who identify as "other Latinxs" (Cuellar, 2019). HSIs also provide access to other minoritized racial and ethnic groups, including Black, Native American, Asian American, and Pacific Islander students (Espinosa et al., 2019). Students at HSIs speak a range of languages, although they are more likely to be nonnative English speakers than those who attend non-HSIs, and they are also more likely to be immigrants (Núñez & Bowers, 2011). Although there are less accurate data available to know the exact number of undocumented and DACAmented students attending HSIs, we can assume that the more than 600,000 active DACA students in the United States are present in HSIs. Moreover, students at HSIs come from a range of socioeconomic backgrounds, although a higher percentage of low-income/Pell Grant-eligible students attend HSIs than non-HSIs (Malcom-Piqueux & Lee, 2011; Núñez & Bowers, 2011). Students who are not academically prepared for college, as indicated by a lower-than-average high school GPA and/or lower standardized math scores, are also more likely to attend HSIs (Cuellar, 2019; Núñez & Bowers, 2011). Much less has been documented about the diversity of students within HSIs by other

* In this book, I use "Latinx" as a professional preference; I acknowledge it is a messy and ambiguous term but defer to it as an accepted term in the most current research within and for the Latinx higher education community. For more on the term "Latinx," please refer to research by Dr. Cristobal Salinas Jr. (Salinas & Lozano, 2019; Salinas, 2020).

social identities (i.e., gender, religion, dis/ability, sexual orientation), but we know students live complex, multiple-issue lives. I call on HSIs to serve, educate, and empower students using an intersectional approach assuming that there is extreme diversity by other social identities. At the same time, I know it's nearly impossible to effectively serve all minoritized groups at the same time using the same approach.

Freedom Dreaming about HSIs

With such a complicated history as a political construct defined only by descriptors and considering the extreme diversity among and within HSIs, it is no wonder that the process of becoming HSIs and defining servingness in HSIs is so difficult. I take a different approach, much informed by my previous work (Garcia, 2017, 2018, 2019; Garcia et al., 2019) but more focused on my hopes and goals for HSIs to become spaces that advance racial equity, social justice, and collective liberation and that commit to enacting a liberatory, humanizing, and emancipatory approach to education. To be clear, the Transforming HSIs Framework is a utopian vision; it's a freedom dream; it's an organization that does not yet exist. Transforming HSIs is no easy feat, and we may never fully see it in our lifetimes, but we must try anyway. I call on educators, decision makers, administrators, governing boards, grant seekers and implementers, policy intermediaries, legislators, and politicians alike to embrace, acknowledge, and elevate the complexities of student identities within HSIs, to recognize the larger systems of oppression that have made the students within HSIs vulnerable within the academic system, to embrace students' collective cultural wealth (Yosso, 2005), and to move HSIs toward a "third space" in which institutional scripts are transformed in order to embrace student knowledge in a way that is valued by the postsecondary field (i.e., the federal government and other HSIs) (Garcia, 2019).

1

Transforming HSIs for Equity, Justice, and Liberation

IN 2005 I WAS HIRED BY CALIFORNIA STATE UNIVERSITY, Fullerton (CSUF), to coordinate its Developing Hispanic-Serving Institutions (HSIs) Title V grants efforts. The focus of the grant was STEM, with joint efforts and commitment from the deans of both the College of Engineering and Computer Science and the College of Natural Sciences and Mathematics. CSUF has a unique model in that each of the eight academic colleges houses an assistant dean for student affairs who reports jointly to the dean of the academic college and the dean of students. My position, which was funded by the Title V grant, reported to two assistant deans for student affairs, one from each of the colleges that were part of the Title V efforts. As such I had an indirect reporting line to the dean of both colleges and the dean of students. I was also fortunate to be part of the Title V efforts, which meant I had an indirect reporting line to the principal investigator of the grant and ultimately to the president of the institution, as the grant resided in the president's office.

For an entry-level student affairs professional, it seemed like an ideal situation. I started the position not knowing how capacity-building grants worked and even less about HSI grants (or HSIs in general). While in graduate school, I learned about HSIs and other Minority-Serving Institutions (MSIs), but I had not spent much time thinking about them. All I knew was that I was working with student affairs professionals to develop retention programming for Latinx students in STEM, and I was excited about that. My master's thesis was about members of Latina Greek Lettered Organizations, their transition and adjustment to campus, and their experiences with the campus environment. I trusted that the college student personnel training I had at the University of Maryland and the master's thesis I had written prepared me to implement Title V programming to retain Latinx students in STEM degrees. I had no idea what the universe actually had in store for me. Little did I know that the position would become the catalyst to my academic career and in many ways this book.

I spent three years passionately developing my position from scratch, despite the fact that I was funded by soft money (i.e., grant money, meaning the position might be eliminated at the end of the grant), a reality that colleagues on campus regularly reminded me of ("You're on soft money; make sure you move into a line item soon"). The younger naïve version of me had no idea what that meant; I just thought it was cool that I got to create my own position. That part of the job was fun. I dreamt up cool things like mentoring programs and intrusive advising and student organizations. I became the founding advisor of the CSUF chapter of SACNAS* after many long discussions with my student assistant, Crystal, a smart, outgoing, fun, big-hearted Latina who was in one of the whitest majors ever: geology. She had moved to geology from civil engineering and shared many stories that I learned from, stories about the machismo within the Latino engineering community and the racism within the geology community. She loved the geologists; they were well-meaning white folks who had no clue that they were "geology so white" and upholding whiteness in their field. But we knew. We founded an

---

*SACNAS is an organization that seeks to expand access to STEM fields for the most underrepresented. https://www.sacnas.org.

organization where she could see herself within the science community. We attended SACNAS conferences and were inspired by scholars like Rochelle Gutierrez, who gave a keynote speech about nepantla (the space in between) in mathematics, drawing on Gloria Anzaldúa's conceptions of the borderlands.

I also used my position to do practitioner-driven research because the amazing faculty at the University of Maryland, Drs. Susan Komives, Marylu McEwen, and Karen Kurotsuchi Inkelas, told me I was a scholar practitioner and that's what scholar practitioners do. I held focus groups and sent surveys to the STEM majors and collected data about retention and student services that I had no idea what to do with. I knew one day I would pursue a PhD and figured data and research would get me there. I also went to conferences, including the Hispanic Association of Colleges and Universities (HACU) conference where I learned more about HSIs and met some of the coolest Latinx professionals I know. But the more I learned, the more I questioned what it meant to be an HSI. I would go to HSI meetings on campus, which were held periodically, and wonder why there were so many high-level administrators at the meetings who talked about HSIs in those one or two hours but never talked to me about what it meant to implement the student support side of the HSI grant.

I had lots of ideas about what it could mean to be an HSI, yet I felt alone in my efforts, lacking the political power on campus to do anything significant. My colleague Victor Rojas managed the grant, and he believed in me and my ideas and let me have fun, as long as my ideas were within the confines of the grant. But the more I read the grant proposal that was submitted and funded, the more I realized that the people who wrote the grant (the inconsistencies in the narrative suggested that multiple people probably wrote the grant) had no clue what an HSI was. There was a huge disconnect between the goals and objectives of the grant, as written, and what I was doing in practice. I enjoyed my professional career as a student affairs professional at CSUF, relished in the creative side of implementing my position, and met many mentors along the way, but the HSI side of my job didn't sit well with me. I regularly asked myself the same question so many others working at HSIs ask, "But what does it actually mean to be Hispanic-*serving*?"

I could see the bigger picture, that there were major issues that needed to be addressed in order to move the institution from Latinx-*enrolling* to Latinx-*serving* (Garcia, 2017). At that time, there was a dearth of HSI research. *Excelencia* in Education had published a series of reports about Latinx student success at HSIs, about the history of HSIs, and about modeling practices that serve students. The late Michael Olivas (Olivas, 1982) and the late Berta Vigil Laden (Laden, 2001, 2004) (rest in power to these early HSI advocates) had also published foundational articles about HSIs, challenging the higher education community to take note of these sleeping giants (my words, not theirs). They saw something that others could not yet see, which was that HSIs were to become essential to the higher education landscape and to Latinx college students. But even those resources did not provide me with the tools I needed to actually move the institution toward Latinx-*serving*. Those were tough times as I struggled to define and enact "servingness" (a term my colleagues and I conceptualized more than ten years later; Garcia et al., 2019) as a Title V coordinator with no real guidance. I became jaded and started to doubt the power of the HSI designation. I knew that enrolling a lot of Latinx students while doing the same things we had always done as white institutions couldn't be the answer.

I didn't have the vocabulary to say that we needed to "decolonize higher education." I couldn't conceptualize deconstructing institutions committed to whiteness and coloniality of power and then reconstructing liberatory and humanizing colleges and universities. I didn't know what decolonial or abolitionist higher education was (see Stein, 2021, for an extensive description of these approaches). In my master's program, Marylu McEwen introduced me to Paulo Freire's *Pedagogy of the Oppressed* and bell hooks's *Teaching to Transgress*, but younger naïve me couldn't comprehend the power of those readings, let alone translate them to practice. I also didn't know the implications of a political construct that was defined solely in legislation with no real guidance or accountability for transforming institutions into spaces of equity, justice, and liberation. As a daughter of ethnic studies, I was already a freedom dreamer, drawing on Black and Chicanx radical traditions about social, political, and educational freedom through activism, self-determination, and community uplift. I had a vision for a more progressive HSI but couldn't clearly articulate it. I knew there was something better, more concrete, more tangible, more centered on Latinx ways of knowing; I knew that structural transformation was necessary for education to become fully emancipatory, but I couldn't find the vocabulary to say that. I could say with strong conviction that we weren't an HSI but couldn't intellectually or concretely conceptualize something better. This book is for those educators like me, trying to find the words and tools to disrupt everything they have ever known about colleges and universities in order to create a more liberatory and humanizing space for students of color.

Reflections on the Decolonizing HSIs Framework

In 2018 I published an article called "Decolonizing Hispanic-Serving Institutions: A Framework for Organizing" (Garcia, 2018), which has been extensively downloaded and cited. As an organizational theorist, I developed the framework for HSI practitioners searching for the vocabulary and tools necessary to deconstruct and rebuild higher education organizations to better serve students of color. The framework was about organizational change, because becoming an HSI is about organizational change. The framework gave educators and decision makers a tangible way to think about that change.

At the time, I was struggling to find an organizational model that acknowledged how organizations reinforced systemic racism. I had not discovered la paperson's (2017) visionary model, *A Third University Is Possible*, which provides a decolonial approach to disrupting colleges and universities founded as colonial projects. By colonial project I mean that our model for higher education in the present-day United States was created and solidified as part of the conquering of Turtle Island (the Indigenous name for North America) when

European settlers viewed Native Americans as hostile and uncivilized and people of African descent were enslaved and dehumanized. As a colonial project, colleges were funded with money from the transatlantic slave trade, governed by enslavers and traders, built by the labor of enslaved people, and with a mission to "civilize" Native Americans (Wilder, 2013; Wright, 1988, 1991). The call to decolonize education acknowledges that "settler colonialism" (the conquering of the land, water, and resources by settlers who remained on the land) and the "coloniality of power" (the racial and economic system of oppression that is set in place as a result of settler colonialism) continue to oppress racial-ethnic-Indigenous people within educational systems.

At the time, Victor Ray (2019) had not published his foundational article, "A Theory of Racialized Organizations," which provides a tangible way to identify whiteness within organizations. By whiteness within postsecondary institutions I mean that present-day practices and policies in colleges and universities were created and standardized by white scholars (of European descent) with white students and white faculty as the normalizing population. Whiteness, which is more accurately described as "systemic racism," affects how students are admitted and educated (Museus et al., 2015). It is also embedded in the curriculum, which elevates and validates white knowledges and white histories, and the cocurriculum, with theories of involvement and engagement standardized based on white students' experiences in college (Bensimon, 2007; Patton, 2016). Whiteness also drives the ways that faculty are rewarded based on their ability to secure external funding and publish in top-tier journals that have normalized white ways of doing research (Garcia, 2019). The decolonizing HSIs framework gave educators a way to understand how HSIs are part of larger systems of oppression including the coloniality of power and systemic racism.

From a justice perspective, however, the decolonizing HSIs framework was flawed. It lacked the depth and complexity necessary to understand the detrimental effects of settler colonialism across the Caribbean and the Americas. It lacked an acknowledgment of the

Afro and Indigenous descendancy in Puerto Rico, Cuba, and the Dominican Republic and across Latin America (Figueroa-Vásquez, 2020). It erased the historical, political, and linguistic realities of the Afro-Latinx and Indigenous Latinx diaspora. By failing to acknowledge Afro-Latinx experiences and identities, the decolonizing HSIs framework reinforced anti-Black racism and perpetuated an essentialist approach to studying Latinidad (Haywood, 2017a). It also lacked full acknowledgment of Latinx Indigeneities, eliminating the historical and present-day experience of Latinxs with Indigenous roots across the Caribbean and the Americas. The decolonizing HSIs framework relied on the analytic tools of mestizaje and indigenismo that are grounded in settler colonial logics that have actively erased Indigenous people and people with Afro descendancy (Calderón & Urrieta, 2019). As a mestiza myself with Mexican American descendancy who benefits from settler colonialism and white supremacy, I elevated an essentialist decolonial HSIs framework that centered Chicanismo and reinforced an approach to serving a monolithic Hispanic/Latinx group that doesn't exist.

Other things to note are that there were aspects of neoliberalism embedded within the decolonizing HSIs framework that were theoretically incompatible.* Neoliberalism is the antithesis of decoloniality, racial justice, democracy, and education as a public good (Giroux, 2014). It is inextricably bound to systems of oppression, including white supremacy and capitalism, that create and re-create inequitable outcomes and experiences for people of color (Museus & Lepeau, 2020). The neoliberal university is less concerned with educational, intellectual, and social interests than it is with commodifying knowledge, generating revenue, privatizing education, managing faculty production, and treating students like customers (Giroux, 2014). Core tenants of the neoliberal university include the commitment to consumerism, competition, surveillance, precarity, and declining morality, all of which work against social justice and equity (Museus &

---

* I would like to acknowledge the undergraduate students at the University of California, Santa Barbara, who called me in and challenged me to consider the incompatibility between decolonial ideologies and neoliberalism; I appreciate you.

Lepeau, 2020). Within the decolonizing HSI framework I included the incentive structure as a dimension that reinforced neoliberal ideals about rewarding people in monetary ways for doing racial equity and social justice work. In reality, these should be core ideals that guide the actions of all members in a decolonized educational structure. Yet colleges and universities as neoliberal machines reward and incentivize people for "doing diversity work," even if it's not part of their core values.

Rather than making incentives a primary dimension in the Transforming HSIs Framework, I address incentives and reward structures in other places where it makes sense, like the fact that women and femmes of color should be rewarded and acknowledged for the extra labor of mentoring students of color, working with local communities, and engaging in service that advances equity and justice for the institution. The reward systems within transformed HSIs must be reconsidered to account for this labor, which is often unaccounted for. I maintain that all members of the organization should be committed to the ideals of racial equity, social justice, and collective liberation. People with dominant identities in higher education (i.e., white, cisgender, men, middle class/wealthy, Christian) should become collaborators working for justice and liberation rather than performing fake or pseudo-allyship. I also removed the restorative justice dimension that was in the decolonizing framework and instead conceptualize a more holistic approach to restoration and healing as part of organizational transformation (Rerucha, 2021).

The Transforming HSIs Framework offered in this book attempts to reconcile some of my own missteps in developing the decolonizing HSIs framework. It also extends the originally proposed organizational dimensions. And although I believe in the core ideologies of decolonizing education, I acknowledge that these efforts in the present-day United States are so entangled in resettlement and reoccupation that they often further the settler colonial agenda (Tuck & Yang, 2012). I have grappled with my own move toward settler innocence and continue this work as a critical organizational scholar of color.

Organizational Theory as a Foundation

I have consistently argued that we must approach the study and practice of HSIs through an organizational lens (Garcia, 2013a, 2015, 2017, 2019). An organizational approach puts the onus on colleges and universities to structurally change the organization in order to produce equitable outcomes for students. It also assumes that the organization needs to change, not the students. Through an organizational lens I ask, "What if the organizational dimensions of HSIs significantly increased the likelihood of students of color succeeding along academic, economic, postgraduation, and liberatory measures?" I also ask, "What changes does the organization need to make in order to ensure success for students of color?"

As an organizational theorist who has drawn on (neo)institutional theory to help make sense of how HSIs become unique organizations with distinct identities within an emerging field, I have relied heavily on macro-level thinking, or field-level thinking about racialization, with the field including all colleges and universities in the United States. Within a highly institutionalized field, organizations are legitimized based on socially constructed myths and ceremonies about how they should act and be held accountable by the rules and regulations developed by the legislators, professional associations, and other legitimizing organizations within the field (DiMaggio & Powell, 1983; Meyer & Rowan, 1977; Suddaby, 2010). The field is shaped by institutional logics that are nested within a larger system of white supremacy that is mostly ignored when conversations about diversity and equity in colleges and university comes up among those with the most influence and power within the field (Ray, 2019). Historically HSIs have been less selective, broad-access institutions that have provided access to students of color, low-income students, and first generation to college students (which is a good thing) but have struggled to adequately serve them because they are traditionally underresourced and undervalued by a field that rewards organizations that perform whiteness rather than rewarding those institutions that advance a racial equity agenda (Garcia, 2019).

In understanding how (neo)institutionalism works, I worry that the most selective, well-resourced HSIs will become the most legitimized within the field of higher education. This has been a fear of mine (and my HSI *hermana* Dra. Marcela Cuellar) for quite some time. We're watching it unfold as the University of California system, which includes some of the most elite public institutions in the United States (UCLA and UC Berkeley), becomes a Hispanic-serving university system (Paredes et al., 2021). I hope that the field will resist the natural progression toward normalizing and legitimizing what these HSIs do while simultaneously undermining what underresourced, less selective, non-research-focused HSIs do. In deconstructing racialized organizations, we must not lose sight of the ways that race-neutral macro-level forces normalize and legitimate what we do, what we believe, and what we value. The most well-resourced and elite organizations in the field should not become the beacon of servingness simply because they perform whiteness better than other HSIs. As an alumna of the UC system, I believe in the system and want other first generation to college women of color like me to have access to the world-class education it provides, I simply acknowledge that a majority of HSIs are not part of the UC system, and that's OK, as all HSIs have the ability to produce equitable educational, economic, postcollege, and liberatory outcomes. I believe in all HSIs and want the field of higher education to believe in them too.

Theory of Racialized Organizations

Guided by theories about racialized organizations, I offer a framework for transforming HSIs (or any racialized college or university) with the goal of elevating racial equity, social justice, and collective liberation. Transforming HSIs will require organizations to decredential whiteness, redistribute resources and power within the institution, couple race and organizational rules, policies, and procedures, and actively empower racial-ethnic-Indigenous groups. The Transforming HSIs Framework attempts to do that, focusing primarily on the meso and macro levels. In centering the meso (organizational) and macro (field) levels, I call on HSIs to address the mechanisms that reproduce racial inequities at the micro (individual) level. Ray (2019) suggests that these mechanisms are related to racial structures and agency, which makes it essential to address racial inequities at the meso and macro levels. Moreover, Ray (2019) argues that "racial structures are produced when central schemas connect to resources" and that "once racial structures are in place, a racial ideology—or racism—arises to justify the unequal distribution of resources along racial lines" (p. 32). In order to transform racialized organizations, racial structures, central schemas, and resources must be carefully scrutinized and deconstructed. Using the four tenets of racialized organizations offered by Ray (2019), I contend that racialized organizations can be transformed and offer a foundation for the Transforming HSIs Framework.

Decredentialing Whiteness by Centering Race

Within racialized organizations, "whiteness is a credential providing access to organizational resources, legitimizing work hierarchies, and expanding white agency" (Ray, 2019, p. 41). Colleges and universities in the United States are no exception, as whiteness is institutionalized in such a way that they appear to be race-neutral in principle, practice, and policy (Cabrera et al., 2017). Whiteness as a social concept allows all members of the organization to operate through a color-neutral lens (i.e., not see race), ignore the systemic nature of racism and white supremacy, and minimize the history and present-day experiences of people of color. This plays out in numerous ways, with whiteness transcending every dimension of college and universities including the racial makeup of educators and decision makers, the curriculum or cocurricular structures, the policies and decision-making, the governance, the reward systems, and the distribution of resources (Garcia, 2018, 2019; Gusa, 2010; Patton, 2016). Whiteness as normative on college campuses leads people to question things like affirmative action and diversity requirements but dismiss racialized events as isolated incidents that are not reflective of the values of the institution (Cabrera, 2019; Gusa, 2010). It also allows people to blame anything but race and racism for the inequities that we continue to see in outcomes and experiences of people of color (Cabrera, 2019). At a systemic level, it allows us to evaluate and rank institutions based on how "smart" their faculty and students are without acknowledging that the measures of smartness are grounded in white standards (Garcia, 2019). Whiteness as a credential must be disrupted or decredentialed in order to transform HSIs.

The Transforming HSIs Framework is grounded in principles of racial equity, social justice, and collective liberation, with race being a fundamental guiding force. Arguably, race and people of color must become central in order to decredential whiteness. Race is the guiding principle in the Transforming HSIs Framework because HSIs enroll a large percentage of Latinx, Black, Indigenous, Asian American, and Pacific Islander students (Espinosa et al., 2019); to enact servingness through a race-neutral lens diminishes this reality, essentially silencing these students and disregarding their experiences with racism and white supremacy and decoupling inequitable outcomes from these systems. To propose a framework that is devoid of race is egregious and reckless. I also acknowledge that besides "Black," the other groups I listed are not races (Latinx, Indigenous, Asian American, and Pacific Islander), yet these panethnic and Indigenous groups are racialized and subjected to the same white logics that criminalize and dehumanize them, which leads to elevated experiences with discrimination, harassment, state-sanctioned violence, and inequitable educational outcomes. I use the term "racial-ethnic-Indigenous" when possible, but the framework is grounded in theories about race, systemic racism, and white supremacy, as well as theories that incorporate race with other minoritized identities such as intersectionality, Chicana feminist theory, and Black radical feminisms. As such, I defer to race throughout the book, accepting that race and the racialization process are messy in the United States (Johnston-Guerrero, 2016). I also acknowledge that racism is central to the educational experiences of these groups as a result of white supremacy. With this in mind, the Transforming HSIs Framework is a racial justice model that theorizes HSIs as a racial justice project.

The unequal distribution of resources is legitimized within racialized organizations (Ray, 2019) and racialized fields (Garcia, 2019). At the macro level, the inequitable distribution of resources to MSIs, or racially minoritized organizations, is historical. HSIs have been underfunded and underresourced since they gained federal recognition (HACU, 2020). As noted by HACU (2020), "as of FY 2016 IPEDS data, HSIs on average received $3,117 per student from all federal revenue sources, compared to $4,605 per student for all degree-granting institutions, just 68 cents on the dollar received by other institutions to educate a disproportionally low-income student population" (p. 9). These inequities affect public HSIs in particular, as they rely heavily on public investments from federal, state, and local contracts and appropriations, with public two-year HSIs receiving 71% of their revenue shares and public four-year HSIs receiving 46% of their revenue shares from these sources (Nellum & Valle, 2015). These public revenue sources have become more unstable in recent years, creating greater challenges for HSIs.

With an average of 30 new HSIs a year, the federal funding to supplement these underresourced institutions has not kept pace. While federal funding to HSIs through the Title V, Part A program grew in the early years, from 1998 to 2004, it leveled off until 2008, when there was a surge of funding through the Title V, Part B and Title III, Part F HSI STEM programs. It again leveled off and in some years decreased despite the continued growth in the number of HSIs each year (HACU, 2020). Ortega et al. (2015) also noted that the competition for federal funds has become fierce, with less than half of all HSIs receiving competitive funding. They commented that "while Title V appropriations have provided HSIs with some financial relief during periods of fiscal constraint, attempts by the federal government to remedy the historic neglect of HSIs by state governments have been unevenly realized, raising concerns over the long-term sustainability of initiatives designed to facilitate the postsecondary success of Latina/o students" (Ortega et al., 2015, p. 159). The Transforming HSIs

Framework addresses these macro-level forces by calling on *external partners and influences* to consider their role in developing mutually beneficial exchanges of servingness that are centered on racial justice and equity (see chapter 6).

At the meso level, Ray (2019) stressed that segregation within racialized organizations is one form of inequitable resource distribution. Racial segregation reveals itself in the inequitable number of educators and decision makers of color within HSIs, with a majority of people of color at the lower levels of the organizational hierarchy and fewer people of color in positions of power (Contreras, 2017; Garcia, 2019; Hurtado & Ruiz Alvarado, 2015; Santos & Acevedo-Gil, 2013; Campaign for College Opportunity, 2020; Vargas et al., 2019). Even when there are people of color in decision-making positions at HSIs, they often feel alone or disempowered (e.g., Doran, 2019b). There is also racial segregation within the curriculum and support services at HSIs, with a majority of the diversity, equity, and justice work occurring in ethnic studies, cultural centers, and TRIO programs (Garcia, 2016b; Garcia & Okhidoi, 2015; Garcia et al., 2018). All physical, capital, human, natural, material, and social resources must be reevaluated and redistributed within HSIs, with the *membership, infrastructure, governance, and leadership* dimensions specifically addressing these resources (see chapters 3–5). Although very little is documented about how organizational budgets reinforce the credentialing of whiteness within HSIs, I urge decision makers to scrutinize their budgets, as budgets are an essential way that colleges and universities enact their *mission, identity, and strategic purpose* (see chapter 2) (Barr & McClellan, 2018). Moreover, the distribution of financial resources within the institution provides power and incentives to those educators, decision makers, and students who receive the resources, and it sends a powerful message about what the institution values and believes in (Barr & McClellan, 2018).

Coupling Race and Organizational Policies and Practices

Racialized organizations decouple stated commitments to diversity, equity, and inclusion (DEI) from formal policies, practices, and procedures

(Ray, 2019). In other words, what colleges and universities *say* about DEI does not align with what they actually *do*. Ahmed (2012) calls it a "non-performative commitment," meaning that institutions name their commitments to diversity without producing the desired effect. A prime example of this is the numerous statements from college presidents and chancellors about their commitment to justice (e.g., Cole & Harper, 2017; Davis & Harris, 2015; Squire et al., 2019). Cole and Harper (2017) found that college leaders tend to focus on individual perpetrators of racists acts but fail to acknowledge the institution's role in perpetrating racism and fail to name the systemic racism embedded in the organization. Within these statements, they may even go as far as dismissing racialized incidents as one-time events while simultaneously moving the perpetrators toward innocence (Davis & Harris, 2015). Squire et al. (2019) found that statements often included "affective shifts," which are emotional pleas filled with sadness, anger, and disappointment that don't become practice or policy. The statements also included "moral slips," that shift the conversation from a moral imperative to legal rationales for the institution's limited ability to actually do something about their stated commitments. Stated commitments to DEI and racial justice are meaningless if they remain decoupled from policies and practices. Yet Ahmed (2012) showed that even when institutions pass policies through the proper channels with the highest level of approval, the practices do not always follow suit due to historical practices that are grounded in whiteness. Ray (2019) also noted that colleges and universities often adopt affirmative action and antidiscrimination policies simply to avoid lawsuits and litigation with little change or substantial transformation occurring to address historical injustices within the organization.

Coupling race with organizational policies and practices necessitates an equity-minded and race-conscious approach. Becoming equity-minded requires educators and decision makers within HSIs to reflect on their own biases, practices, and judgments; analyze the structures, policies, and practices that create inequities; and take action to mitigate inequities within the institution rather than blaming or placing the onus on students (Bensimon, 2012). Grounded in theories about race and racial justice, the Transforming HSIs Framework also mandates race-consciousness, forcing educators and decision makers to notice how race is embedded within the daily processes and practices of the institution and how racism affects the experiences and outcomes of all people of color within the institution (Bensimon, 2012). Being both race-conscious and equity-minded requires a disconnected attachment from diversity and inclusion, as diversity and inclusion are simply "feel good" words that do not call for the decredentialing of whiteness, the redistribution of resources, or attachment to policies and practices (Ahmed, 2012). The Transforming HSIs Framework calls on the organization to become antiracist by elevating the experiences and outcomes of people of color, dismantling whiteness, redistributing human and economic resources, and enacting policies and practices that align with the organization's commitment to racial equity and justice. Antiracist work within a transformed HSI requires the constant recognition of institutional whiteness and institutional racism and the active enactment of policies and practices that disrupt them. This is hard work, but it will take the organization much further than the "feel good" diversity and inclusion efforts that are exhausting for the people of color who are often charged with this work and rarely rewarded for it.

Actively Empowering Racial-Ethnic-Indigenous Groups

Individual agency, or the ability to act, is tied to the racialized structures of an organization that actively subordinates racially minoritized people to the lower levels of the hierarchy, thus inhibiting their agency (Ray, 2019). Agency is controlled through organizational actions such as the regulation of time and differential wages for equally qualified people of color and women. Moreover, there is little recognition or reward for the emotional labor that Latinx, Black, Indigenous, Asian American, and Pacific Islander workers contribute in order to advance the organization (Ray, 2019). People of color who are committed to advancing racial justice and equity within the organization are often faced with resistance, have limited budgets to do the work, and face emotional costs and risk of burnout (Jones,

2019). Yet change within racialized organizations often comes from social movements led by those with the least amount of agency within the organization but who can clearly see the ways that whiteness is a credential, the differential distribution of resources, and the ways that race is decoupled from all policies and actions (Ray, 2019).

Resistance is a key tactic for those who lack agency within the organization. There are numerous stories of faculty of color enacting their own agency within racialized organizations. A group of Chicana/Latina faculty at one HSI established a research collaborative called "Research for the Educational Advancement of Latin@s (REAL)" as an active form of transformational resistance to racism and sexism within the institution (Ek et al., 2010). In noticing that their institution was steeped in values of whiteness, manhood, and Eurocentric ideals, despite the fact that it was an HSI by enrollment, they formed the research collective in order to advance their scholarship and mentor each other into and through the tenure and promotion process. They also grappled with their own racialized and gendered identities, discussed tactics for teaching racially and economically minoritized students, and advocated for themselves (Murakami-Ramalho et al., 2010). There are also stories of staff of color enacting their own agency. Abrica and Rivas (2017) detailed the ways in which their human agency was diminished working as Chicana/Latina institutional research staff at Hispanic-serving community colleges. They talked about the ways that administrators upheld whiteness in the organization by remaining politically neutral and complacent with the race-neutrality inherent in their number crunching and data reporting. Yet they resisted, asking critical questions about students' backgrounds, experiences, and aspirations while simultaneously asking what the institution was doing to support students.

Students also resist and enact agency, demanding recognition and educational structures that serve them (e.g., Comeaux et al., 2021). Students at one emerging HSI formed coalitions across racial-ethnic groups in order to challenge the systemic racism they saw within the institution and manifested by administrator decision-making (Aguilar-Hernández et al., 2021). Aguilar-Hernández and colleagues provide a detailed historical account of how students of color were met with resistance and defeat in their efforts to demand that the institution increase enrollment of Latinx students, hire key administrators of color who would better serve them, and establish a "Raza Center" to support them. The students were successful in gaining an ethnic-specific space to meet their needs, but the resistance from faculty and alumni intensified, which often occurs when people feel that whiteness within the organization is threatened. Although resistance and social movements within organizations often leads to organizational change (Zald et al., 2005), the Transforming HSIs Framework calls on HSIs to empower racial-ethnic-Indigenous groups to lead the change.

Transforming Hispanic-Serving Institutions Framework

The Transforming HSIs Framework includes nine dimensions: (1) mission, (2) identity, (3) strategic purpose, (4) membership, (5) infrastructure (which includes four subdimensions), (6) governance, (7) leadership, (8) external partnerships, and (9) external influences (visually represented in figure 1). The framework is a guide to help organizations address transformation one dimension at a time, with each dimension being equally important. It is a tool to support organizational change in practice, although it could guide research and assessment too. I encourage readers to find their place in the framework based on their position within higher education and start the transformation process there. I also want to remind readers that the framework is not all-inclusive, so some might not see their position or work within it. There are many things I could have included and will likely include in future iterations of the framework. For example, I don't mention marketing and public relation, but I do know that HSIs need to do a better job of creating awareness of their HSI status and what that means. There is also more work to do with language, bilingualism, and biliteracy within HSIs, and undocumented and DACAmented students in HSIs, yet the research and evidence of what this looks like in practice is still emerging. With a little creativity and imagination, the framework can be useful to all.

Figure 1. Transforming Hispanic-Serving Institutions Framework

In chapter 2, I outline mission, identity, and strategic purpose focusing on individual and organizational outcomes and experiences (also known as "indicators of success" or "measures of success" for both students in HSIs and the HSIs themselves). I call on HSIs to decredential whiteness, starting with these core organizational elements, centering a mission that is antiracist and antioppressive, enacting an organizational identity that elevates liberatory outcomes and empowering experiences for people of color and mapping out strategic purposes that ground racial equity and racial justice in all policies, procedures, and practices. These dimensions cut across and drive the other six dimensions of the framework. The mission, identity, and purpose represent *who we are* and *what we value* as an organization.

In chapter 3, I focus on membership, which is the heart of the federal definition of HSIs based solely on the enrollment of Hispanic and low-income undergraduate students. I call on transformed HSIs to include families, graduate students, educators (faculty and staff), and decision makers (administrators and boards of trustees) in their definition of members, as undergraduate students should not be the sole determinant of what it means to be an HSI. The membership dimension represents the *people who do the work* to enact the mission, identity, and purpose. I challenge us to complicate the "H" in HSIs, as the Hispanic and Latinx umbrellas are not monolithic. In theorizing membership, we cannot rely on an essentialist approach that elevates anti-Blackness and anti-indigeneity and/or ignores the intersectional identities that further marginalize and exclude multiply minoritized people of color (Haywood, 2017a; Kendall, 2020; Núñez, 2014).

In chapter 4, I talk about centering racial-ethnic-Indigenous members and ways of knowing in the infrastructure, which includes the curriculum, cocurriculum, support structures, and physical infrastructure. This dimension was originally called, "technology" in the decolonizing HSIs framework, as technology in an organizational model refers to the ways that inputs and all forms of delivery manifest the intended mission, identity, and purpose of the organization. In other words, it represents *how we do* what we proclaim to do and value. In this framework I use to the term "infrastructure" and defer to terms that are germane to higher education: "curriculum," "pedagogy," "cocurricular activities," "involvement and engagement," and "student support services." I also added physical infrastructure as an important dimension, particularly as HSI federal grants allow for transformation of the physical infrastructure. I call on all members to innovatively rethink this dimension of servingness. Importantly, there is a focus on centering race, ethnicity, and indigeneity in all aspects of these higher education functions, calling us to actively disrupt race-neutral and dehumanizing approaches to delivering education. The tangible dimensions of the infrastructure are often the place where race is decoupled from the rules, regulations, and policies of the organization.

I extend the how of enacting the mission, identity, and strategic purpose to chapter 5, where I talk about how transformed HSIs should be formally governed and informally led by people of color with multiple minoritized identities that center their ways of knowing in their grassroots efforts to change the institution. I call governance "the glue that holds the framework together" but believe that grassroots leaders are often the most committed to disrupting systemic racism within higher education despite the fact that they are often disempowered to do this work. Specifically, I talk about the redistribution of resources and power and call for an elevated level of agency among the grassroots leaders of the organization. *In chapter 6, I talk about how transformed HSIs should engage with external partners and external influences* in order to create a mutually beneficial relationship of servingness.

HSIs as Liberatory Educational Spaces

This book is about creating liberatory and humanizing futures for HSIs. Liberation from a Freirean perspective calls for an approach to education that is both reflective and action oriented ("praxis"). Freire (2018, originally published in 1970) argued that educational practices should acknowledge the historical and cultural ways that the oppressed have been dehumanized and exploited. He also argued that education should allow the oppressed and the oppressor to work collectively toward freedom, revolution, transformation, and collective liberation. This approach becomes humanizing because it allows oppressed students to feel human, be seen, and feel valued in educational spaces. I draw on the principles of liberatory and humanizing education to advance an organizational framework. In this sense, liberatory education is more of a philosophical and ontological way of being (e.g., Dale & Hyslop-Margison, 2010) that extends into all aspects of the postsecondary setting. Liberatory education at a transformed HSI should have the stated goal of achieving equity and justice for students, families, and communities by disrupting historical and structural understandings of knowledge and centralizing the cultural and community knowledge of minoritized people (Jefferson et al., 2018). Moreover, the goal of liberation must be to allow students to have full control over decisions and conditions that affect their lives, families, and communities (Bale & Knopp, 2012). Finally, creating joy and enacting love within educational spaces must be viable goals of liberatory education (Love, 2019). Drawing on these principles, I outline various ways that HSIs can be transformed into spaces of racial equity, social justice, and collective liberation.

I also defer to the concepts of race-consciousness and equity-mindedness throughout this book. Race-conscious, equity-minded educators and decision makers accept that institutions of higher education were built on a foundation of white supremacy (Patton, 2016), settler colonialism (la paperson, 2017), and anti-Blackness (Dancy et al., 2018). They also acknowledge that the entire infrastructure embodies whiteness, as do the traditional processes, practices, and approaches to organizing. The coloniality of power embedded within the structures of the institution drive neoliberal decision-making and the tendency to advance science and technology, entrepreneurialism, and social progress that are tied to economic outcomes and social reproduction rather than racial and social justice (de Oliveira Andreotti et al., 2015). Race-conscious and equity-minded educators and decision makers within a transformed HSI understand how racial and colonial structures affect student outcomes and experiences; make connections between racial inequities and white supremacy, settler colonialism, and anti-Blackness; and seek to reform the organization for greater racial equity and social justice (Bensimon, 2012; Felix, 2021).

This book is also informed by my own experiences and *praxis* (critical reflection and action) within HSIs as well as my own research and active engagement with HSIs. The solutions in this book draw on transdisciplinary analytic tools about organizations and race that come from organizational theory, urban education, sociology, business management, ethnic studies, race studies, endarkened feminisms, and decolonial studies. These tools are not perfect, but they allowed me to conceptualize a utopian educational space. I contend that transformed HSIs should produce equitable outcomes and experiences for people of color (racial equity); should redistribute resources and power to allow people of color to lead, heal, and thrive within colleges and universities (social justice); and should advance an intersectional approach to coalition building and solidarity (collective liberation). This book is about transforming colleges and universities from the ground up. It's about disrupting the historical and structural schemas that reinforce racialized inequities in outcomes and experiences. This book is about abolishing educational systems that oppresses people of color and rebuilding liberatory educational spaces that advance equity, justice, liberation, solidarity, love, joy, and healing. This book is *not* about diversity and inclusion. It's also *not* about integration or assimilation or sense of belonging. It's about transforming institutions to meet the needs of people of color, not vice versa.

This Book Is for the People

This book is for college presidents/chancellors, vice presidents/vice chancellors, deans, directors, professors, postdocs, student affairs staff, Title V grant implementers, and boards of trustees. It's also for classified staff, administrative assistants, maintenance staff, institutional advancement staff, and campus police. The book is also for alumni, parents, families, community members, private foundations, policy intermediaries, politicians, and everyone who advocates for better education and a better society. It's for people who believe in the power of HSIs and for those who don't yet believe. (I didn't always believe, despite being an alumna of an HSI.)

This book is for racial-ethnic-Indigenous minoritized students: Latinx, Black, Indigenous, Asian American, Pacific Islander, and Mixed Race. It's for students at the intersections of minoritized identities in colleges and universities: low-income students, undocumented and DACAmented students, students from mixed-status families, students from the Latin American and Caribbean diaspora, multilingual students, non-Christian students, students with dis/abilities, students with neurodivergent ways of processing the world, students with social/emotional needs, gender nonbinary students, queer students, Trans* students, former foster youth, parenting students, formerly incarcerated students, veteran students, and so many others who are excluded or on the margins of education. It's for the people who have been excluded from HSI research and practice, despite being part of the "H" in HSI. It's for students who are struggling in ways that must be acknowledged, students who have family members in immigration centers, students who are sex workers, students who are homeless or food insecure, students who have been rejected by their families because of their sexual orientation or gender identity, students who are migrant workers, students who do not have access to health care, students with incarcerated family members or who are system impacted.

This book is for the educators and decision makers who are tired of elusive narratives about diversity and inclusion, educators who know firsthand the injustices and oppression that students at HSIs are facing, and educators who want to support their students. This book is for those of us who believe that a "third university" is possible, a postcolonial institution that deconstructs systemic settler colonialism and white supremacy (la paperson, 2017). It's for those of us who understand that systems of oppression create inequities and who want to disrupt those systems. It's for the grassroots leaders who start movements from within HSIs in order to transform them (Kezar & Lester, 2011). It's for the freedom dreamers who are brave enough to envision liberation in education, even if they have never experienced it or seen it, and struggle and fight for it, even if it seems impossible (Kelley, 2002).

Transformation Is Imperative: A Call to Action

I call on readers to freedom dream with me. I call on you to imagine what could be, unrestricted by what currently is. We know that colleges and universities are slow to change, but they do change. They are changing. This is your call to action, a call to do something. We owe it to the Latinx, Black, Indigenous, Asian American, Pacific Islander, and Mixed-Race people at the intersections of minoritized identities who are entering our colleges and universities and changing them, simply by their presence. We owe it to the people of color on campus who do not feel a sense of belonging to a campus that was never made for them (us). We don't feel like we belong. We are not satisfied with our experience. We don't want to simply be tolerated or celebrated for one month a year. We don't want to help others learn about diversity and multiculturalism. We don't want to be othered. We don't want to experience microaggressions. And no, the campus climate is not chilly; it's oppressive, racist, sexist, heterosexist, capitalist, toxic, and often violent. We also owe it to the families and communities that students come from. HSIs should serve all members, including families, alumni, and local communities.

HSIs must become educational spaces that not only acknowledge but disrupt inequities, oppression, and trauma, that actively work toward justice, healing, liberation, and joy. Transformed HSIs must commit to serving, educating, and empowering minoritized groups within HSIs. HSIs must critique the injustices faced by students who attend HSIs while centering their overall experiences, histories, and identities. Transformed HSIs must work toward racial justice and collective liberation. This book is not only a call to action; it's a toolbox for acting. To read it and do nothing would be egregious.

2

Committing to Mission, Identity, and Strategic Purpose

THE MISSION, IDENTITY, AND STRATEGIC PURPOSE are the foundations of the Transforming HSIs Framework that drive the actions of the organization. In the framework, the *mission* represents who we serve and what we value as an organization, the *identity* reflects who we are and what we do, and the *strategic purpose* describes how the mission and identity are enacted, measured, and assessed. The mission, identity, and purpose should lay out both a commitment to and actions toward equity, justice, and liberation for Latinx, Black, Indigenous, Asian American, Pacific Islander, and Mixed-Race students, families, and communities. These dimensions should go beyond *valuing* compositional "diversity" and elusive "inclusion" and move toward *action and disruption* of the systems of oppression that reinforce whiteness and anti-Blackness within educational spaces, exclusion, inequitable outcomes, and unwelcoming college environments. Since *becoming* an HSI is about organizational *change*, transformed HSIs must be willing to adapt to their students, not vice versa.

In my work with HSIs, I have found that many are unwilling to change their mission, identity, and purpose, unwilling to add terms like "HSI," "race," "racial justice," "Latinx," "antiracism," or "social justice," to their stated commitments, often driven by fear of suggested exclusion. But it's essential to grapple with how the institution's history is connected to systemic racism and coloniality of power and the various ways that history oppresses and excludes people of color within the institution. Transformed HSIs should acknowledge and apologize and redress for higher education's participation, complicity, and advancement of Black enslavement, Indigenous genocide, stolen land, and Japanese internment, to name a few historic atrocities in the United States (de Oliveira Andreotti et al., 2015). They must also reflect on contemporary policies and practices and question whether they have embodied and enacted a racialized HSI mission, identity, and purpose since meeting the federal designation requirements. Beyond the enrollment criteria, transformed HSIs can and should commit to fulfilling a mission, identity, and strategic purpose that advances equity, justice, and liberation. They should commit to equitably graduating students in a reasonable amount of time and with low debt while advancing their economic and social mobility. But for transformed HSIs that seek to abolish inequitable systems and advance a more liberatory and humanizing education, there should also be measures of liberation, or what I call "liberatory outcomes." The call for HSIs to do more than simply enroll a large percentage of Latinx students is loud, yet the guidelines and accountability are nearly nonexistent. The Transforming HSIs Framework provides structure, with the mission, identity, and strategic purpose being foundations for change.

Centering Equity and Justice in the Mission

Stated simply, "the mission of an organization defines its purpose" (Austin & Jones, 2016, p. 7). It's a philosophical commitment to what we want and ought to do while concretely stating who we serve. The mission reflects the values of the institution and creates a shared vision and sense of purpose for organizational members (Kezar & Lester, 2009). Members look to the mission to understand the priorities, values, and norms of the organization. It provides direction and urgency for the work we do and sheds light on the meaning and character of the organization. The mission also reflects the current needs and challenges of society as the institution adequately responds to the environment. It includes micro- and macro-level meaning and direction for the institution and evolves over space and time.

Contreras et al. (2008) challenged the higher education community to think about the mission of HSIs, arguing that the designation implied a special mission. They claimed that the mission is important enough to prompt institutional leaders and decision makers to "enact policies and practices, allocate resources, and take other steps to meet [the HSI] priority" (Contreras et al., 2008, p. 75). Yet when they reviewed the mission statements of 10 two-year and four-year HSIs, they found that none mentioned being an HSI in their mission statement. Instead, these institutions relied on words such as "diversity," "culture/multiculturalism," and "access" to express their commitment to serving a large percentage of Latinx and other students of color. They further searched the institutional websites for any indication of HSI designation and found that all but one had links to a page that stated that they are an HSI. Contreras et al. (2008) speculated that the mission presents an opportunity for colleges and universities to state their commitment to serving Latinx and low-income students. Andrade and Lundberg (2016) replicated the work of Contreras and colleagues with 70 Hispanic-serving community colleges (HSCCs) that had received Title V grants. They too found that none of the HSIs directly noted their HSI designations in their mission statements and instead deferred to "culture" and "access." These authors noted the complete disregard for race and ethnicity and omission of terms such as "Hispanic" and "Latinx" in the mission statements.

Malcom-Piqueux and Bensimon (2015) expanded their review to 103 HSI mission statements and still found that none talked about being an HSI. They did find, however, that some institutions mentioned being an HSI in their strategic plans and accreditation self-studies, but not many. They concluded that being an HSI did not play a prominent role in mission statements, strategic planning, or accreditation self-studies but argued that it should. They provided guidance for HSIs to consider as they revisit their mission statements, stressing that being an HSI that successfully serves and educates Latinx students is an imperative goal for society as a whole, particularly as we consider the exponential growth of this population in the United States.

Drawing from this work, I called for an HSI mission that is grounded in antiracist and antioppressive ideologies within the decolonizing HSIs framework. In this way, the mission of HSIs can support the education and liberation of all racially and ethnically minoritized people, not just Latinxs. I remain committed to this call yet am reminded that college and university missions are often laden with neoliberal ideals despite their stated commitments to diversity and inclusion (Museus & Lepeau, 2020). Transformed HSIs should focus less on neoliberal logics and more on race-conscious and equity-minded actions. This will require HSIs to center people of color in their mission and specifically name the racial-ethnic-Indigenous groups they are committed to serving. It is egregious for HSIs, designated as such because they enroll a large percentage of students of color and often receiving competitive federal funding as a result of the HSI designation, to be race-, ethnicity-, and identity-neutral within their mission statement. The HSI designation is connected to the racial-ethnic-Indigenous identity of students and should be acknowledged.

Transformed HSIs must also state their committed actions for advancing racial justice, collective liberation, and healing for the students, families, and communities they serve. In grounding the mission on equity and justice *with and for* minoritized communities, colleges and universities can avoid doing this work for self-serving, missionary, or altruistic reasons (Edwards, 2006). Acknowledging the needs of society is also necessary, as HSIs should embrace the fact that they are educating students that have been discriminated against and oppressed throughout their educational pathways; providing access to education and empowering minoritized groups can contribute to a better society and should not be understated. In preparation to change the mission, a vision statement is a good place to start, which paints a picture of what the organization wants to become in the future (Wessling, 2015). As part of the process of *becoming* an HSI, the vision statement can move the organization toward a more transformative mission in the future. Moreover, the mission alone, no matter how critical and transformative, is insufficient for moving an HSI toward full transformation, with empirical evidence suggesting that stated commitments to equity and justice within missions are often not enacted or embodied by decision makers, leaders, and educators (e.g., Aguirre & Martinez, 2002; Ahmed, 2012; Museus & Lepeau, 2020; Zerquera et al., 2017).

The neoliberal logics of higher education are manipulative because they sound ideal; transformed HSIs should be critically cautious when creating their mission. For example, institutions often commit to providing a "cutting-edge" and "world class education" by offering "high quality, rigorous, and superior" courses and programs. Transformed HSIs may instead commit to providing an education that "advances critical consciousness and an understanding of social injustices across the world." Research institutions often tout their advancement of knowledge and contributions to the scientific community. Transformed HSIs alternatively may commit to "producing knowledge that advances various forms of justice, from environmental justice for minoritized communities to criminal justice for people of color." Liberal arts colleges often express their commitment to "developing critical thinkers and global citizens"; the language, however, is often race and identity neutral. Transformed HSIs instead may seek "to develop race-conscious, antiracist critical thinkers who understand transnational social issues." Community colleges often commit to workforce development, which is an essential and historic mission. Transformed HSCCs instead may commit to "advancing a more diverse and equitable workforce that is committed to equity, justice, and liberation for the communities that students come from." Language matters, including the language used in mission and vision statements.

Enacting an Intersectional Racialized Organizational Identity

I began my HSI research journey grounded in organizational theory and specifically organizational *identity* theory. After studying identity development models in my master's program, I hypothesized that the HSI organizational identity was like the racial-ethnic identity of individuals, which requires the organization to take a journey to better understand itself, similar to the way people go on a journey to learn about their unique social identities. In reality, colleges and universities have a white racial identity, from the infrastructure to the governance and decision-making structures, everything is white normative and guided by historically white ways of being (e.g., Cabrera et al, 2017; Garcia, 2019; Patton, 2016). This does not change simply because they enroll a large percentage of students of color. The challenge to *become* an HSI beyond the enrollment of students and beyond the federal designation is an organizational identity issue. The process of *becoming* an HSI requires the institution to understand, embrace, and enact its racialized identity.

Guided by theories of organizational identity and organizational culture, I proposed the Typology of HSI Organizational Identities (Garcia, 2017). With the typology, I argued that the HSI organizational identity is enacted within an organizational *culture* that is centered on Latinx identities and ways of knowing. I extend this thinking in the Transforming HSIs Framework to include the institutional *environment* and call for an inclusion of racially and ethnically minoritized students, with their identities and ways of knowing being acknowledged and elevated. In other words, enacting an HSI identity does not have to be "exclusive to Hispanics or Latinxs"; rather, to be an HSI can include an intentional enactment of an identity that centers all students of color at the intersections of minoritized identities. In the typology I further note that an HSI organizational identity includes a focus on *outcomes*, with a call to produce equitable outcomes for Latinx students. The Transforming HSIs Framework extends this to call for the production of equitable outcomes for racially and ethnically minoritized students. This convergence of organizational *culture* with student-level *outcomes* produced the Typology of HSI Organizational Identities, with four identity types emerging: Latinx-enrolling, Latinx-producing, Latinx-enhancing, and Latinx-serving. Although the typology is not intended to be a stage-based model of organizational identity development, it does provide a framework for institutions to determine what their current identity is and what their ideal identity is, with no hierarchy of identities. In other words, all four types of HSIs are important, and institutions can move among and through these identities.

Organizational identity is best understood as a collective understanding of how members of the organization make sense of the question "Who are we as an organization?" (Albert & Whetten, 1985). For HSIs undergoing an organizational identity change, the question should be "Who are we as an organization that enrolls a predominantly Latinx and racial-ethnic-Indigenous population of students?" The extreme diversity of students *within* HSIs and *within* the "H" presupposes that the HSI organizational identity ought to embrace the intersections of identity, as students of color at HSIs are likely to also be low-income, first generation to colleges, and/or embody other minoritized identities. The question is further complicated to "Who are we as an organization that enrolls students of color *at the intersections* of multiple minoritized identities?"

The extreme diversity *among* the population of college and universities that meet the HSI eligibility also suggests that the HSI organizational identity is one of multiple organizational identities (i.e., two-year, religious, liberal arts, research, technical, etc.). HSIs should also ask, "What does it mean to be a ___ HSI?" Scholars have begun to conceptualize the intersection of multiple organizational identities (i.e., Catholic HSIs, Hispanic-serving research institutions [HSRIs,] HSCCs) stressing that institutions do not have to lose their historic identity in order to embrace an additional HSI identity. Moreover, some have begun to conceptualize the intersection of student identities with organizational identities (i.e., *Queer* HSI), although there is more work to be done here.

Garcia et al. (2021) proposed a *Catholic* HSI (C-HSI) identity maintaining that the historical mission of the 226 Catholic colleges and universities in the United States to carry out the Catholic intellectual tradition can and should align with an emerging HSI mission to serve low-income first generation to college Latinx and other students of color. They found that as of fall 2020, 14% of Catholic colleges and universities were HSI eligible and 16% were emerging HSIs, stressing that these institutions should embrace an organizational identity that is both Catholic and Latinx. Yet Catholic colleges and universities must disrupt the theopolitical, social, historical, and economic histories that have subjugated Latinxs. Moreover, the C-HSI identity ought to be race and identity conscious as well as faith based, or Catholic HSIs run the risk of upholding a white normative identity that erases and harms the people of color they seek to serve. They draw on Latinx theologies, arguing for a C-HSI identity that centers *lo cotidiano* (the daily) and traditioning, which Latinx theologians assert is part of the way that Latinxs transmit faith and commit to Christian values on a daily basis through their racialized and cultural lived experiences.

Marin and Pereschica (2017) advanced an HSRI identity, stating that a focus on the research aspect of HSIs should be distinct. With less than half of all HSIs offering graduate programs (42% of 569 HSIs in fall 2019; *Excelencia* in Education, 2021c) and even fewer being research-specific institutions conferring doctoral degrees (24% of 569 HSIs in fall 2019) the distinct identity of HSRIs is important. Marin and Pereschica (2017) interviewed graduate students at one emerging HSRI who suggested that the role of graduate students as teaching assistants and lab instructors made them natural mentors and teachers for undergraduate students at these institutions. Yet Garcia and Guzman-Alvarez (2021) found that there are disparities in the number of graduate Latinx students at HSIs compared to undergraduate Latinx students. This elevates the need for a distinct HSRI identity that includes (1) increased enrollment of Latinx graduate students, (2) increased engagement of Latinx graduate students in the HSRI identity development process, and (3) an assessment of the campus climate for Latinx graduate students. Marin (2019) extended the idea of becoming an HSRI by interviewing administrators at an emerging HSRI, who stated that the internal and external context of the university is essential to this identity. An important part of the HSRI identity is the surrounding community, with efforts to increase research-driven solutions to some of the most pressing community issues such as sustainability in food and housing production and environmental concerns affecting the local community. HSRIs should not carry out a race- or identity-neutral mission, as they are uniquely positioned for knowledge creation with and for surrounding communities of color.

Doran (in press) called for a specific HSCC identity that centers the community college function and Latinx students, yet she acknowledged that there is much work to be done to bring this identity into fruition. In fall 2019, 44% of the 569 HSIs were community colleges (*Excelencia* in Education, 2021b). Like all community colleges, HSCCs are broad-access institutions with multiple missions including (1) preparing students to transfer to four-year institutions, (2) offering development education to prepare students for college-level work, (3) preparing students for vocational jobs (often referred to as Career and Technical Education [CTE]), and (4) offering community-based courses to serve the region (Cohen & Brawer, 2008; Núñez, et al., 2015). Martinez (2020) added that HSCCs have an emerging baccalaureate-producing mission. As such, the HSCC identity and mission must include each of these functions but with a focus on students of color, low-income, immigrant, and first-generation colleges students who enroll in HSCCs at high rates (Núñez et al., 2011).

The transfer function of HSCCs is essential to the identity and mission, with Núñez et al. (2015) noting that Latinx students who successfully transferred from HSCCs to four-year institutions in comparison to those that did not transfer were more academically prepared (according to GPA and math preparation), received higher amounts of financial aid, remained continuously enrolled, had plans to transfer, and had higher degree aspirations. The developmental education function is also vital to the HSCC identity and mission, especially since Latinx and Black students have high enrollments in developmental courses at HSCCs but low completion (Felix & Fernandez Castro, 2018). Yet researchers have found that students who enroll in developmental courses at HSCCs report feeling academically invalidated in these courses, both in the initial reality of having to enroll in courses that do not count toward a degree and in interacting with faculty in these courses, who are often deficit minded (Acevedo-Gil et al., 2015; Doran, 2017, in press). The HSCC identity must include efforts to validate and empower students, with research suggesting that there are faculty and counselors at HSCCs who take time to provide feedback and care to students and serve as guides to students as they move through the community college curriculum (Acevedo-Gil et al., 2015; Alcantar & Hernandez, 2020; Doran, in press). Jimenez Hernandez (2020) also found that intrusive advising can be effective with students at an HSCC, increasing their semester-to-semester persistence.

Doran (in press) notes that there are fewer studies about Latinx students and CTE programs at HSCCs and cautions practitioners from overemphasizing this dimension in the HSCC identity and mission, as research indicated that Latinx students are less likely to gain high-skill and high-wage jobs following completion of CTE programs. The community-focused function of HSCCs is also underresearched, yet Doran states that HSCCs have the ability to respond to changing regional workforce needs and should continue to think about this dimension of their identity and mission. Of final note, Doran suggests that HSCCs keep financial considerations at the forefront of their work with Latinx students, as affordability is a key reason why students choose the community college postsecondary pathway.

Intersecting Student and Organizational Identities

Cataño and González (2021; González & Cataño, 2020) advocated for a *queer* HSI (Q-HSI) identity that considers the sexual orientation and gender identity of LGBTQ+ students at HSIs. Their work to conceptualize a Q-HSI identity has mostly been within the context of community colleges, yet four-year institutions should also consider their queer organizational identity. Of importance they note that LGBTQ+ Latinxs experience high rates of violence, depression, and attempted suicide both on and off campus, are often unable to find adequate mental and physical health support on campus, and continue to be invisible on campus. In conducting an environmental scan of 14 HSCCs in California, they found that only one had a queer student resource center and none had a Latinx resource center. In reviewing the HSI grants for these institutions they discovered that proposed support for these students was mostly academic, with little concern for the intersectional identities of the students. In conducting a critical policy analysis at two HSCCs, they also found a higher number of noninclusive language references about LGBTQ+ Latinxs. Across these two studies, they proposed seven dimensions to consider in the process of queering the HSI identity: (1) include intersectional LGBTQ+ Latinx initiatives in HSI grant initiatives; (2) hire LGBTQ+ Latinx staff and leaders on campus; (3) align campus, district, and state initiatives around servingness with efforts to serve LGBTQ+ Latinx; (4) increase training and development for professionals on campus about what it means to serve LGBTQ+ Latinx students; (5) add identity-specific outcomes for LGBTQ+ Latinxs; (6) increase budget allocation for LGBTQ+ Latinx initiatives; and (7) collect LGBTQ+ Latinx data for better decision-making.

Jones and Sáenz (2020) called for a Latino male–serving HSI identity (LMS-HSI), drawing on their work with Latino male initiatives within HSCCs. This is a notable organizational identity considering the persistent educational attainment gaps by gender from high school graduation through enrollment in graduate programs (Sáenz et al., 2016). Núñez et al. (2011) also found that Latino men were more likely to enroll in HSCCs than non-HSCCs. In addition to acknowledging the dangers of overemphasizing outcomes in the HSI identity due to the racialized nature of these normative measures, Jones and Sáenz (2020) contend that an LMS-HSI must center gender and draw on critical theories about gender expectations, roles, and masculine ideologies. In accessing data from three HSCCs and 72 participants within these sites, they conceptualized an LMS-HSI identity that is embedded in the culture and practices of the institution and reflected in equitable outcomes for Latino men. Importantly, participants stressed the need for data-driven decision-making that disaggregates multiple types of outcomes by race, ethnicity, and gender. They also talked about the need for a college-wide commitment to the success of Latino men, which includes disrupting deficit thinking and shifting toward a culture that celebrates and encourages Latino men while enhancing their academic self-concept and efficacy. The authors also envisioned an approach to serving Latino men across the educational pipeline by building partnerships that would enhance their college going and access.

Although other scholars have not fully conceptualized the intersection of student identities with the HSI organizational identity, the possibilities are unlimited, with each transformed HSI needing to address the specific needs of its students. For example, transformed HSIs may explore what it means to be a Chicana HSI, Afro HSI, Indigenous HSI, Boricua HSI, or Fronterizo HSI. Elevating the intersectional identities of students as part of an HSI organizational identity is necessary for full justice, liberation, joy, and healing for minoritized students.

Conceptualizing Justice and Liberation as Strategic Purpose

Colleges and universities develop and implement strategic plans, usually every five years, to determine the measurable ways that they will move toward fulfilling their purpose. Strategic planning is a process that institutions of higher education adopted from corporations as a result of the accountability and assessment movement of the 1980s (Hinton, 2012). The adoption of strategic planning has become common for colleges and universities, with institutions developing a set of goals and objectives and an implementation plan based on their mission, values, and vision statements. There is typically a planning process inclusive of organizational members who develop assessment metrics and outcomes used to determine how the goals and objectives will be met (Hinton, 2012). The strategic plan is an ideal place to operationalize the institution's commitment to an HSI mission and identity grounded in equity and justice while conceptualizing a race- and identity-centered strategic purpose. Although some HSIs have begun to include their plans to enact their HSI mission and identity in practice, most have not (Flores & Leal, 2020; Malcom-Piqueux & Bensimon, 2015). Moreover, most HSIs have not considered their distinct mission, identity, and purpose within their accreditation self-studies (Fernandez & Burnett, 2020; Malcom-Piqueux & Bensimon, 2015).

The strategic purpose should be documented in the institution's strategic plan and should include measurable ways the institution will fulfill its mission and enact its identity as a transformed HSIs. In this section I talk about "indicators of serving" students that can be used to assess the strategic purpose of a transformed HSI. Garcia et al. (2019) argued that the most measurable way to assess serving-ness is with academic outcomes, nonacademic outcomes, validating experiences, and racialized experiences. I extend that thinking to talk about *equitable academic outcomes, liberatory outcomes,* and *validating experiences.* I also talk about creating an *institutional environment that is free of racism, microaggressions, and discrimination.* Overall, the strategic purpose should drive institutional actions and be well articulated within the strategic plan for each of these measures.

Educational Purpose: Equitable Academic Outcomes

Academic outcomes such as persistence, graduation, and degree attainment are what I call "normative outcomes." I use the term "normative" because they are essentially made "normal" or "normalized" by the general public. Normative academic outcomes are also legitimized by federal and state governments, accreditation boards, policy intermediaries, and the Department of Education, as they hold postsecondary institutions accountable for delivering these normative outcomes (Espinosa et al., 2014). Beyond these normative academic outcomes, institutions of higher education are also pressured to deliver *neoliberal outcomes* such as upward mobility, workforce development, and the ability to pay back debt, thus reducing the government's social commitment to its people and elevating the economic viability and capitalist foundations of the country (Jankowski & Provezis, 2014).

Yet institutions of higher education have historically delivered both academic and neoliberal outcomes inequitably to students of color. Black students exhibit the lowest persistence and completion rates of all groups, and when they do graduate, they have the highest debt, have the highest unemployment rates, and earn less than other college graduates in their cohort (Espinosa et al., 2019). Indigenous students, including American Indians, Alaska Natives, and Native Hawaiians, also have inequitable academic and neoliberal outcomes, although the data are inconsistent (Espinosa et al., 2019). Latinx students are showing hopeful outcomes, with six-year completion rates (150% completion rates) higher than Black and Indigenous students, but they are still completing degrees at lower rates than white students (Espinosa et al., 2019).

The educational purpose of transformed HSIs will require a stated focus on advancing equitable academic outcomes for students of color at the intersections of minoritized identities. By definition, HSIs are required to address the long-term educational inequities of students with federal grants earmarked for HSIs, calling on them to expand educational opportunities and improve degree attainment of Latinx students (US Dept of Education, 2022). Transformed HSIs must commit to redesigning the infrastructure of the institution in order to produce equitable academic outcomes including GPA, DFW rates, course completion, semester-to-semester persistence, 150% graduation rate, associate's and bachelor's degree attainment, successful transfer from two-year to four-year institution, and STEM degree completion (Garcia et al., 2019). Desired academic outcomes should be stated in the strategic plan for the institution and ought to be specific to the historical mission of the institution (e.g., HSCCs desire to increase equitable transfer rates).

For transformed HSIs pursuing racial equity as part of their mission, the specific minoritized groups must be named in the strategic plan. This will require the use of disaggregated data to first identify inequities and then name the goals and objectives for addressing these inequities (Bensimon, 2007, 2012). At minimum, data should be disaggregated by race and ethnicity to reveal inequities by racial-ethnic groups. For transformed HSIs, income or Pell Grant status should also be important forms of disaggregation, since HSIs, by definition, are supposed to serve low-income students. Paredes et al. (2021) found that when they compared 150% graduation rates for all Latinxs in the University of California system to those who are Latinx, first generation to college, and Pell recipients, the rates were slightly lower for those with multiple minoritized identities (first generation and low income). As noted by Bensimon (2012), advancing racial equity in academic outcomes will require educators and decision makers to acknowledge that inequities are the result of failed institutional policies and practices and not the result of students' characteristics, backgrounds, effort, and motivation. As such, disaggregated data must be used to identify inequities and goals for addressing them, but this process must be done through the lenses of race-consciousness and equity-mindedness in order to disrupt deficit thinking about student achievement in the strategic planning process. Identifying inequities in academic outcomes is important, but educators and decision makers must be trained to ask questions about the socio-historic factors that have affected students of color's educational experiences, including their preparation for college and the structural factors that are hindering their success (Bensimon, 2007, 2012).

Job attainment and upward mobility, or the ability of college graduates to have stronger economic futures than their parents, is recognized as an important indicator of serving, with HSIs shown to be effective at advancing the social mobility of their students (Espinosa et al., 2018). Yet this is arguably an individual benefit grounded in neoliberal ideals. Transformed HSIs must acknowledge that individual upward mobility of Latinx, Black, Indigenous, Asian American, Pacific Islander, and Mixed-Race students may also lead to greater economic mobility for their families and communities and make this a part of the strategic goals. Transformed HSIs should seek to enhance academic outcomes that also advance collective liberation and healing for students and their families and communities. For example, an HSI in central or northern California may partner with organizations supporting migrant communities in the Central Valley as well as corporations in Silicon Valley as part of their workforce development goals. Workforce development must not be viewed through the eyes of the corporations and business but rather from the perspective of students who may want to give back to their communities while also fulfilling their upward mobility and advancing their economic futures. In other words, transformed HSIs should support students' upward mobility while also supporting their desires to contribute to the local job market and invest in their home communities.

Social Justice Purpose: Liberatory Outcomes

The purpose of this book is to advance a social justice purpose and liberatory approach to education at transformed HSIs. By definition, the federal government never imagined that HSIs would become spaces of justice and liberation (that's my freedom dream, not theirs). As a scholar who believes in socially just approaches to education, I think they should become spaces of racial justice, healing, joy, and liberation. Transformed HSIs must commit to redesigning the infrastructure of the institution in order to produce liberatory outcomes in addition to equitable academic outcomes. Garcia et al. (2019) argued that nonacademic outcomes are important indicators of serving, including outcomes that scholars have found to be enhanced within HSIs: academic self-concept (Cuellar, 2014), social agency (Cuellar, 2015), racial identity development (Garcia et al., 2018; Guardia & Evans, 2008), civic engagement (Garcia & Cuellar, 2018), and leadership (Onorato & Musoba, 2015).

In thinking about how best to measure justice and liberation for minoritized students, I argue for liberatory outcomes to become essential indicators of servingness within transformed HSIs. Guided by Freirean (2018) ideologies about liberatory education, including the development of students' civic mindedness, democratic participation, and community engagement, liberatory outcomes for students are the measurable ways to assess learning and engagement in curricular and cocurricular experiences that enhance a critical understanding of the world. Liberatory outcomes necessarily include racial-ethnic-Indigenous identity development as well as development of intersectional identities, such as jotería identity (Tijerina Revilla & Santillana, 2014). These outcomes presuppose that students of color with multiple minoritized identities enter the institution not having had the opportunity to explore their racial-ethnic-Indigenous identity or other intersectional identities in formal educational settings and, even further, may hold internalized notions about who they are as racialized and minoritized individuals (Camacho Parra, 2012; Salazar, 2013). Research has shown that college students can and often do explore their racial-ethnic-Indigenous identity while in college, with many contexts contributing to their development, including courses, student organizations, the internal and external college environment, and critical incidents such as experiences with racism and discrimination (e.g., Garcia et al., 2018; Guardia & Evans, 2008; Keeton, 2002; Keeton et al., 2021; Torres & Hernández, 2007; Torres et al., 2019).

Liberatory outcomes also include antiracist orientation, social justice orientation, critical consciousness, political participation, civic engagement, and social activism, all of which are important indicators of serving and all of which can be measured (Garcia, 2021). Keeton and colleagues (Keeton, 2002; Keeton et al., 2021) further contend that racial-ethnic-identity development is often connected to the development of other proposed liberatory outcomes, including critical consciousness, social justice orientation, and social activism. Cuellar et al. (2017) also suggest that liberatory outcomes, or what they termed "empowering outcomes," for students at HSIs should include positive academic self-concept and aspirations for graduate school. These are grounded in humanizing educational practices, as students of color are too often told they are not capable of academically succeeding in college and beyond (e.g., Conchas & Acevedo, 2020; Means et al., 2019; Salazar, 2013). Transformed HSIs must engage in asset-based language that empowers students. A less explored liberatory outcome in HSI research that is becoming more relevant is the need to ensure the mental and emotional health of students of color as a form of liberation and humanization.

Importantly, these liberatory outcomes should be included in the strategic plan and connected to the infrastructure in order to conceptualize how the curriculum, cocurriculum, support services, and physical infrastructure elevate a humanizing and liberatory education. Liberatory student-level outcomes can be named and prioritized within the strategic plan, as well as organizational- and community-based outcomes (Garcia, 2021). Organizational outcomes may include more direct work with and for social justice, which can include the pursuit of external funds intended to advance justice, empowerment, and liberation. Many foundations such as the Ford Foundation, W. K. Kellogg Foundation, David and Lucile Packard Foundation, Bill and Melinda Gates Foundation, William T. Grant Foundation, and Spencer Foundation have turned a focus on identity-based and social justice funding with a commitment to racial justice, educational equity, access to health care, environmental justice, reproductive rights, and training future scientists of color (Foundation Center, 2009).

A commitment to addressing issues in the local community should also be a part of the strategic purpose of transformed HSIs. For example, HSIs may be situated in communities facing extreme environmental conditions, food deserts, housing and homelessness, and crises such as water and contamination, which often affect low-income communities. Transformed HSIs, within their strategic purpose, must commit to graduating students with the tools necessary to work toward justice around issues faced by communities of color and low-income communities, including poverty, homelessness, joblessness, lack of access to health care, and inadequate water and food sources. Important community and societal outcomes may also be connected to language, with a growing need to graduate multilingual students who enter professions that are community facing such as law, health care, social work, education, and more. Some HSIs, such as the University of Texas at El Paso, have begun doing this work, recognizing the problem of patient-provider language discordance in health care (Summer et al., 2017). They have addressed this problem by incorporating Spanish language into the introductory curricula in pharmacy, physical therapy, and speech-language pathology (Summer et al., 2017). These types of efforts can in fact advance students' liberatory outcomes (advancing translingual development within the professions) and community-based liberatory outcomes (a growing number of professionals with advanced multilingual skills).

Humanizing Purpose: Equitable Experiences

A final dimension of the purpose that should be thoroughly conceptualized in the strategic plan of transformed HSIs is the organizational culture and environmental climate that fulfills a humanizing purpose. It's not enough to produce equitable academic and liberatory outcomes; transformed HSIs must also provide equitable and humanizing experiences for all its members. Garcia et al. (2019) argued that validating experiences are important indicators of serving at HSIs and stated strongly that racialized experiences are indicators of *not* serving. In other words, if members of the organization experience racism, discrimination, harassment, or microaggressions on campus, then the organization has not fulfilled its purpose as a liberatory and humanizing space. Experiences are a direct reflection of the organizational culture and environmental climate, which must become a part of the strategic plan, stated as intentional actions to disrupt a racialized and discriminatory culture and create a humanizing and validating environment.

The persistence of racialized and oppressive experiences at HSIs has been well documented and cannot be ignored. Cuellar and Johnson-Ahorlu (2016) found that Asians and Asian Americans reported the highest level of experiences with discrimination and bias on a campus climate survey compared to Latinx and white students at one HSCC in the western United States. Yet when they interviewed participants, Latinx students described an unwelcoming campus climate, stating that there were spaces on campus where they had witnessed staff members ignoring Latinx students, specifically Spanish-speaking students who staff members claimed they could not help due to their own language barrier. Latinx students also felt discriminated against for certain jobs on campus, including the computer center and the cafeteria, where they stated that a majority of the student workers were not Latinx. These findings suggest that there is a greater need to address campus climate issues outside of the classroom and within student support programs where students described the most negative and racialized experiences. Of note, classified staff must be a part of the strategic purpose and the collective effort to support and serve students of color at an HSI.

Sanchez (2019) described the racialized experiences of Latinx students at three types of HSIs, including a high Latinx-enrolling HSI, an HSI with nearly half the population identifying as Latinx, and an emerging HSI. Although there were fewer instances reported at HSIs with higher numbers of Latinx students, students at each type either experienced firsthand microaggressions or witnessed them. Examples included stereotypes about Latinxs not being born in the United States and having family members in drug cartels. Students also described deficit views held by perpetrators, including suggestions that Latinx students were admitted because of affirmative action and perceptions that Latinx students are not as smart as white students. Some participants also noted their experiences with segregation on campus, oftentimes unexplained and intentional, with students and faculty creating separation between white students and students of color. Participants shared that faculty, staff, and students were all perpetrators of microaggressions, and although most of the time it was white people, there were reported instances of Latinx people committing the microaggressions. This suggests that within the strategic purpose, there must be intentional actions to address racialized incidents, including training all members to notice and disrupt microaggressions.

Latinx students at one emerging four-year HSI in the Southwest described in detail the various ways that they heard deficit views of Latinxs and experienced microaggressions and racialized aggressions. Importantly, Cuellar and Johnson-Ahorlu (2020) distinguished between racialized experiences outside of the university and within, noting that some students talked about their junior high and high school experiences as well as those within their local communities and their places of employment. Participants in their study talked about teachers, community members, and supervisors who questioned their ability to succeed in education and work because of their dark skin (race), their language (Spanish), and their overall academic abilities. They stated that the deficit views and racialized experiences sometimes played out on campus too but often in less severe ways. This is hopeful, suggesting that emerging HSIs and HSIs are taking steps to disrupt deficit narratives and racialized experiences on campus, but they still have a long way to go. One student described her frustration with the campus's inability to understand Latinxs beyond Mexicans, while another talked about her experience being falsely accused by white students of stealing and receiving little support from staff on campus. Importantly, these findings show that the strategic purpose also requires deliberate plans for disrupting racism and oppression that students experience outside of campus.

Serrano (2020) found that Black and Latino men experience the racial climate in unique ways at a four-year HSI in California. Within the large campus environment, Latino men felt a positive sense of belonging, since they are part of the largest racial-ethnic population on campus, while Black men said they felt isolated, as they were mostly surrounded by non-Black people of color. They critiqued the idea of "diversity" at an HSI, stressing that having a majority Latinx population (58.4%) does not make the campus diverse. Within smaller microclimates, however, Latino men and Black men equally shared frustrations with the persistence of microaggressions such as having to speak on behalf of their entire communities, since they often found themselves to be the "only one" in their classes. Specifically, they referred to the classroom as a space where they experienced microaggressions and talked about how they did not have any faculty of color in classes outside of ethnic studies (Serrano, 2020). These findings support the idea of developing a distinct HSI identity and strategic purpose that considers the race and ethnicity, as well as the sex and gender of students at HSIs.

Abrica et al. (2020) similarly found that Black men had negative racialized experiences at a two-year HSCC. The 15 men in their study experienced forms of anti-Blackness that were distinct from racism and racial microaggressions. Participants described how their Black intellect had been rejected, questioned, and appropriated. One engineering major said that his peers accused him of cheating because he got the highest grades in class, while a computer science major said that a white student copied his essay after he specifically asked him not to. Other participants described their feelings of invisibility and simultaneous hypervisibility as often the only Black man in classes who is never called on or included in peer groups. Participants also talked about the anti-BLM and simultaneous anti-Black violence they saw on campus, with BLM posters being defaced with words like "all lives matter" and posters of Black boys and men such as Mike Brown and Trayvon Martin being torn down altogether. These studies highlight the importance of assessing the racial climate and documenting the experiences of Black students on campus and intentionally naming the need to disrupt racism and anti-Blackness toward Black students at HSIs within the strategic purpose. This includes specifically documenting and addressing the needs of Afro-Latinx students at HSIs in the strategic purpose.

Desai and Abeita (2017) centered the experience of one Native American woman, Joy, who identifies as Diné (Navajo) and who grew up on the Navajo reservation before attending one four-year HSI in the Southwest. She was a student activist on campus who focused on Native American issues and social justice. Her experiences on campus were influenced by her experiences off campus and specifically by her growing up within a liminal space as a member of a racialized group subjected to problematic federal policies such as the blood quantum requirement and continual violence as part of settler colonial logics. Within the institution, she described institutional microaggressions that marginalize Native American students, including the university seal that depicts a negative portrayal of "a 'rifle-toting' frontiersman and a 'sword-carrying' conquistador" (Desai & Abeita, 2017, p. 282). Joy also talked about the commodification and exploitation of native culture that the university enacted by displaying traditional objects such as totem poles, drums, and dolls that are sacred and ceremonial. Joy also described murals on campus that reinforce racist perceptions of white people (settlers) as doctors and scientists and Native Americans and people of color as farmers and laborers. The importance of this article is that it specifically describes institutional microaggressions toward Native Americans that are inappropriate for transformed HSIs.

Kovats Sánchez (2021) shared testimonios of Indigenous Ñuu Savi, Bene Xhon, and Nahua students with direct ties to the Mexican states of Oaxaca and Guerrero attending HSIs in California. She found that although students felt somewhat validated when they saw course offerings about pre-Columbian Ñuu Savi and Mesoamerican Oaxaca, they felt microinvalidated and invisible as the focus of these courses were solely on pre-Columbian history. In other words, they felt like their identities were seen as distinctly historical or past tense with little effort to elevate their present-day voices. They also felt invalidated in Latinx- and Chicanx-centered spaces, which also excluded present-day Indigenous experiences while elevating a mestizo (mixed Spanish and Indigenous) narrative. Students described their interactions with other students on campus who had a romanticized understanding of Indigenous identity, which further created feelings of invalidation. One participant described her frustration and anger with the self-proclaimed and proud Latinx-serving institution that had a problematic Indigenous mascot that brought pain and dishonor to her Indigenous identity. Transformed HSIs must take a critical approach to addressing and dismantling racism, discrimination, microaggressions and, importantly, anti-Indigeneity in their strategic purpose. A "proud HSI" simply cannot reinforce false narratives about Indigenous communities.

This well-documented empirical research reinforces the need for transformed HSIs to disrupt the historical and oppressive environment and to create validating and empowering experiences. These experiences include interactions with same-race-ethnicity peers, cultural validation, Spanish-speaking peers and educators, and mentoring and support groups (Garcia et al., 2019). Validating experiences at transformed HSIs must combat the negative interactions with peers and educators, cultural invalidation, microaggressions, and deficit thinking about students at HSIs. The need for more validating experience stems from validation theory, developed by Rendon (1994), who has been arguing for the disruption of a college environment not adequately designed for students with minoritized identities since before HSIs were formerly recognized. She argues that validation consists of six dimensions: (1) confirming and supportive processes both in and out of the classroom that are created by educators; (2) students' feeling of self-worth and academic ability; (3) validation as a prerequisite to student development; (4) validation from many sources, including educators, administrators, families, partners, and classmates; (5) validation as a development process; and (6) validation being most effective when offered early in the college career (Rendon, 1994). Transformed HSIs must provide these types of validating experiences with an intentional effort to center students racial-ethnic-Indigenous identities and other social identities in the process, and it must be stated in the strategic plan for the institution.

There is plenty of HSI research that demonstrates these validating experiences. Cuellar and Johnson-Ahorlu (2020) found that students' positive interactions with faculty and administrators at their emerging HSCC combatted some of the deficit views they had heard throughout their educational careers prior to college. Students shared that faculty were genuinely concerned with their well-being and found ways to learn with them. They said the campus was inviting and supportive, and one student described an administrator on campus who encouraged him to get involved in leadership opportunities and nominated him for an award as a result of his involvement. Similarly, students at another HSCC with a predominantly Black, Latinx, and Afro-Latinx population described numerous examples of faculty and staff who validated them both in and out of the classroom (Alcantar & Hernandez, 2020). In the classroom, faculty cultivated their academic and linguistic abilities. Faculty said things like "I see potential in your future" and used students' work as an exemplar for other students to learn with, which increased students' academic self-concept (Alcantar & Hernandez, 2020, p. 7). The students also talked about interpersonal validation, with faculty being genuinely concerned about their personal and family lives. Others said faculty continued to care about them even after they completed the course and helped them navigate other educational experiences such as transferring. Garcia (2016a) talked to students at an HSI in the Southwest who said they felt culturally validated in the classroom simply because their professors looked like them and had similar cultural and racial-ethnic backgrounds and experiences. Faculty brought those experiences into the classroom, from food and music to the Spanish language, as ways to connect with and validate students as racialized and cultural beings. As part of the strategic purpose, these types of validating experiences must become the norm at transformed HSIs.

Conclusion

Transformed HSIs can become spaces of liberation and justice, starting with the mission, identity, and purpose. This will require an approach to education that abolishes the white normative structures that continue to re-create exclusion and that rebuilds the institution as guided by equity, justice, liberation, solidarity, love, joy, and healing. The process of becoming a transformed HSI must start with the mission, identity, and strategic purpose; however, statements about who we are and what we value should not be philosophical in nature. Instead, they should be objective and actionable. This includes an intentional focus in the campus strategic plan about how to move the institution toward the goals of equity, justice, and liberation. Decision makers and leaders must scrutinize their budgets as part of the strategic planning process, determine how to distribute financial resources to support their transformed HSIs mission and purpose, empower those who are already doing racial equity and justice work, and provide incentives to those educators, decision makers, and students most committed to the mission, identity, and purpose. The redistribution of resources and power within the institution is necessary for racialized organizations seeking to advance equitable educational outcomes, liberatory and humanizing experiences, and complete validation of the students, families, and communities they serve.

3

Extending and Complicating
Membership

MEMBERSHIP IS AN ESSENTIAL ORGANIZATIONAL DIMENSION in
the Transforming HSIs Framework. HSIs came into existence as a result of the compositional diversity of the undergraduate members,
yet in early conversations about the HSI designation, there was no
mention of other members. By focusing solely on undergraduate students in the definition, the federal government's HSI competitive
grant processes have been centered on the educational success of
students, with no accountability for addressing the institutional
membership beyond the students. In seeking to decredential whiteness, redistribute resources and power, and empower people of
color, within the transformed HSIs framework I extend membership to include educators (faculty and staff) and decision makers
(administrators and trustees), as well as graduate students and families. I call on all members to commit to advancing social justice and
collective liberation within the institution and in the community,
with educators and decision makers responsible for carrying out the
mission, identity, and strategic purpose of the organization. These
members also lead and govern the institution and create the infrastructures that enhance servingness.

The HSI definition also fails to account for membership beyond the federal government's reified definition of "Hispanic." The term "Hispanic" rose to prominence in the United States between the 1960s and the 1980s as Latinx political activists advocated for a panethnic label that would capture the political, social, health, and educational needs of a growing population that was in some ways similar based on historic roots, language, and culture, but quite different by region, diasporic experiences, language, race, phenotype, and overall needs as subethnic communities (Mora, 2014). The federal government and media also had interests in categorizing this group as its political influence and economic power rose. By 1980, after multiple attempts to develop an inclusive panethnic category, the Census Bureau solidified the "Hispanic" category, despite its major flaws, mainly that it was tied to the notion of "Hispano," which had been embraced by self-proclaimed descendants of Spanish people (colonizers) who wanted to distance themselves from their Indigenous and African roots (Mora, 2014). Hispanos also wanted to distance themselves from poor and undocumented people. The term "Hispanic," therefore, has always been exclusionary, particularly for Latinx people who don't speak Spanish, identify as Afro-Latinx, and/or are members of Indigenous groups across Mexico, Latin America, and the Caribbean.

To many, the term "Hispanic-Serving Institution," is also exclusionary, and in many ways HSIs have excluded most minoritized groups in their efforts to define servingness. I contend that the term "HSI" and all efforts to enact this identity should not be exclusionary. Alternatively, I advance a liberatory agenda with regard to HSI enactment, calling for HSIs to disrupt whiteness and moves toward innocence in order become racially just organizations as part of their HSI grant implementation efforts (Petrov & Garcia, 2021). Transformed HSIs must make a concerted effort to reconcile all forms of exclusion within their definition of membership. As a political construct backed by the Higher Education Act, the term "HSI" may not change, but as a social construct, the meaning making attached to the term can be defined by the students, families, educators, and decision makers shaping the HSI identity. In other words, transformed HSIs can use the acronym and apply for federal funding as a result of this designation while also attaching deeper meaning to this identity as they implement their federally funded grants (e.g., "HSI: Racially Just Institution"). Rather than assuming that "Hispanic-serving" implies "Hispanic-only," the term "HSI" must become a construct that allows members to embrace and enact a racialized identity, organizational mission, and strategic purpose that ensures that all people of color with multiple minoritized identities are equitably educated, served, and empowered within the institution.

The diversity within the "H" must be complicated and the exclusion within the "H" must be reconciled. To this point, much of the research and practice has elevated a Mexican American or Chicanx centered agenda. An antiessentialist approach to servingness is necessary, which will require transformed HSIs to reject a monolithic, simplistic definition of "Hispanic" or "Latinx" that erases and disregards the experiences of those outside a reified understanding of these terms and instead centers the complexities of intergroup experiences (Haywood, 2017a). Transformed HSIs must also grapple with the omission of other racial-ethnic-Indigenous groups on campus that do not fall under the "H," including Black, Indigenous, Asian American, and Pacific Islander people. Membership should acknowledge all minoritized racial, ethnic, and social identities in a way that acknowledges the intersectionality of identities present within the institution.

This includes but is not limited to racial-ethnic-Indigenous people who may also be low income, undocumented, mixed status, Trans*, nonbinary, queer, dis/abled, multilingual, and non-Christian. A focus on intersectionality here requires a deeper analysis of the ways that people with multiple minoritized identities experience exclusion and inequitable outcomes as a result of systems of oppression and dynamics of power that prevent them from achieving liberation and justice within institutions that were never for them (Núñez, 2014). Liberation in this sense is interconnected and intertwined among multiple groups within the organization. True solidarity and justice require an understanding that not all racially and ethnically minoritized people experience the same struggles, as extreme differences lie at the intersections of race, class, sex, gender, sexual orientation, immigration status, religion, spirituality, and ability (Kendall, 2020). These intersections lead to great inequities in the fulfillment of basic needs such as livable wages, food, and housing, as well as access to health care, education, and legal representation.

Extending Membership beyond Undergraduate Students

A majority of HSI research has highlighted the lack of racial-ethnic-Indigenous diversity among educators and decision makers within HSIs, stressing the need to increase the number of Latinx and other racially and ethnically minoritized groups that work in HSIs. Although I agree that transformed HSIs should diversify the racial-ethnic-Indigenous composition of faculty, staff, administrators, and trustees, they must acknowledge that the agency of people of color in racialized organizations is often diminished (Ray, 2019) and instead seek to empower Latinx, Black, Indigenous, Asian American, Pacific Islander, and Mixed-Race educators and decision makers. Moreover, all members should commit to the principles of racial equity, social justice, and collective liberation, as being a person of color does not ensure this commitment.

Transformed HSIs should start by documenting their own racial-ethnic-Indigenous disparities among all members of the institution before taking action to address these disparities. Since the HSI designation is achieved with the enrollment of 25% or more Latinx (and 50% or more low-income) undergraduate students, a majority of the compositional diversity in HSIs is seen only at the undergraduate level. Across four-year public, two-year public, and two-year private HSIs, white students only represent about 25% of the population, while Latinx students represent nearly 50%, with Black and Asian students embodying another 17% (9% and 8%, respectively) (Espinosa et al., 2019). Moreover, four-year private HSIs enroll even greater percentages of Latinx students, 65%, compared to white (17.3%) and Black students (6.6%). HSIs are arguably the most racially and ethnically diverse institutions in the United States at the *undergraduate level*.

Beyond racial-ethnic-Indigenous diversity, HSIs also enroll a higher percentage of low-income students, first- and second-generation immigrant students, and nonnative English speakers (Núñez & Bowers, 2011). Less is documented about the enrollment of undergraduate students of color with intersectional identities such as those with dis/abilities, those who identify as Trans*, nonbinary, or queer, and those from minoritized religious groups. These and other social identities must be accounted for, as well as groups that are increasing in number in HSIs, including former foster youth, formerly incarcerated people, and parenting students. HSIs ought to document the diversity of the student body across intersectional identity groups and see them as essential members of the organization working toward collective liberation and healing.

Graduate Students at HSIs

The compositional diversity at HSIs typically stops at the undergraduate level, with research showing that the number of Latinx students enrolling in graduate programs at HSIs between 2005 and 2015 was modest at best, and in some cases flat, while the enrollment of Latinx undergraduates in HSI soared in the same time period (Garcia & Guzman-Alvarez, 2021). The difference between the percentage of Latinx undergraduates enrolling in HSIs and Latinx graduates enrolling in HSIs increased significantly over the 10-year period, showing swelling inequities between the two groups. These inequities were most pronounced at Hispanic-serving *research* institutions, which is alarming, since they have the greatest potential for increasing pathways of educators and decision makers of color into HSIs.

Graduate students are important members, serving as teaching assistants, lab assistants, and mentors to undergraduate students at their institutions (Marin & Pereschica, 2017). Gonzalez et al. (2020) found that graduate students saw their role as mentors to undergraduates at HSIs as essential, especially at large HSIs, where undergraduate students can easily get lost. Marin and Pereschica (2017) discovered that graduate students wanted to be engaged in the process of becoming an HSI, yet they recognized that they needed to learn more about what it means to be an HSI beyond the enrollment criteria. Outside of these few studies, there is little empirical evidence of diversity in other forms at the graduate level. Transformed HSIs must acknowledge that graduate students are important members of the institution, actively seeking to increase the enrollment of graduate students of color with multiple minoritized identities and engaging them in the HSI meaning-making process.

Faculty at HSIs

Faculty diversity at HSIs is also insufficient, with numerous scholars highlighting the extreme disparities between faculty of color at HSIs and students of color at HSIs (Contreras, 2017; Gonzales, 2015; Santos & Acevedo-Gil, 2013; Vargas et al., 2019). Vargas and colleagues reported that at HSIs that were awarded Title V Developing HSI grants between 2009 and 2016 ($N = 167$), on average, 67% of tenured or tenure-track faculty were white, 14% Latinx, 5% Black, and 8% Asian American. There wasn't much variation by institutional type, except at private HSIs, where 75% identified as white and 10% as Latinx. This is an important distinction, since private HSIs, on average, enroll a greater percentage of Latinx students (Espinosa et al., 2019). The size of the undergraduate population must also be accounted for when thinking about the percentage differentials of tenured and tenure-track faculty. In comparing the co-ethnoracial student to faculty ratios, Vargas et al. (2019) documented that the Latinx student to Latinx faculty ratio at HSIs awarded Title V grants was 146:1, while the white faculty to white student ratio was 10:1. At private HSIs it was much higher at 264:1. These data suggest that there is a dire need to increase faculty of color at HSIs, especially Latinx faculty.

Diverse faculty members are essential at HSIs for a number of reasons. Latinx students want to see themselves in the faculty at HSIs, as it is motivating to see successful Latinxs with terminal degrees on a daily basis (Gonzalez et al., 2020). Moreover, Latinx students at HSIs feel like they can relate to Latinx faculty, personally, culturally, and linguistically (Garcia, 2016a; Gonzalez et al., 2020; Guardia & Evans, 2008). Yet with so few Latinx faculty at HSIs, opportunities for meaningful connections are often missed, especially in areas such as STEM where there are even fewer (or no) Latinx faculty (Contreras Aguirre et al., 2020). Diverse faculty teaching at HSIs are also more likely to develop pedagogical skills that recognize the unique ways of knowing and being that students at HSIs bring to the institution. For example, the writing composition faculty at New Jersey City University ask students in a developmental writing course to write translingual autoethnographies that allow them to interrogate privileged forms of English while encouraging them to use multiple languages in their writing (Corcoran & Wilkinson, 2019). The need for transformed HSIs to change the faculty composition cannot be understated, yet they must also hire faculty who can enact socially just, culturally relevant, liberatory, and humanizing curriculum and pedagogy (see chapter 4).

Staff and Administrators at HSIs

Data suggest that Latinx representation among staff and administration is also inequitable at HSIs. Hurtado and Ruiz Alvarado (2015) reported that in 2006–7, 36.9% of people in executive/administration and managerial positions in HSIs identified as Latinx, compared to 53.4% of students who identified as Latinx. Moreover, 43.4% of other professional staff positions in HSIs identified as Latinx. These statistics suggest that there is a slightly greater number of Latinxs in staff and administrative positions at HSIs than Latinx faculty, although there is great range at individual institutions. In fall 2009, for example, 22.37% of people in executive/administration and managerial positions at California State University, San Bernardino, identified as Latinx, compared to 58.23% of first-time full Latinx undergraduates (Santos & Acevedo-Gil, 2013). Similarly, in fall 2013 Latinxs represented only 11% of the administration, compared to 27% of Latinx undergraduates at one small private HSI in the Midwest (Garcia, 2019). Staff and administrators of color at HSIs are critical, as they have the power to serve as institutional agents and grassroots leaders who utilize applied critical leadership, Latino educational leadership, and decolonizing leadership practices to enact change with and for minoritized students (see chapter 5). Transformed HSIs must increase the compositional diversity of staff and administrators who are also committed to the HSI identity, mission, and strategic purpose and who are race-conscious, socially just, and antiracist in their decision-making.

Governing Boards at HSIs

Very little has been written about the membership of governing boards at HSIs, despite the fact that governing boards have a high level of decision-making power, including hiring, advising, and assessing university presidents, upholding the institutional mission, providing strategic direction for institutions, and determining policies that affect students (Association of Governing Boards [AGB], 2010; Kezar, 2006). Research has shown that governing boards at Historically Black Colleges and Universities (HBCUs) have a significant influence on choosing presidents that have similar values and personality traits as board members, signifying that board makeup is important (Commodore, 2018). The Campaign for College Opportunity (2020) highlighted the compositional diversity of the four governing boards of the California public postsecondary systems, all of which are appointed by the governor of the state. They reported that while the four boards have a significant amount of racial and gender diversity and are becoming increasingly more equitable in alignment with the undergraduate population within the three state systems in California, there are still inequities. In particular, they recommended the need for more Latinx, Asian American, Native Hawaiian, Pacific Islander, American Indian, and Alaskan Native board members, which makes sense considering a majority of the colleges and universities in all three California systems are HSIs or emerging HSIs, and several are also Asian American and Native American Pacific Islander–Serving Institutions (AANAPISIs). Transformed HSIs must embrace governing board members as essential members in their pursuit of servingness, not only increasing the diversity but recruiting board members who understand and are committed to the HSI identity, mission, and purpose and who will elevate important conversations about racial equity, social justice, and liberatory education.

Families at HSIs

Families have not been thoroughly considered within HSI research, yet families may be some of the most important members that a transformed HSI can embrace. Students of color are often socialized by their families and communities to value education and pursue advanced educational opportunities and often remain committed to their families throughout their educational journeys, making it nearly impossible to exclude families from the college experience (Covarrubias, 2021). Families are an important part of the educational process, often disrupting dominant ideologies about education and imparting culturally and community-specific knowledge by way of legends, storytelling, and corridos (Delgado Bernal, 2001). Families pass down knowledge from elders and ancestors that would otherwise be lost in the US colonial educational system and elevate students' bilingual and bicultural experiences beyond what they would otherwise get through formal education (Delgado Bernal, 2001).

Moreover, a liberatory educational philosophy specifically calls for the integration of students' funds of knowledge, which is often connected to their families. Moll et al. (1992) first introduced the idea of funds of knowledge as a way for teachers to value and use the knowledge, skills, and resources that students bring to the classroom setting with the goal of disrupting deficit thinking about student achievement. Funds of knowledge hypothesizes that the families and communities that students come from possess a tremendous amount of knowledge that arises from lived experiences (Moll et al., 2013). Theses lived experiences are abundant and may include those gained from household practices; jobs (e.g., farming, construction, migrant labor, household maintenance); involvement in community organizations; and/or experiences connected to socio-political-legal contexts (e.g., immigration law). Engaging families as members of transformed HSIs can support students' use of funds of knowledge in order to navigate and disrupt systems of oppression and power within the educational system (Castillo-Montoya & Ives, 2020).

Some HSIs have implemented family orientations that access family funds of knowledge, including their language and culture. These programs consider family members beyond the dominant white nuclear structure and are often held on weekends or in the evening hours, taking into consideration the needs of families. University of California, Santa Cruz (UCSC), for example, implemented a Regional Family Conference (RFC) supported by one of its federally funded HSI grants (Covarubbias et al., 2020). The RFC is free to all students, has a broad definition of family, and focuses on topics germane to first-generation and low-income students including financial aid literacy, being the first to go to college, and being undocumented in college. Responding to conference evaluations, UCSC improved conference logistics, adding a second location in one of its feeder regions and shortening the program to better accommodate families that worked on the weekend. In engaging families and inviting them to become members of the campus community, transformed HSIs must meet families where they are, understanding that they have a range of economic, language, and social needs. Families must be seen and valued as essential members of transformed HSIs, as they are vital to the success of racially and ethnically minoritized students and transmit essential funds of knowledge that align with the institution's commitment to a liberatory and humanizing education.

Changing the Composition of the Membership

In order to change the composition of the membership within HSIs, intentional race-conscious and equity-minded processes and practices must be in place. Although the focus should be on increasing the racial-ethnic-Indigenous composition of members, there should also be an effort to increase the number of members who have other minoritized identities in order to reach the desired composition of people who can support and serve multiply minoritized students at HSIs through an intersectional lens. For example, recruiting members who speak multiple languages and identify as Trans* or queer, who are Muslim, or who have invisible dis/abilities is desirable and justified as transformed HSIs work toward radical liberation and collective healing. There must also be a concerted effort to increase the number of people committed to the HSI identity, mission, and purpose and who can enact racial equity, social justice, and collective liberation in policy and practice. The goal must be to develop active strategies that will lead to long-term and sustainable changes in the compositional diversity of all members as well as the philosophical beliefs and values of members. Empowering those who have lacked the power to make change in racialized organizations should also be a priority (Ray, 2019).

Audit Current Membership

Institutions should conduct an audit of the various social identities of all members (e.g., race, ethnicity, gender). The goal of the audit is to understand the places and spaces where compositional diversity is present within and across the membership. Institutional research professionals can be a part of this process, as they tend to be the keepers of the data and they know how to disaggregate them. Disaggregating data by race and other social identities can help members see how inequities transcend the membership dimension. Disaggregated data will better equip decision makers with knowledge of the lack of representation within and across the membership. Institutions should conduct an audit of all members including undergraduate and graduate students, faculty, staff, administrators, and their boards of trustees, yet here I focus on the educators and decision makers.

For faculty, staff, and administrators, membership data should be disaggregated (at minimum) by race/ethnicity and sex across departments and disciplinary areas. Data may also be disaggregated by job families, such as facilities, maintenance, administrative support, secretary, student services, and administrator, and by job classifications, such as facilities I–IV, administrative support I–IV, student services I–IV, and so on. This level of disaggregation across positions and classifications will provide the most accurate picture of the places and spaces on campus where diversity is most present. For faculty, there must also be an accurate picture of the diversity among full-time, part-time, and adjunct professors and across academic ranks including assistant, associate, and full professor. For the board of trustees, efforts should be made to collect social identity data, which may require trustees to disclose these data. These data can help the presidents and/or chancellors make decisions about future invitations for board members. The data collected through the audit should help decision makers determine the human resource needs of the institution as it moves toward transforming itself.

Rethink Hiring Practices

There is a need to rethink the hiring practices utilized by HSIs. Although much of the research focuses on hiring diverse *faculty*, the existing literature can be used to develop tactics for increasing the compositional diversity of all educators and decision makers within HSIs. Of importance, it is necessary to acknowledge that race plays a role in the hiring process, including the way that whiteness is valued. In naming race, there is also recognition that racism and white supremacy negatively affect the institution's ability to hire people of color. Myths about diversity that emerge during the hiring process must be disrupted, including the myth that there is a lack of racially and ethnically diverse candidates in the applicant pool and the myth that candidates of color are only interested in prestige and money when selecting an institution to work at (Liera & Ching, 2020). The idea of "good fit" must also be challenged, as it is racially coded and is not the best criteria when evaluating candidates (Liera & Ching, 2020). But if we are going to defer to "fit" in hiring, a "good fit" for an HSI includes having experience teaching, mentoring, and advising students of color, being committed to the values of racial and social justice, and having the ability to enact an educational experience that aligns with the transformed HSIs framework.

The recruitment process should begin with a well-developed recruitment plan that includes the appointment of a search committee that has expertise in hiring for racial equity and justice, and if they don't, they should be trained (Zambrana et al., 2020). This includes white people in order to reduce the service load placed on people of color on campus (Sensoy & DiAngelo, 2017). Although implicit bias training should be provided, as it is unconscious and often emerges while committee members review applications, the topics of equity-mindedness and race-consciousness should also be included in the training. Committee members should be trained to use language that is asset based as they discuss candidates. Deficit language is often attached to words like "merit" and "fit," which are racialized and grounded in white normative measures of excellence, rigor, and epistemology (Liera & Ching, 2020). A well-developed recruitment plan may also include the appointment of equity advocates on the committee who are responsible for minimizing bias and developing strategies to ensure equity-minded and race-conscious approaches are used, which may include developing the job announcement, evaluation rubric, and interview questions (Liera, 2020).

The committee should develop a job announcement that will support its efforts to change the racial-ethnic composition (Zambrana et al., 2020). The job announcement should express the institution's desire to hire people who are committed to working at an HSI and who value equity and justice in education. HSIs should state clearly that they are HSIs and lay out the qualities and skills for members seeking employment. For example, California Lutheran University stated in its job announcement the desire to hire people who can mentor Latinx, Black, and Native American students (Tugend, 2018). The use of specific language in the job description also matters, including words such as "racial justice" and "racial equity" rather than words such as "multicultural," "diversity," and "cultural awareness." The job announcement should be shared and promoted through organizations that are committed to advancing the careers of people of color in higher education as well as diversity-related publications such as *Diverse Issues in Higher Education* (Liera & Ching, 2020). Other active recruitment tactics may include outreach to other MSIs that enroll larger percentages of people of color who may fill positions (Liera, 2020).

The committee should decide the application materials that are needed in the first round in order to make an informed decision and be intentional about minimizing potential barriers in the process. For example, asking candidates for multiple statements about teaching, research, advising, mentoring, and the like and requiring three letters of recommendation at the point of application could be a huge barrier for candidates, especially candidates of color and first-generation scholars, and it may deter them from submitting their application altogether. Moreover, letters of recommendation are often filled with normative assumptions about excellence and merit (Zambrana et al., 2020). For the first round, candidates should be asked to submit a cover letter outlining their qualifications for the job, resume/CV, and one statement about their commitment and actions toward advancing racial equity, social justice, and collective liberation for communities of color. The prompt should ask candidates to express their *demonstration and examples* of racially just and equitable actions in their statement. The guidelines may also ask candidates to discuss what it means to work at an HSI and about their knowledge for educating Latinx, Black, Indigenous, Asian American, Pacific Islander, and Mixed-Race students as well as other minoritized students at HSIs (e.g., low-income students). Letters of recommendation and other statements (e.g., teaching statement) should be requested at a later point in the process once candidates are being strongly considered.

The review of application materials must be intentional and systematic. As noted by Liera and Ching (2020), a focus on merit and fit often occurs because members are asked to subjectively evaluate candidates' accomplishments and potential with no clear guidance on how to operationalize these measures when hiring for equity and justice. Committee members must be trained to review cover letters, CVs/resumes, and statements in a way that does not reinforce normative standards of excellence (Sensoy & DiAngelo, 2017). The review of applications should also decenter "counting" things like years of experience or number of publications or grants and instead focus on experiences and actions that center, support, and uplift minoritized students and communities. Although the use of a rubric is debatable among social justice educators and equity scholars, I advocate for the use of a rubric that can make a seemingly subjective process of reviewing applications more objective. The rubric must have specific measures for assessing a candidate's actions toward advancing racial equity and social justice. Words such as "racial equity," "social justice," and "empowerment" should be in the rubric.

For faculty candidates, the rubric might have prompts such as "Candidate shows evidence or potential of engaging in research activities that center racial equity and justice" or "Candidate shows evidence or potential of engaging in racial equity and justice pedagogy through class assignments." For staff candidates, the prompts may be "Candidate shows evidence or potential of developing campus programs that center racial equity and justice for students" or "Candidate shows evidence or potential of supporting and mentoring racially and ethnically minoritized students." For administrator candidates, prompts may include "Candidate shows evidence or potential of implementing policies that advance racial equity and justice," "Candidate shows evidence or potential of making decisions that reduce inequities in outcomes and experiences for minoritized students," or "Candidate shows evidence or potential of redistributing resources and power to better support people of color in the institution." Rather than giving candidates a numeric score, the rubric should allow committee members to provide descriptive evidence of their commitment to racial equity, justice, and liberation.

The interviews, both virtual and on campus, are important moments to evaluate candidates, but there must be structured interview questions and standardized evaluation measures that minimize quantification and maximize narrative feedback (Zambrana et al., 2020). Structured interview questions should ask candidates to describe actions that show their experience with or potential for educating for equity, justice, and liberation. For example, faculty may be asked how they teach antiracism in the classroom or to name guiding theories and exemplar books used in their courses. Staff may be asked to demonstrate a program on campus that they created that advances racial justice, or administrators may be asked to provide evidence of decision-making and policy implementation that is antiracist. The on-campus visit is also an opportune time to have candidates demonstrate their values and practices that align with the mission, identity, and purpose of a transformed HSI that centers racial equity, social justice, and collective liberation for students of color, their families, and the communities they come from. They should be invited to discuss these values with various people they interact with while on campus, and these people should be adequately prepared to have these conversations and assess the candidate's responses. All people who interact with the candidate should complete an evaluation, and the evaluation should prompt respondents to evaluate the candidate's values, actions, experiences, and potential for being an educator or decision maker who is committed to equity, justice, and liberation. There are numerous resources for hiring for diversity, equity, and antiracism, but the bottom line is that the process *should not be race-neutral*, as that will reinforce white dominance in the process.

Cluster Hiring

There are programmatic initiatives that HSIs may implement as active recruitment strategies. Institutions may consider cluster hiring, which involves hiring educators into cohorts across departments based on interdisciplinary topics or "clusters" (Urban Universities for Health, 2015). The clusters can and should be innovative and may focus on increasing excellence across disciplines, topical areas, institutional vitality, community engagement, racial diversity, diversity of ideologies, or other goals that the institution has. HSIs could consider topics such as "HSIs," "Latinxs" "antiracism" or "social justice education," and encourage the hiring of educators and decision makers that focus on these efforts. Although cluster hiring is typically done to increase racial and ethnic diversity and interdisciplinary collaborations of *faculty*, HSIs should consider making these hires more complex by including *staff and administrators* in the cluster, particularly when aiming to increase diversity of academic leaders such as deans and provosts.

Institutions should express explicit goals and expectations for the cluster, gain early buy-in from department and division leaders across the institution, engage current members in the process early on, provide sufficient rewards and recognition for members who participate in the cluster hiring process, and establish long-term goals for sustaining the cluster, including financial commitments (Urban Universities for Health, 2015). The first cluster hire program was launched at the University of Wisconsin–Madison in the late 1990s and had significant financial support ($15 million raised), which is vital to the success of these programs (Urban Universities for Health, 2015). The Urban Universities for Health (2015) found that cluster hiring can be effective for increasing the racial-ethnic-Indigenous diversity of faculty on campus, changing the administration's perceptions of diversity, and implementing practices such as training requirements for search committees. Muñoz et al. (2017) also documented their success in hiring four racially and ethnically diverse faculty through a "cluster hire focused on diversity, equity, and inclusion" (p. 8).

Grow Your Own Program

A less talked-about method for increasing diversity of educators and decision makers in HSIs is a "grow your own program." This type of program may work best for training (or growing) future staff and administrators at HSIs. It is not uncommon for staff and administration positions at a university to be filled by alumni of the institution. Freeman (2015) described how the Higher Education Administration and Leadership program at Adams State University, an HSI in Colorado, was redesgined to include two tracks for people seeking master's in education degrees: one for early career professionals working at HSIs and one for midcareer professionals at HSIs. The program offers courses such as "Leadership in Minority-Serving Institutions" and "Leading for Student Success in Minority-Serving Institutions." Using seed grant monies, the program was created in response to the growing need for Latinx leaders on campus and has been recognized by *Excelencia* in Education as a model of success (Barnett et al., 2016).

For instutions that do not have master's or doctoral programs in education, other bachelor's and graduate programs can be charged with developing curriclum that is specific to training future staff members for HSIs. Counseling and social work programs, for example, may train future college advisors, counselors, and general student services peronnel with a specific focus on understanding the needs and experiences of Latinx and other minoritized groups. Masters of business administration and other bachleor's and master's programs that emphasize leadership development may also be charged with re-desgining curriculum specific to training future leaders at HSIs. Specific internship programs or practica should also be instituted to help future leaders learn about what it means to work at an HSI before they graduate.

Building an Intentional Pathway

Creating a pathway program is another way to increase the number of racially and ethnically diverse educators in the institution. As noted by Tugend (2018) some institutions have created postdoctoral fellowships within departments that expect to have open faculty lines within the next few years. This is one way to develop career pathways, but HSIs that are two-year institutions, comprehensive universities, or liberal arts institutions that may not hire research postdocs must be more creative. Some HSIs may offer teaching postdocs if that is their focus or need as an institution. These HSIs may develop collaborations with the research institutions in the area, as their applicants can come from these surrounding institutions. Moreover, they may need to develop collaborations with other HSIs; yet as noted, the enrollment at the graduate level is not nearly as diverse as it is at the undergraduate level. Although there is very little research about this idea, transformed HSIs can be creative in their efforts to transform the composition of their educators and decision makers and an intentional pathway could be beneficial.

Retaining Members of Color

Retention of educators committed to equity and justice within HSIs is also an issue that must be discussed. The focus in research has primarily been on the need to recruit and hire more educators of color in HSIs (e.g., Contreras, 2017; Gonzales, 2015; Santos & Acevedo-Gil, 2013; Vargas et al., 2019), with little attention paid to retention as an additional issue. Yet retention may be the core reason for the lack of educators of color at HSIs, and institutions must develop a plan for disrupting the revolving door. When educators of color are heavily recruited, they often enter an institution where racism continues to exist and manifest in multiple ways. For example, faculty of color may feel like they have to prove themselves; support students of color at greater levels than their white colleagues, despite the fact that this is not valued in the promotion and tenure process; and work within a contentious racial climate that is unsupportive (Kelly et al., 2017). Latina faculty, specifically, may experience isolation as "the only one" in their department; feel left out of institutional opportunities due to minoritized identities connected to race, class, and gender; and feel tokenized, often serving the campus as the representative of her entire racial-ethnic-Indigenous and gender group (Gonzales et al., 2015). These experiences may be exacerbated by the same cluster hires touted as effective ways of increasing diversity of educators at HSIs, as those hired as part of the cluster may be perceived by members of dominant groups as (unqualified) "opportunity hires" (Kelly et al., 2017).

At HSIs, educators continue to face a contentious racial climate despite the fact that the student population is racially diverse. Zaragoza and Garcia (2022) found that retention of faculty of color was a major issue at one small Catholic HSI in the Midwest where white faculty represented approximately 70% of the faculty population, compared to nearly 60% of Latinxs at the undergraduate level. Participants in their study were concerned that several faculty and staff of color, and specifically Latinx-identified faculty and staff, had left the institution as a result of a toxic racial climate. Students also noticed that educators of color were leaving the institution due to a toxic racial climate, writing a letter to the administration expressing their concerns about the issue of retention of educators of color and demanding that the institution hire more, stressing that they serve as important role models and mentors to students of color. B. A. L. (2019) also described in detail their own experiences with racialized and gendered micro- and macroaggressions at their HSI. The author recounted their experience with a white male student accusing them of hating white men and their experiences with a Latino man questioning their authority in front of a large lecture-sized class. They also talked about the apathy of an administration who only saw the students as customers, rather than people, with little recognition of students' racialized experiences prior to entering the institution and often reinforcing deficit narrative about students' academic abilities.

Venegas et al. (2021) similarly described these types of experiences for Black and Asian American faculty at three HSIs with over 50% Latinx student populations. Aubree, a Black professor in the study, said that she experienced sexist attitudes and colorism in the classroom and a lack of departmental and institutional support to deal with the issues. All the participants in the study cited a lack of support for their research and teaching and for dealing with racialized experiences. Several participants also said that they experienced racism, discrimination, and exclusion among colleagues and administrators, with one describing a situation where colleagues spoke Spanish in front of her even though they knew she didn't speak Spanish. Experiences with racism, sexism, and exclusion among non-Latinx women of color educators is not acceptable for a transformed HSI and completely counters any efforts to build solidarity and collective liberation across minoritized groups. Martinez et al. (2017) reported similar experiences among a group of 16 Black, Asian American, Pacific Islander, Latina, and Mixed-Race women at three institutions, one of which was an HSI. Importantly they noted that "working at an HSI did not appear to lessen or eliminate instances of marginalization or discrimination" (Martinez et al., 2017, p. 702). Although less has been documented in research, staff at HSIs also experience a contentious campus racial climate, although as noted by Garcia (2016b), experiences with racism and microaggressions may vary based on the compositional diversity of the department that staff are in. A predominantly white space on campus may lead people of color to feel tokenized and disempowered regardless of the overall racial composition of the HSI. Importantly, decision makers need to acknowledge that there is a racial climate issue that is affecting the retention of educators of color and must be willing to intentionally address and disrupt the issues.

One suggestion is to implement and sponsor identity-based affinity groups for educators. It is common for institutions to host affinity groups such as a Black faculty and staff association, a Latinx faculty and staff association, and a LGBTQIA faculty and staff association. These types of associations can serve as counterspaces, which can lead to greater retention of minoritized educators and decision makers. Racial affinity groups can also serve as important spaces of healing, critical camaraderie, and resistance (Pour-Khorshid, 2018). These types of spaces allow members to share their experiences and strategize ways to become better educators in the shared fight for social justice. For a group of Latina faculty members at two HSIs in Texas, the interdisciplinary research collaborative known as REAL (Research for the Educational Advancement of Latin@s) served as an agency for transformational resistance, allowed Latina faculty to challenge racism and sexism in the academy, and became a source of muxerista mentoring between and among Latina faculty and ultimately students on campus (Ek et al., 2010; Murakami & Núñez, 2014). Support for these types of affinity groups should be monetary, with transformed HSIs providing budgets to be used for programming and other means of addressing the contentious racial climate for all students and educators. Although research shows that educators of color at the intersections of minoritized identities at HSIs often resist, create their own spaces for collective healing and support, engage in strategic service work, and mentor each other (i.e., Ek et al., 2010; Martinez et al., 2017; Murakami & Núñez, 2014; Venegas et al., 2021), the institutions themselves should actively redistribute resources and empower educators of color as an essential retention tactic.

Moreover, HSIs need to assure that the reward structures in place adequately recognize and account for the specific labor of educators working toward the HSI mission, identity, and purpose (Garcia, 2018). For faculty there must be recognition of the development and implementation of curriculum and pedagogy that are grounded in racial justice and liberatory ideologies and that promote the development of critical consciousness. For example, faculty may be required to show evidence of implementing courses that center racially minoritized ways of knowing, enhance students' knowledge of inequities by race, require service learning with the local Latinx, Black, or Native American populations, and promote action for justice and equity. Faculty should be recognized for the pursuit of community-engaged research and/or increased service obligations to minoritized communities on campus. Whether tenure stream or not, these efforts must be utilized in a formal evaluation system.

Staff and decision makers also need to be evaluated, promoted, and rewarded for their efforts to implement programs and services that center racially minoritized students, that advance justice in local Latinx and low-income communities, and that support the development of liberatory outcomes for students. Decision makers should also be evaluated, promoted, and rewarded for eliminating policies that reinforce inequitable outcomes and implementing policies that lead to great racial equity across the institution. In every review process, educators and decision makers must be able to demonstrate that their work is grounded in mission, purpose, and strategic objectives of the transformed HSI in measurable ways and foregrounded in racial equity and social justice.

Training and Professional Development for All Members

A final dimension of membership for transformed HSIs to consider is the need to equip members with knowledge and skills for serving minoritized students, which requires long-term training and development. This includes members with minoritized identities and from dominant groups (e.g., white, cisgender, men, heterosexual, Christian) who all must be trained to enact the organization's HSI mission, identity, and purpose through the lens of equity, justice, and liberation. All members of the organization, regardless of racial and social identities, need tools and frameworks to assist their development as social justice educators. There are numerous options for training; some HSIs have participated in the W. K. Kellogg Foundation's Truth, Racial Healing, and Transformation training, others have started antiracism book clubs on campus, while many now require unconscious bias trainings. Petrov and Garcia (2021) argued that Title V and Title III grant monies can and should be used to hire trainers of color who utilize critical theories and frameworks in their workshops and trainings. They stressed that training and professional development is an essential step toward disrupting whiteness and coloniality of power within HSIs and crucial for becoming a racially just HSI, with funding from the federal government often being used for these efforts. Importantly, training and development must be longitudinal and ongoing.

Of note, educational practices transcend the curriculum and the classroom, crossing into the cocurricular structures. As such, all educators and decision makers should be trained to enact educational experiences and make decisions that are race-conscious and equity-minded across the curriculum, from STEM to humanities, across the campus, from residence life to service learning, and across decision-making, from the provost's office to the institutional governing board. University of California, Santa Cruz, implemented a Multicultural Advising Conference (MAC) in response to feedback that they received from students about the number of instances of microaggressions happening within advising sessions (Sánchez Ordaz et al., 2020). Students also reported a low level of satisfaction when interacting with offices such as financial aid. With the support of Title V grants for developing HSIs, the campus launched the MAC in order to support the advising staffs across campus in their development of strengths-based advising practices, which included training on how to recognize microaggressions and how to utilize microaffirmations in advising sessions. Importantly, the campus assessed the racial climate for students through focus groups in order to develop training and development that was specific to the campus and the students at UCSC. These types of trainings should also be added to the reward structure, with active participation required to be promoted in the institution.

Training and development should help all educators and decision makers center people of color within the institution and elevate their voices across campus. Centering the experiences of Latinx, Black, Indigenous, Asian American, Pacific Islander, and Mixed-Race students requires educators and decision makers to get to know their students' journeys and histories, acknowledge and affirm students' language preferences, understand the students' familial traditions and practices, know how governmental policies affect and influence the daily lives of students, and acknowledge the intersectional identities of students (España & Herrera, 2020). Members should also engage in critical discourse about the normalizing and privileging of white, cisgender, heterosexual, middle-class, able-bodied, Christian men across the institution. Every member of the institution must learn how to disrupt the white normative bodies of knowledge, policies, and practices that are historically engrained within the institution, asking, "Whose history, voices, and knowledge have been excluded from the educational practices, processes, and policies?" This may require the support of external consultants and organizations. Springfield Technical Community College (STCC) utilized the expertise of ESCALA Educational Services, a national organization that provides pedagogical training and development to faculty at HSIs (ESCALA Educational Services, 2022; Griffin-Fennell & Lerner, 2020).

Training and development should also be multidimensional, as research shows that even when college educators feel like they have the knowledge to educate racially/ethnically minoritized students at

HSIs, they feel less confident about their skills or ability to do so (Koren et al., in development). As such, training and development must go beyond enhanced knowledge to increased skills for educating minoritized students. Within training and development, educators must be encouraged to think about their own social identities and their positionality within the institution and society ("awareness of self") and grapple with how their identity and positionality influence their epistemology and approach to education (Takacs, 2003). There should be plenty of opportunities for self-reflection on both privileged and minoritized identities, and educators and decision makers should consider the socialization process that has led to their current understanding of various minoritized groups and their intersectional identities (Sensoy & DiAngelo, 2012). STCC sponsored staff and administrators to attend the Unidos Equity Leadership Institute, developed and sponsored by Adams State University, a small HSI in Colorado (Adams State University, 2018; Griffin-Fennell & Lerner, 2020). Self-awareness, exploration of identities, and understanding epistemologies are core concepts that participants grapple with.

Beyond self-awareness, educators and decision makers must come to understand the historical experiences of various racial and ethnic groups in the United States, including their historical connections to settler colonialism and chattel slavery (Garcia & Natividad, 2018). The historical mistreatment of people of color in the United States, dating back to the founding of the country, must not be dismissed, as it has affected the educational experiences of students of color across their educational experiences. Educators should also acknowledge the present-day educational experiences of students of color, including their likelihood of being disciplined at higher rates, being diagnosed with a learning dis/ability, being an English-language learner, and/or not being considered for gifted education (Love, 2019). Members may also be prompted to evaluate deficit language that may evolve from their own belief systems about the types of students that are likely to succeed in college and the ones that aren't. This includes a disruption of the rationalization that often happens when educators and decision makers search for answers to racial-ethnic inequities they see in outcomes and experiences (Malcom-Piqueux & Bensimon, 2015). Within a transformed HSI, students should never be blamed, and instead the institution should search for answers to how the structures for serving students have been inadequate. Overall, training and development should be grounded in race-consciousness, social justice, and collective liberation and healing; it must encourage participants to move beyond valuing difference; it should push educators and decision makers to disrupt oppression within their educational practices, within their evaluation and assessment of students, and within their educational policies and decision-making.

Conclusion

The main organizational dimension that drives the HSI designation is membership, yet it is underdeveloped as a concept for becoming a transformed HSI. A majority of attention has been paid to the compositional diversity of the undergraduate membership, with a loud call for increased compositional diversity of the faculty at HSIs. Yet the focus on undergraduates and faculty is insufficient, as all members are essential to the organization, each playing a different role. Transforming HSIs requires focused attention on changing the composition of all members called upon to carry out the mission, identity, and purpose of the HSI, including staff, decision makers, and leaders of the institution. To elevate servingness, transformed HSIs must also pay attention to how inequities play out for all members of the organizations in enrollment, hiring, experiences, and outcomes. This requires a race-conscious and socially just approach to changing the composition while also working to retain current members of color and training all members of the institution to enact the HSI identity, mission, and purpose. Moreover, transformed HSIs should support and serve all members within and beyond the "H" that have not been a part of the HSI conversation, including but not limited to Afro-Latinxs, Indigenous Latinxs, Queer Latinxs, Muslim Latinx, Neurodivergent Latinxs, and beyond. Membership is a complex dimension and must be treated as multidimensional.

4

Developing Infrastructure

INFRASTRUCTURE IS ARGUABLY THE MOST TANGIBLE DIMENSION of the Transforming HSIs Framework. It includes the subdimensions of curriculum, cocurriculum, support services, and physical infrastructure. The mission, identity, and strategic purpose are enacted within the infrastructure by the members. In essence, it's the "what we do" as organizations committed to serving Latinx students and other students of color at the intersection of minoritized identities. With the reauthorization of the Higher Education Act of 1992, HSIs came into existence with no direct guidance on how to transform the infrastructure for serving Latinx students. Yet the US Department of Education's Title V Developing HSIs program allows institutions to pursue competitive grants to develop their infrastructure for serving students, suggesting that it is an essential endeavor for becoming an HSI. Moreover, investment in the infrastructure will enhance the educational outcomes of students enrolled in HSIs, with Garcia (2013b) finding that institutional expenditures, including instructional, academic support, student support, and institutional support, positively influence the graduation rates of Latinx students at HSIs.

There are 16 allowable activities within the Title V program, with a majority focusing on the infrastructure (Santiago et al., 2016). As documented by Santiago et al. (2016), most Title V recipients have invested in curriculum development and student support services. Boland (2018) also found that successful grantees seek to enhance advising, counseling, and academic support. These findings indicate that grantees are addressing the infrastructure dimension most directly. Vargas and Villa-Palomino (2018), however, reviewed 220 successful Title V grant application abstracts and discovered that 85% of grantees proposed race-neutral programs and initiatives, while only 10% took a Latinx-centered approach to serving students. I call on transformed HSIs to discontinue the use of race- and identity-neutral practices and offer numerous suggestions throughout this chapter and book.

The students who enroll in HSIs deserve an educational infrastructure that acknowledges their sociohistoric contexts, centers their identities and ways of knowing, and is validating, humanizing, and liberating. The infrastructure and overall approach to education must acknowledge that Latinx students and other students of color who enroll in HSIs have experienced discrimination, harassment, and racialized aggressions within school settings. We must acknowledge that they have endured K–12 educational systems that have "murdered their spirits" (Love, 2019). We must acknowledge that they have been asked to check their racial and social identities, community cultural wealth, and funds of knowledge at the door while investing in learning intended to assimilate them to mainstream US white ways of knowing (Conchas & Acevedo, 2020; de los Ríos, 2013; Garcia, 2018; Salazar, 2013). We must acknowledge that they may have internalized racism and oppression as a result of their schooling, which causes them to devalue their minoritized identities and overvalue white Eurocentric dominant identities (Camacho Parra, 2012; Salazar, 2013). At the same time, we must understand that internalized racism and oppression is often "safe," as the weight of being a person of color or a person with minoritized identities in the United

States is often so overwhelming that it's easier to blend into mainstream culture and society, particularly for those who have experienced success along normative metrics (Sensoy & DiAngelo, 2017). As such, providing students with liberating and humanizing educational experiences may come with resistance. We must do it anyway.

Curriculum and Pedagogy: Liberation in the Classroom

I discuss curriculum and pedagogy together since they are intertwined but acknowledge that they are distinct from one another, particularly on college and university campuses where curriculum is clustered within departments and often delivered as a unit, guided by the disciplinary needs of the academic program. I consider the curriculum to be the content that is delivered by faculty in the classroom; oftentimes it is determined by core faculty within the department. Alternatively, I use the term "pedagogy" to describe the philosophies, principles, and practices that guide educators' decisions about the content and mode of delivery. Pedagogy can be more individualistic than the curriculum, with each faculty member delivering the departmental content (or curriculum) through their own philosophical lens. I encourage educators to think about the ways that curriculum and pedagogy diverge and converge in various ways as they develop their own philosophies about how to best educate students in HSIs. I also consider curriculum and pedagogy to be aspects of the formal classroom, which are often under the purview of faculty, yet I encourage faculty to work with staff in cocurricular programs and student support services in order to integrate aspects of engagement and support that can enhance students' liberatory and humanizing experiences. Although scholars have argued that the curriculum and pedagogy at HSIs must be culturally relevant (Garcia et al., 2019), the HSI literature is underdeveloped when thinking about transformation toward racial equity, social justice, and collective liberation. Within a transformed HSI, the curriculum and pedagogy must be grounded in these principles.

Faculty at transformed HSIs should assess, audit, and redesign the curriculum to ensure that it aligns with the mission, identity, and purpose of the institution. Banks (2010) proposed four approaches to curriculum redesign: (1) contributions approach, (2) additive approach, (3) transformation approach, and (4) social action approach. The curriculum remains virtually unchanged within the *contributions approach* except for the inclusion of racial-ethnic-Indigenous heroes and artifacts. The success of these heroes is often celebrated and attributed to the process of acculturation with little emphasis on the oppressive structures and systems that they had to overcome in order to succeed in mainstream America. With the *additive approach*, teachers add concepts, themes, or perspectives of minoritized or racialized individuals, often through the addition of a book or unit focused on these groups. With this approach, minoritized communities are still viewed through the eyes of the mainstream population and often interconnected to the experiences and histories of dominant groups. With the *transformation approach*, the fundamental goals, structures, and perspectives of the curriculum are changed, allowing multiple perspectives and voices to emerge as significant, including those of dominant and minoritized groups. With the *social action approach*, students take control of the curriculum, making decisions about who and what should be included in the course. This approach is an interdisciplinary, fluid, and progressive approach to curriculum development that centers student voices. These four approaches can be used by educators at transformed HSIs seeking guidance on curriculum reform, specifically minimizing the contributions and additive approaches, and elevating the transformative and social action approaches.

Few studies have documented curriculum approaches at HSIs. Garcia and Okhidoi (2015) found that the ethnic studies curriculum at one HSI in the Southwest was salient to participants' understanding of servingness, stressing the need to institutionalize ethnic studies curriculum within HSIs. Ethnic studies at this HSI were embedded within the general education requirements, which allowed students to take courses that counted toward their degree requirements, an important step toward overall curriculum and general education redesign. Ethnic studies, by design, incorporate a transformative and social action approach, as they center the ways of knowing and identities of racially and ethnically minoritized groups, allow students to examine how US colonialism and white supremacy transcend all aspects of society thus creating inequities, and elevate the study of students' communities, histories, arts, and science (Sleeter, 2011). Although much of the research about the outcomes of ethnic studies has been within K–12 schools, the evidence is clear that ethnic studies have the ability to academically engage students of color, increase their learning, enhance their sense of agency, and take action on a position in their communities (Sleeter, 2011). As argued by Garcia and Okhidoi (2015), ethnic studies curriculum should be centered at HSIs as an essential aspect of the infrastructure.

Yet the curriculum at HSIs cannot rely solely on ethnic studies programs and faculty (Garcia, 2020a). All departments and academic programs must take responsibility for delivering the same type of transformative and social action experiences that ethnic studies deliver. In particular, there must be a focus on core courses that serve as gateways into quantitative-based majors, where there are often inequities in outcomes for students of color and low-income students. Redesigning these courses through a transformative and social action approach can directly address the goals of the Developing HSIs Title III, Part F program and the National Science Foundation's Improving Undergraduate STEM Education: HSI Program, which focus directly on addressing inequities in STEM degree achievement and success for students who attend HSIs. Redesigning quantitative-based courses should address both social justice pedagogical goals and mathematical pedagogical goals (Gutiérrez, 2002; Gutstein, 2006; Kokka, 2019). In other words, course redesign should allow students to develop positive social and cultural identities, critically analyze society in order to take action to change it, and become competent users of mathematics as assessed by dominant measures. Castillo-Montoya and Ives (2020) contend that liberatory educational praxis requires faculty to expose students to dominant and critical disciplinary knowledge while allowing them to envision academic content as a tool for self-growth, contributions to community and society, and critical examination of the discipline or field itself. These are important aspects of curriculum redesign at transformed HSIs.

Bhattacharya et al. (2020) described the mathematics curriculum redesign process at one HSI in the Southwest, which was the focus of their Title V, Part A grant. In analyzing academic outcomes data through a racial equity lens, the grant team found that the college algebra course on campus was preventing students of color and low-income students who wanted to pursue STEM degrees from successfully entering those programs (what is often referred to as "weeding out"). Before the redesign, the course used a remedial approach and was lecture and exam based, with little effort to build students' foundational knowledge of algebra. The course redesign was asset-based, with the instructor assuming that all students could succeed in quantitative-based majors with the proper foundations and support. The instructor picked a new book that would build foundational knowledge; incorporated active learning strategies, innovative prelecture videos, and formative feedback; and embedded peer collaboration, tutoring, and advising. Although these substantive changes to the course do not align with Banks's (2010) approach and do not engage with social justice mathematics approaches, they do actively incorporate aspects of culturally relevant teaching, including believing that all students can succeed, developing a community of learners, encouraging students to learn collaboratively, scaffolding knowledge, and incorporating multifaceted assessment (Ladson-Billings, 1995a, 1995b), which is also important within the HSI curricular structures.

Beyond addressing inequities in STEM, transformed HSIs must also think about their role in training future professionals through schools of education, social work, law, and public health. Again, little research has documented how HSIs are doing this work, yet the work is being done. Ginsberg et al. (2018) explored the California Mini-Corps

(CMC) Program, housed at Fresno State in their study but found at many HSIs across the state of California. The CMC program is a unique teacher preparation program grounded in the ways of knowing, language, and culture of migrant students, families, and communities. The CMC program connects future teachers who are undergraduate students with K–12 students who have similar experiences as migrants and bilingual speakers. The program also cultivates future teachers who have a social justice orientation and who extend these practices to the families they serve. The CMC is a good example of how transformed HSIs can train future teachers to serve their communities, while simultaneously serving the students they enroll through a transformative and social action approach. Regardless of the specific approach that faculty at transformed HSIs take, curriculum redesign through a social justice and racial equity lens is vital to the infrastructure.

Pedagogical Development at HSIs

Faculty at transformed HSIs should develop their own pedagogical principles and philosophies grounded in liberatory and humanizing education (see figure 2). Professional development opportunities for faculty should address the gaps in pedagogical training, as most postsecondary faculty are not trained how to teach (Mora & Rios-Aguilar, 2017). This may include a reflection on pedagogical approaches and practices, either through journaling or in dialogue with other faculty. Faculty teaching in a teacher education program at an HSI in Texas participated in a book study about culturally sustaining pedagogies and met weekly to discuss core concepts such as reflecting on their own identities, how to decenter whiteness and recognize white gaze, and how to disrupt dominant and deficit narratives about students (Leija et al., 2020). Another approach is to ask faculty peers to observe teaching and provide feedback, focusing specifically on liberatory praxis. Peer evaluation is a core feature used by ESCALA Educational Services, which is a consortium of educators who support the pedagogical development of faculty at HSIs (ESCALA Educational Services, 2022). ESCALA also believes in faculty mentoring to support

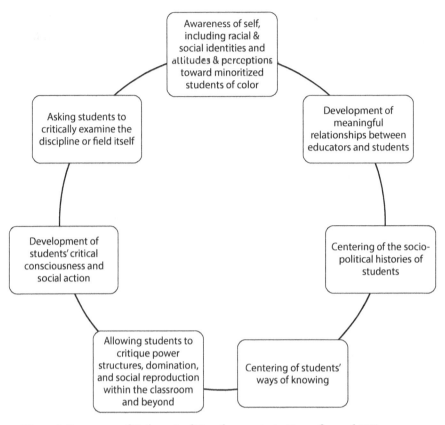

Figure 2. Processes of Pedagogical Development at a Transformed HSI

pedagogical development, with the main focus on increasing retention and success of Latinx and low-income students at HSIs.

Awareness of self, including identities, attitudes, and knowledge, is essential to developing liberatory pedagogical philosophies. Faculty
should reflect on their own social identities, both privileged and minoritized, paying attention to how their identities are similar to and
divergent from those of the students they teach. Murakami-Ramalho
et al. (2010) found the process of understanding their own social identities and experiences in relation to those of the students they teach
valuable for developing their liberatory approach to pedagogy at an
HSI. As part of the process of becoming aware of self, faculty at transformed HSIs should also reflect on their own feelings and perceptions

about students' ability to learn and succeed, paying attention to the ways they assume deficiency. Ching (2019) found that STEM faculty at HSIs made assumptions about Latinx students, stating that students lacked self-esteem and confidence and feared authority, which made it difficult for them to ask for help. Even those faculty with similar racial-ethnic backgrounds developed assumptions and perceptions of Latinx students' ability to succeed. Disrupting deficit thinking is an important part of developing a liberatory pedagogical philosophy, especially at HSIs, where students are likely to enter college academically underprepared as determined by normative measures such as standardized tests (Cuellar, 2019). Garcia et al. (2020) also suggest that faculty teaching at HSIs assess their understanding of institutional discrimination and blatant racial issues, as these are indicators of faculty members' level of race-consciousness and/or race-neutrality. They found that faculty's race-consciousness is positively correlated with faculty knowledge and skills for teaching through a culturally relevant lens.

Liberatory education involves the *development of meaningful relationships* with students and the acknowledgment of socioemotional experiences in students' lives (Salazar, 2013). For students of color with multiple minoritized identities at HSIs, socioemotional experiences may include housing and food insecurities, joblessness, challenges of being in a mixed status family, illness, caring for family members, among others, many of which were exacerbated with the COVID-19 pandemic. Faculty must understand that these experiences may affect student success and engagement in the course, taking the time to develop relationships with students in order to offer support and guidance. Students at one two-year HSI said that when they were struggling with personal issues and felt like they needed to drop out, they trusted the faculty who had taken the time to develop relationships with them and felt that those faculty guided them through tough situations (Alcantar & Hernandez, 2020). Meaningful, stable relationships between educators and students are associated with learning and academic success and should not be undermined (Osher et al., 2019). Moreover, building relationships and getting to know students is an important step in moving toward centering students' ways of knowing and funds of knowledge in the classroom and curriculum (España & Herrera, 2020). Faculty with similar backgrounds and experiences can develop relationships with students based on their similarities, while those with divergent experiences must acknowledge how differences shape the way they view students' abilities and skills (Ching, 2019). Building strong relationships can also help educators disrupt the dehumanization of minoritized students that often happens within the curriculum and formal classroom (Salazar, 2013).

Dehumanization typically occurs within the curricular structures as educators passively teach topics that ignore and erase the existence of people of color and other minoritized groups. Alternatively, a humanizing approach includes *centering the sociopolitical histories of students*. Núñez et al. (2010) found that an effective pedagogical tool for teaching at an HSI was allowing students to explore inequities in their local communities. Since HSIs are often situated within low-income and underserved communities, faculty should provide opportunities for students to critically examine and address sociopolitical inequities within their own communities. Faculty at transformed HSIs should also provide course content that helps students understand systemic level social inequities (Núñez et al., 2010). This should include a transnational lens, recognizing that the lived experiences of students at HSIs include living in the borderlands, living in mixed status families, or being part of the Latin American or Caribbean diaspora. de los Ríos (2019) highlighted the power of music, specifically Mexican corridos, in her study, in showcasing the sociopolitical realities of a transnational experience for Latinx students. Music, art, and spoken word should not be undermined as powerful pedagogical tools for elevating issues of social justice through a decolonial lens for racial-ethnic-Indigenous students at HSIs (Cervantes & Saldaña, 2015). Humanizing pedagogy not only promotes students' consciousness around sociopolitical issues, but it also elevates their engagement in learning.

Similarly, educators should *center students' ways of knowing*, which requires them to understand students' cultures, languages, and families (España & Herrera, 2020). Doran (2019a) found that faculty teaching developmental education courses at a two-year HSI in Texas regularly engaged with students' families and learned about students' familial origins as part of their pedagogical practices. Multiple studies have also highlighted the importance of elevating students' linguistic ways of knowing in the HSI classroom (e.g., Corcoran & Wilkinson, 2019; Garcia, 2019; Venegas et al., 2020). Translanguaging, or the practice of accessing a holistic repertoire of communication, is a powerful way to disrupt false notions of "proper" and "improper" English embedded within a colonial education (Corcoran & Wilkinson, 2019). Faculty at HSIs across the country are using translanguaging practices in composition classes, developmental writing courses, and teacher education programs as a way to disrupt deficit thinking about students' linguistic and writing abilities (see Baca et al., 2019; Kirklighter et al., 2007; and Schall et al., 2021, for numerous examples). Yet translanguaging practices should be used in all classrooms at HSIs. There is an emergence of programs that are incorporating Spanish language in the curriculum at HSIs, from health care programs to journalism and social work (Summers et al., 2018; Garcia, 2013a, 2019). Yet in acknowledging the extreme diversity within and beyond the Latinx community at HSIs, Spanish should not be the only language that educators bring into their curriculum and pedagogy. In working with Indigenous Latinx students, Kovats Sánchez (2018) found that finding courses in their native language on campus (Tu'un Savi, spoken by Ñuu Savi people) was a liberating and validating experience for them.

Rios-Aguilar and Marquez Kiyama (2017) challenge postsecondary educators to develop pedagogies and educational practices that *critique power structures, domination, and social reproduction within the classroom and beyond.* Salazar (2013) stressed that liberatory educational principles include an individual and collective journey toward critical consciousness and critical reflection with the goal of transforming oppressive structures and facilitating liberation of the minoritized. Freire (2018) argued that a foundation of liberatory education includes the development of conscientização, or the ability to understand the historical, social, political, and economic ways that oppression is engrained in society and to take action to eliminate these forces. Numerous educational scholars have conceptualized critical consciousness as the ability of minoritized students to "critically analyze their social conditions and act to change them" and have stressed the importance of elevating critical consciousness as part of a pedagogical philosophy (Watts et al., 2011, p. 44). Watts et al. (2011) proposed three core components of critical consciousness, including (1) critical reflection (the ability to critically analyze social inequities and see them as systemic); (2) political efficacy (the perceived ability to engage in individual or collective activism); and (3) critical action (the process of acting in order to change inequities in society). Educators at transformed HSIs must consider the most effective ways to *develop critical consciousness and promote social action*, which includes developing assignments that encourage and enable action as a critical step.

Scholars have also stressed the importance of exposing students to both dominant and critical disciplinary knowledge as a way to elevate their consciousness (Castillo-Montoya & Ives, 2020). *This includes asking students to critically examine the discipline or field itself.* In writing about the area of mathematics education, Gutiérrez (2013) argued that although educators have begun to critically examine the ways that knowledge, power, and identity are interwoven within the discipline, this task must be for the sake of creating new meanings of mathematics and understanding new connections between the discipline and students' worldviews rather than simply critiquing the white normative ways that mathematics has traditionally been taught. This requires a strong relationship between faculty and students at HSIs. Castillo-Montoya (2019) found that sociology professors teaching predominantly racially and economically minoritized students at an HSI developed disciplinary knowledge by using "interim" points, defined as "an intermediary position whereby the professor converts subject-matter ideas ostensibly dissimilar from students' everyday knowledge into personal or practical ideas familiar to students" (p. 212). These interim points were often connected to culturally and sociopolitically relevant concepts and real-life examples developed through the professors' relationship building techniques. Allowing both faculty and students to critique the discipline is essential and can be done through a variety of perspectives. In surveying faculty and students in natural science majors at one Puerto Rican HSI, Delgado et al. (2019) found that Spanish-dominant speakers struggled in natural sciences because the field itself valued English over any other language. Making this discovery is a powerful way for these students to critically examine the field itself for the sake of challenging and changing it.

Cocurriculum: Liberation beyond the Classroom

Transformed HSIs must address the "beyond the classroom" experiences and educational opportunities that are part of a liberatory and humanizing approach to education. I use the term "cocurricular" to emphasize that these experiences are part of the curricular educational mission of the university and support the advancement of student academic outcomes, yet they are usually offered beyond the classroom. Within the literature, cocurriculum has been theorized as *involvement* and *engagement* in out-of-class experiences, with higher education scholars stressing that involvement and engagement increase student persistence, retention, and academic success (e.g., Astin, 1984, 1993; Kuh, 2009; Tinto, 1993). Opportunities for involvement and engagement include student organizations, Greek organizations, internships, study abroad, on-campus employment, residence life, college athletics, and numerous other experiences. Kuh (2009) further argues that engagement activities are often embedded within the curricular structures, including first-year seminars, learning communities, service learning, senior capstones, and undergraduate research experiences. The correlations between involvement and engagement and desired postsecondary outcomes have been well documented (e.g., Association of American Colleges and Universities

[AAC&U], 2005; ACPA, 2008; Astin, 1993; Kuh, 2009; National Survey of Student Engagement [NSSE], 2007).

Although the concepts and theories of involvement and engagement remain relevant to all college students, the work of Alexander Astin, Vincent Tinto, George Kuh, John Weidman, and other white men has been highly criticized for being based solely on the experiences of traditional 18- to 24-year-old, full-time enrolled, white male students (e.g., Bensimon, 2007; Harper & Quaye, 2008). In other words, they are white normative, or made normal based on white populations, which can have detrimental consequences for HSIs that embrace these concepts without being critical of involvement and engagement opportunities for students of color. Bensimon (2007) argued that operating through a race- and class-neutral lens inevitably promotes a deficit perspective in which students of color and low-income students are assumed to be unmotivated and uninterested in engagement opportunities, without accounting for their lived experiences. Moreover, a liberatory educational experience must account for systems of oppression that minoritized students deal with on a daily basis. Garcia et al. (2020), for example, criticized Weidman's model of socialization for not accounting for socializing contexts such as racism and white supremacy that students of color must contend with every day, both on and off campus.

Based on extensive research, Astin (1984) posited five basic postulates of student involvement: (1) involvement includes an investment of physical and psychological energy; (2) involvement happens along a continuum; (3) involvement has both quantitative and qualitative features; (4) quantity and quality of involvement is directly related to student learning and development; and (5) an increase in student involvement is correlated with the effectiveness of policies and practices. The first postulate is particularly important for educators at transformed HSIs to grapple with, as scholars have stressed that time on task and quality of effort are essential for increasing desired educational outcomes (Kuh, 2009). Time, however, is a privilege afforded to students who do not have to work or manage other responsibilities while in college. With over 50% of students at HSIs identifying as low income, transformed HSIs ought to think creatively about how to offer cocurricular experiences to students who may not have the time to engage in experiences beyond the classroom. The fifth postulate is particularly salient within the transformed HSIs framework, as it places the onus of responsibility for providing opportunities on the institution rather than the student.

Enhancing Structures for Liberation

Within a transformed HSI, involvement and engagement in beyond-the-classroom experiences can be considered a mediator of academic outcomes. In other words, participation in liberatory cocurricular structures will enhance academic outcomes in the long run (e.g., AAC&U, 2005; ACPA, 2008; Astin, 1993; Kuh, 2009; NSSE, 2007). Yet research shows that student engagement at HSIs is slightly lower than student engagement at other types of MSIs, even after controlling for student characteristics (Fosnacht & Nailos, 2016; Nelson Laird et al., 2007). This suggests that transformed HSIs must actively redesign the infrastructure in order to enhance engagement and involvement in liberatory experiences while accounting for the realities of students of color, low-income students, and students at multiple intersections of identity. Much like a liberatory curricular experience, the cocurricular experience at transformed HSIs must also center the sociopolitical histories of students; center students' ways of knowing; promote a critical critique of power structures, domination, and social reproduction; develop critical consciousness; and promote social action. Time spent with faculty and peers is also an important aspect of engagement (Astin, 1984; Kuh, 2009), while Cuellar et al. (2017) argued that validating interactions and mentorship with staff on campus can also lead to greater engagement. Cocurricular experiences should allow for interactions between students and all educators on campus, not just in the classroom faculty. Here I briefly describe *structures for liberation* as both *physical spaces* and *involvement opportunities* based on a few examples within HSIs. Although

I acknowledge that there are numerous examples that have been documented at Predominantly White Institutions (PWI), this book is about HSIs and therefore the focus is on research with HSIs.

Liberatory Spaces at HSIs

Liberatory spaces on campus can enable students to explore their identities and interact with peers, mentors, and educators like them. Some HSIs are utilizing their Title V funds to create these spaces where students can feel validated and supported. Roberts and Lucas (2020) described the power of a Title V center at one dually designated HSI and AANAPISI (Asian American and Native American Pacific Islander-Serving Institution) in California, where there were already established cultural centers for Latinx and AAPI students. The Title V center supplemented those cultural centers with a core mission to promote the success of first-generation college students by providing study space, tutoring, mentoring, and special programming to promote engagement with peers and faculty. Roberts and Lucas (2020) interviewed student users, peer mentors, and staff in the center who described it as a counterspace where they received both academic and nonacademic support, including referrals to other services on campus and food vouchers to support students' basic needs. As more students at HSIs are experiencing food and housing insecurities, transformed HSIs must find ways to address these needs through the structures for serving (Duran & Núñez, 2020). Importantly, the Title V centers can serve students at the intersections of oppression, supporting first-generation to college students and low-income students with basic needs.

University of Texas at San Antonio (UTSA) similarly used Title V funds to create a center for first-generation college students and transfer students (Rodriguez & Gonzales, 2020). The goal of the center is to increase persistence and retention of first-generation and transfer students on campus by providing mentorship and a space of validation. Although the center's mission is to support first-generation and transfer students, the space also reflects students' ethnic and cultural ways of being, by design. Rodriguez and Gonzales (2020) described the center as "an obvious departure from most offices in the university. The center is carpeted in patterns and tones reminiscent of the Southwest, while its walls are brightly painted in colors that speak to an aesthetic that is reminiscent of a vibrant México in its bright yellow, blue, and orange" (p. 299). The center has served close to 800 students with the support of 27 peer mentors and 22 faculty coaches, with mentorship and validation being important mediators of academic outcomes, as the data show that students who participated in the center's programming had slightly higher first-year persistence rates than the general university population.

California Lutheran University used Title III, Part F HSI funds to create a space on campus to support the academic outcomes of students with a focus on STEM students at the intersections of race, ethnicity, and income. The ALLIES in STEM initiative has a summer bridge program to support the transition of students to campus, an undergraduate research component, and peer and faculty mentoring (Masters et al., 2020). One of the main goals of the program is to increase students' science identity and academic self-concept, which can be considered liberatory outcomes, especially as students of color often enter college with lower academic self-concept and confidence than white students as a result of educational systems (and teachers and counselors) that have made them feel academically inadequate. Students in the ALLIES in STEM program showed increased confidence in their ability to do well in their STEM classes and their ability to be STEM professionals after participating in various aspects of the program. The data show that providing academic and personal support, mentoring, and racial-ethnic-cultural validation are important structures for serving that have the ability to enhance liberatory outcomes for students in HSIs.

These examples show the broad ways that HSI federal funds can be used to establish centers and spaces on campus that address the academic, cultural, and liberatory needs of students at HSIs through an intersectional lens, rather than focusing solely on one dimension of identity. Before establishing centers to meet students' multidimensional needs, transformed HSIs that do not have established cultural centers should first consider the importance of these spaces, which serve as "counterspaces, a home away from home, and a haven in a hostile territory" for students of color (Patton, 2010, p. xiv). Although many cultural centers are rooted in the 1960s and 1970s civil rights struggle, when there were no HSIs and a majority of colleges and universities were predominantly white, minoritized students at HSIs still want these spaces. Latinx and undocumented students at Dominican University, a small private HSI in Chicago with a predominantly Latinx student population, demanded a multicultural center in the year 2020 (and were successful in their demands, with the president providing a space and hiring a full-time director for the Center for Cultural Liberation) (Petrov & Garcia, 2021). The commitment of financial and human resources to spaces of racial liberation is a powerful way to transform racially white organizations. Yet spaces and centers that only focus on race-ethnicity-Indigeneity are insufficient for addressing the full needs of students of color at HSIs, as their intersectional needs must also be accounted for.

Liberatory Opportunities at HSIs

Racial-ethnic-Indigenous student organizations at transformed HSIs may also be essential for enhancing liberatory engagement. Latinx Greek organizations and organizations that have historically served and empowered Latinx college students at PWIs (e.g., MEChA [Movimiento Estudiantil Chicano de Aztlán], SACNAS, SHPE [Society of Hispanic Professional Engineers]) are still relevant within the HSI context. Guardia and Evans (2008) found that Latino men in a Latino Greek organization at one HSI in the Southeast developed their racial-ethnic identity through their involvement. Participants stressed that being involved in their racial-ethnic-based organization led to involvment in other campus-based activities, further enhancing their leadership development. They also talked about the importance of language preservation, which they experienced as a result of being involved in an organization where a majority of the members used Spanish as a form of bonding and communication.

Alternatively, Onorato and Musoba (2015) found that Latina women in their study who attended a predominantly Latinx-enrolling HSI in the Southeast were involved in student organizations that were not racial-ethnic specific. With such a large population of Latinx students on campus, mainstream student organizations had a large population of students of color too, making involvement and engagement opportunities more accessible. The women in their study experienced leadership development as a result of involvement and also had opportunities to discuss race, ethnicity, and gender with other members in their organization. These examples are important within the context of transformed HSIs as they suggest that racial-ethnic-Indigenous-specific organizations and involvement opportunities are *still relevant* at HSIs, even if the majority of the student population is students of color; at the same time, opportunities that are not racial-ethnic-Indigenous-specific may also cultivate conversations about race, gender, sexual orientation, and other intersectional identities because these identities are important to students at HSIs. Transformed HSIs should cultivate and enhance identity-specific involvement and engagement experiences for students as an essential part of the infrastructure.

Of final note, liberatory experiences and opportunities at transformed HSIs should be dynamic and innovative and account for the barriers and challenges to involvement and engagement that students at HSIs may face. Many experiences and opportunities for supporting students at HSIs have not been documented, but it doesn't mean they aren't occurring at HSIs. I encourage readers to dream about the possibilities rather than reinventing the same experiences that have been created and re-created for decades. Students need to know that the institution understands them and their families and communities' experiences with injustice. Providing cocurricular opportunities for students to focus on various dimensions of collective liberation and healing, even if it is not grounded in their own struggles, is imperative. Examples are numerous and include fighting for justice and liberation for women and children in immigration centers, mixed-status families negatively affected by Immigration and Customs Enforcement, DACAmented and undocumented students, day laborers, farm workers, factory workers, union workers fighting for basic worker rights, queer and Trans* people facing violence and death at high rates and legislative bills that seek to erase and harm them, sex workers who are stigmatized and criminalized, incarcerated people who have been wrongly accused and sentenced, Muslims and Jews who face violence in their place of worship, and Palestinians struggling for liberation, among many others not mentioned here. Although students at transformed HSIs can learn about these struggles for justice within the formal classroom, they can act and fight for justice through out-of-the-classroom experiences and involvement opportunities. This is part of collective liberation within transformed HSIs.

Support Services through a Justice Lens

A third dimension of the infrastructure is the support services that are generally offered at all colleges and universities. These services include academic advising, counseling and psychological services, academic support services, career services, and technology support among others. Many campuses also offer support services for students with dis/abilities, former foster youth, veterans, and students with varying religious needs. There is also an emergent focus on supporting students with food and housing insecurities and those that have faced extreme loss due to COVID-19. Mental health is also front and center, with college and university presidents reporting that student mental health needs are a top concern (Turk et al., 2020). Although it is common practice to provide support services for students, I encourage educators at HSIs to evaluate and assess their structures for serving students through a race- and identity-centered approach, which is still not common across HSIs. After reviewing student equity plans and other relevant policy and practice documents of nine Hispanic-serving community colleges (HSCCs) in California, Felix and Fernandez Castro (2018) found that only 16% ($n = 28$) of all identified activities for addressing equity explicitly named Black (9%) or Latinx (7%) as a focus of the activity. Of the 28 activities, only six described explicit plans to address the structures by creating or integrating new offices, units, or rolls on campus for attending to racial identity-specific needs.

A look at the list of demands made by students of color at 80 institutions across the nation in response to systemic and structural racism on campus (https://www.thedemands.org) shows that students want more specific support for minoritized students. This includes mental health support, career support, and legal support, in addition to an increased demand for academic support and campus activities (Chessman & Wayt, 2016). Students of color want mental health professionals, career advisors, legal consultants, and academic advisors that look like them, including professionals of color with multiple minoritized identities. Students need to feel safe when they seek out services on campus. For example, students of color need mental health professionals that understand their experiences with everyday racism, discrimination, and microaggressions, someone who can validate their experiences as racialized people who are often criminalized on campus, in the classroom, and at the hands of campus police (Jenkins et al., 2021; Smith et al., 2007). Since students of color have experienced long-term trauma because of systemic racism, educators at transformed HSIs must address mental health concerns and center healing in their practice (McGee & Stovall, 2015). Students of color also need career advice that acknowledges their needs, not only for themselves but for their families. For example, students may not want to leave their families and communities to pursue career opportunities, regardless of how beneficial those opportunities are or how upwardly mobile they become as a result. Students of color also need legal advice without fear of repercussion. Undocumented students, for example, should not fear that they might put themselves or their families in harm if they seek out legal advice on campus. Students also want to visit academic advisors without the fear of being microaggressed, yet there are documented experiences of that being the case at HSIs (Sánchez Ordaz et al., 2020).

Transformed HSIs, as racialized institutions serving a majority student population of color, must actively develop support services that center students' race and intersectional identities. Moreover, there is a need to hire race-conscious, equity-minded, abolitionist student services professionals who will not reinforce deficit understandings about students' abilities, needs, and experiences (Felix, 2021; Maldonado, 2019). Student services personnel, and all classified staff at transformed HSIs, also need training and professional development to enhance their ability to serve students through a race-conscious and socially just lens. University of California, Santa Cruz, for example, utilized Title V federal funding to implement a campus-wide advising conference to help advisors develop humanizing approaches to serving students that included the disruption of implicit bias and the enhancement of microaffirmations (Sánchez Ordaz et al., 2020). Here I provide ideas for developing student services through a justice-centered approach.

Principles of a Justice-Centered Approach

Patty Berne and Sins Invalid (n.d.), a dis/ability justice performance project that centers people of color, queer, Trans*, and nonbinary people with dis/abilities (https://www.sinsinvalid.org), developed 10 principles of dis/ability justice that offer an excellent example of how to center race and intersectionality through a justice lens. Their approach is particularly powerful, as they call for justice around a topic, dis/ability, which higher education has essentially ignored as an equity and justice issue and instead treats as a compliance concern (Evans et al., 2007). As noted by Evans et al. (2007), "from a social justice perspective, it is important to understand the law is an incomplete method of social change, and equity cannot be achieved through legal measures only" (p. 92). Patty Berne and Sins Invalid call for dis/ability justice that includes (1) intersectionality, (2) leadership from those most impacted, (3) anticapitalist politics, (4) cross-movement solidarity, (5) recognizing wholeness, (6) sustainability, (7) commitment to cross-dis/ability solidarity, (8) interdependence, (9) collective access, and (10) collective liberation. Although they are referring specifically to dis/ability justice, I find these principles particularly powerful when thinking about student services transformation toward justice. Based on these principles,

Are students of color with multiple minoritized identities *utilizing* the services?	Are student services identity neutral? Are race and other intersectional identities of students at the core of support services?	Are students served through a normative, white, traditional college student approach?
Are students of color with multiple minoritized identities asked to be leaders and help provide direction for services?	Are people of color with intersectional identities leading these services?	How are students informed about available student services?
Are approaches to student services guided by law and compliance rather than equity, justice, and liberation?	Are student services cross-functional to allow for collective liberation?	Are students served through a deficit lens?

Figure 3. Questions to Guide the Development of Justice-Centered Support Services

I offer a set of guiding questions for support staff to consider (see figure 3). Although there are few examples of liberatory approaches to student support services in the HSI research, the principles and guiding questions I offer should be considered by all student support units across campus, including those areas not typically considered "support services," such as campus police.

Abolish Campus Police and Campus Conduct

With the number of Black people in the United States disproportionately killed by police officers, there is a loud call to abolish police both on and off college campuses. The call to divest, dismantle, and delegitimize police is a socially just solution, as it challenges the power and resources that have historically, politically, and economically legitimized state-sanctioned violence toward people of color in the United States (Akbar, 2020). An abolitionist approach essentially calls for a disruption of the economic and legal system that contributes to inequities in the carceral state. Of importance, an abolitionist approach does not call for more DEI, implicit bias, and antiracist training but instead calls for a completely new method. Transformed HSIs committed to racial equity and justice must acknowledge that students of color, and particularly Black students, are regularly subjected to state-sanctioned violence and surveillance on campus (Jenkins et al., 2021; Smith et al., 2007). As transformed HSIs challenge the neoliberal hold on higher education, the call to abolish police on campus is aligned, as policing and incarceration are fundamental tools in a neoliberal society (Akbar, 2020). A more equitable, just, and liberatory approach to policing and campus conduct, therefore, is crucial within a transformed HSI.

A call to abolish police on college campuses would mean a reduction in police budgets and an increase in resources for student-centered and community-based approaches to address noncriminal matters (Davis, 2020). An abolitionist approach also requires colleges and universities to discontinue the use of local police for support with noncriminal situations such as large-scale events and gatherings on campus (Davis, 2020). Divestment from police would disrupt the carceral logics that have been embedded within institutions of higher education since the inception of campus police in 1894 at Yale University (Davis & Matias Dizon, 2020) and aligns with the call to transform HSIs at the structures. Transformed HSIs that commit to divesting in police should instead elevate the use of trauma-informed care, mediation, and restorative justice, particularly in the conduct system. While campus police mirror and mimic the racially unjust policing system in society, so too does the traditional conduct system within colleges and universities.

In the decolonizing HSIs model, I called for the use of restorative practices on campus (Garcia, 2018). Although "justice and accountability" is no longer a core dimension of the transformed HSIs framework, the ideological practice of restorative justice emerges, particularly when it comes to judicial hearings and campus conduct. Restorative practices have been adopted by urban schools as an alternative to "zero tolerance" rules that disproportionately criminalize, isolate, and remove students of color from the classroom (Winn, 2018). Some colleges and universities have also adopted restorative justice to resolve conflict (Lipkin, 2009). As a humanizing process, restorative justice combines mediation with responsibility, placing relationship building at the center by allowing those who have been harmed to discuss solutions for repairing damage with those responsible for the harm (Winn, 2018). The adoption of restorative practices in judicial and conduct hearings at transformed HSIs is an intentional way to reject and disrupt carceral logics embedded within the educational system. The goal of a restorative process shall be healing for the students, the institution, and the larger community (Rerucha, 2021). In a transformed HSI, this can be powerful for situations related to racism and intersectional discrimination, as there can be active work toward solidarity and liberation in the process of healing.

Physical Infrastructure

A final element of infrastructure is the *physical* infrastructure. Despite the fact that Title V grants allow for expansion and improvement of the physical infrastructure, it has not been an important facet of servingness. Yet the physical infrastructure can be vital to transformed HSIs as institutions move toward developing spaces and places that evoke feelings of humanization, racial equity, social justice, collective liberation, and healing. When I conducted my dissertation study, participants brought attention to the physical infrastructure; notably they said that the murals in the building that housed ethnic studies made the institution feel like an HSI (Garcia, 2013a). I visited the building and spent time with the murals; I took note of the feelings that I had in the space, and, yes, I felt what my participants meant. That space felt like an HSI, and I could see myself there. Most places on campus do not make people of color feel like they belong, and some spaces feel exclusionary, including those that have statues or building names that memorialize historically racist or colonial figures. The finding about the murals was powerful, and although I haven't published that aspect of my dissertation, I often talk about the importance of place and space on campus.

I call on organizational members to address the physical infrastructure as an important endeavor in transforming the institution, as campus artifacts send powerful messages about the campus culture and values regarding equity and justice (Banning & Bartel, 1997). These messages may be about belonging, safety, equity, and role behaviors for certain groups (Banning & Bartel, 1997). They may also elicit emotional responses, ranging from overtly positive, meaning the artifacts are consciously and actively designed to create a significant positive message, to overtly negative, which occurs when the message is so strongly negative that there is little room for interpretation about its intent to harm members of certain social identity groups.

As suggested by Banning and Bartel (1997), campus artifacts include art, statues, paintings, signs, graffiti, and architecture. Alcantar et al. (2020) added that digital platforms and campus geography are also important aspects of the physical infrastructure. Digital platforms include websites and social media posts, while geography is about the physical location of services, departments, and programs that center people of color and other minoritized identities (e.g., Educational Opportunity Program, ethnic studies) (Alcantar et al., 2020). Each of these elements should be a part of the campus shift toward becoming a transformed HSI, which may include investing in artifacts, art, and architecture that are socially conscious, about and for people of color, and created by artists of color. Garcia and Zaragoza (2020) confirmed the importance of these artifacts when they talked to students at two HSIs in the Midwest who were asked to take pictures of artifacts that represent diversity on their campuses. Several students took pictures of art, including sculptures and murals, while others took pictures of signs on campus and door decorations on faculty members' doors, which conveyed powerful messages to students about diversity. Several students took pictures of the cultural center, which to them embodied the campus's commitment to diversity.

Arguably, spaces and places that represent and center people of color are important dimensions of the physical infrastructure and architecture, including cultural centers, which have historically served as counterspaces and spaces of resistance for students of color (Patton, 2010). Transformed HSIs must establish spaces where students can gather and find community with same-race and social identity peers, remembering the need to redistribute power and resources as a part of decredentialing whiteness. Campuses must also ensure adequate funding for the people who work within spaces where equity, justice, and liberation are at the center. Although participants in Garcia and Zaragoza's study (2020) were told not to take pictures of people, students stressed that people are a vital indicator of servingness at an HSI, reinforcing the need to increase the compositional diversity of educators and decision makers on campus. Yet as noted by Jenkins (2010), educators who work within spaces that center minoritized students often face an uphill battle as they navigate a larger campus climate that is frequently unsupportive of efforts to empower racial-ethnic-Indigenous communities and other minoritized groups. Transformed HSIs must fund and support physical infrastructure and the people who work within these spaces.

Transforming the physical infrastructure should be intentional, fluid, ongoing, and reflective to ensure that artifacts continue to send the originally intended message about equity and justice. One student in Garcia and Zaragoza's (2020) study noted that although art may represent diverse cultures, races, or ethnicities, it could also be exclusionary to groups that are not represented. This also suggests a growing need to elevate intersectionality and solidarity through campus artifacts. Transformed HSIs should also evaluate the campus artifacts to determine if they counter the campus's commitment to racial equity, social justice, and liberation. Examples may include buildings named after (in)famous people who historically opposed justice and civil rights for minoritized groups and statues of real or mythical heroes that reinforce dominant narratives about history, whiteness, and settler colonialism. This includes art, statues, and pictures of campus mascots that reinforce these narratives, including pioneers, patriots, frontiersmen, and Indigenous people. Desai and Abeita (2017) found that for Native American students at one HSI, the university seal was microaggressive at an institutional level, while Kovats Sánchez (2021) documented how one Indigenous student described the campus mascot as harmful. Banning et al. (2008) suggested that campus artifacts be assessed for their messaging, ranging from negative or null to contributions/additive and transformational/social action. A microaggressive university seal or campus mascot is an example of a negative symbol that may elicit feelings of exclusion and outright violence.

Using Banning et al.'s (2008) taxonomy, Alcantar et al. (2020) assessed the campus artifacts of three dually designated HSIs and AANAPISIs in the West to understand the implicit and explicit ways that the campuses communicated their enactment of servingness. They observed architecture, building locations, signage, artwork, sculptures, digital platforms, and campus geography, noting how commitments to racial-ethnic-Indigenous equity were communicated at four levels: negative, null, contributions/additive, and transformational/social action. They found notable ways that the three campuses addressed the physical infrastructure as they strived to become HSIs/AANAPISIs. They emphasized that a transformational shift of the physical infrastructure may include the central relocation of student services specifically for students of color (e.g., cultural centers), increased signage that indicates the campus's designation as an HSI, the inclusion of HSI status and commitments on the campus's webpage, and the installation of permanent art collections centering communities of color and by racial-ethnic-Indigenous artists. Simultaneously, they urged transformed HSIs to remove artifacts that are outright racist (including campus mascots), celebrate whiteness (including pictures of predominantly white male founders, boards of trustees, or prominent alumni), are English only, and that police students (including those that restrict movement or usage of campus facilities or equipment) (Alcantar et al., 2020).

In addition to assessing artifacts through the lens of racial equity and antiracism, Davila and Montelongo (2020) stressed the importance of HSIs, acknowledging their commitment to serving low-income and first-generation students. They described the technological renovation at one HSCC in Texas that addressed the digital divide that low-income and first-generation students faced. Taylor and Burnett (2019) also examined digital equity across a sample of 217 HSIs, specifically asking questions about accessibility to websites. They found a wide range in website accessibility, with some institutions having thousands of errors across their institutional sites, meaning that students with dis/abilities may not be able to access some pages using Voiceover, a robust screen-reading assistive technology. Importantly, only 7.8% of all HSI websites in the sample were accessible enough for students using Voiceover to navigate their way to the admissions and application page. This presents a huge concern about accessibility to HSIs for students with dis/abilities. Multiple dimensions of identity should be part of the artifact assessment, including race, ethnicity, gender, income, dis/ability, and religion (Banning & Bartel, 1997). Spaces and artifacts at transformed HSIs must be grounded in equity, justice, and liberation for students of color at multiple intersections of identity.

Conclusion

Transformed HSIs can and should utilize federal funds to develop infrastructures for serving minoritized students of color (Garcia & Koren, 2020). Yet a redistribution of current economic, human, and social resources is also essential. Policies and practices about what is taught (curriculum), how it is taught (pedagogy), and how learning is supported beyond the classroom (through engagement, involvement, support services, and the physical infrastructure) must de-credential whiteness, be coupled with race (and/or center race), and seek to empower people of color. In other words, there should be a concerted effort to redesign the infrastructure that centers on the identities and experiences of students of color at the intersections of minoritized identities. But there are no one-size-fits-all approaches. Educators at transformed HSIs must consider the various dimensions of identity and experiences that students arrive to campus with, which is different at every institution, depending on regional location and type of institution.

Transformed HSIs must invest resources in curriculum and beyond the classroom experiences that will elevate the institution's commitment to racial equity, social justice, and collective liberation of all minoritized groups and advance the practices that support equitable academic and liberatory outcomes and humanizing and validating experiences. The approaches, philosophies, and practices outlined in this chapter just touch the surface of the level of deep reflection and change that must occur at transformed HSIs in order to provide an experience that centers racial-ethnic-Indigenous students' ways of knowing and elevates their critical consciousness while also advancing their learning and academic success. Of final note, campuses should also engage various members to determine their needs and desires for the infrastructure, including students, families, and external partners. Engaging students in the process is important, as they will be honest about how the infrastructure does or does not represent their reality.

5

Rethinking Governance
and Leadership

IN THE TRANSFORMING HSIs FRAMEWORK, governance and leadership connect all the dimensions, with members (see chapter 3) working with external influences (see chapter 6) to make decisions and develop policies that fulfill the mission, identity, and purpose of the organization (see chapter 2) by developing the infrastructure (see chapter 4). Governance and leadership were not considered by Latinx advocates who fought vehemently for the HSI designation; instead, they focused on the enrollment criteria for becoming an HSI and sought to secure federal funding for these resource-deprived institutions (Valdez, 2015). As such, governance and leadership are often ignored dimensions of HSI grant getting and implementation (Santiago et al., 2016), with little efforts to train and develop decision makers who can lead for equity, justice, and liberation. The governance and leadership dimensions should become a part of the process to convert HSIs into liberatory spaces. Decision makers and leaders at HSIs must believe in this goal and actively work toward it.

The Transforming HSIs Framework is about organizational *change*, which requires strong leadership and decision-making (e.g., Kezar & Eckel, 2002a, 2002b; Petrov & Garcia, 2021). Yet the change is grounded in decolonial, abolitionist, social justice principles and guided by the assumptions that the organization is racialized, which necessitates a different level of commitment and action on the part of decision makers and leaders. An abolitionist approach to transformation is not about destroying current structures but rather redesigning for justice by analyzing and reconciling the ways that the organization has been oppressive and harmful (Kaba, 2021). With this institutional reckoning comes the requirement for healing and growth as part of transformation (Rerucha, 2021), which should be guided by the governance and leadership dimensions. An active move to transform the institution requires a disruption of the power structures that dominate most institutions of higher education, with mostly white people having authority and decision-making power and governing through the lens of white normative standards (Ledesma & Burciaga, 2015). Transformed HSIs must redistribute power and resources by investing in infrastructures, policies, and practices that are grounded in liberatory and humanizing approaches to education.

A redistribution of resources includes human resources, with a need for professional development for educators and decision makers. All leaders and decision makers should reflect on their personal beliefs about racism and oppression and equity and justice (Garcia & Natividad, 2018). We must remember that we are entrenched in the organizations and systems that we seek to change and that we require a personal transformation too (Kaba, 2021). Training and development should also provide decision makers and leaders with tools for disrupting the deficit thinking about students that is rampant in colleges and universities (Bensimon, 2007; Mora & Rios-Aguilar, 2017; Maldonado, 2019). This deficit thinking is directly connected to whiteness, as educators and decision makers actively blame students of color for their own struggles rather than acknowledging the various ways that educational systems themselves are flawed (Bensimon, 2012). Resources, power, and budgets must be coupled with race, or they run the risk of becoming race-neutral and insufficient for addressing inequities in outcomes and experiences for students of color at the intersections of minoritized identities.

Within the Transforming HSIs Framework, governance and leadership are conceptualized separately, although they work in conjunction in order to create change. Kezar and Eckel (2002a, 2002b) argued that comprehensive, deep-seated, structural change within institutions of higher education requires the support of senior administration, collaborative leadership, a robust design for change, staff development, and visible actions. The Transforming HSIs Framework itself is a robust design for change that calls on all members of the organization to commit to and act upon becoming an HSI. As conceptualized in the original decolonizing HSIs model, I believe that governance and leadership at transformed HSIs should be decentralized and communal. Within a transformed HSI, governance and leadership shall be truly shared, with intentional efforts to elevate the voices of historically minoritized members, including people of color with intersectional identities across gender, sexual orientation, religion, and ability.

Rethinking Governance for Equity and Justice

Governance is a concept as old as colleges and universities themselves, with the enduring need to determine who has the authority to make decisions, manage the organization, develop policies, allocate resources, and strategically plan for the future of the institution (Austin & Jones, 2016; Marginson & Considine, 2000). Yet governance must be defined within the context of HSIs, as decisions within higher education are always context specific (Posselt et al., 2020). The HSI context includes the sociohistoric context of the institution, including the regional and local communities surrounding the institution. It also includes the sociohistoric contexts from which members of the organization come and participate in. This includes an acknowledgment of the racialized nature of the HSI designation and a consciousness of the racial-ethnic-Indigenous and intersectional identities of the students who attend HSIs.

Governance is a complex concept that occurs at the micro level (departmental) and meso level (organizational) of the organization, with decisions being made that affect the day-to-day functioning and overall organizational performance (Austin & Jones, 2016). At the micro and meso levels, the structures must allow for decision-making, policy development, and resource allocation that fulfill the mission, identity, and purpose of the organization. Individual departments and programs should have full autonomy to determine the best way to do this while simultaneously working toward equity, justice, and liberation. Micro- and meso-level decisions and policies are abundant and include those that pertain to student admissions, faculty and staff hiring, tenure and promotion, and curriculum review. Decisions and policies are also made to address every aspect of student life, from residence hall and fitness center policies to rules governing student organizations and student conduct. Through the lens of equity, justice, and liberation, these decisions must be made while simultaneously asking if and *for who* they are fair, equitable, and just (Kezar & Matias Dizon, 2020). Within a transformed HSI, micro- and meso-level decision-making must center the ways of knowing and being of people of color with multiple minoritized identities. This includes a critical analysis of how policies and decisions directly and indirectly affect minoritized students (España & Herrera, 2020).

Governance also includes responsiveness to the macro level (state, federal, and system level) structures that influence the organization and fulfillment of the HSI mission, identity, and purpose (see chapter 6). The macro-level structures often determine funding for the institution and stress accountability, affordability, and quality assurance, making them essential to govern and manage (Austin & Jones, 2016). Yet they often do this in race-neutral ways, meaning they do not adequately account for racial inequities and injustices in making decisions (Jones et al., 2017). Institutional decision makers at transformed HSIs should work with policy intermediaries and legislators to elevate the focus on race-conscious state- and federal-level decision-making and enhance efforts to diversify state governing boards, which remain predominantly white. Governance at the macro level also includes a relationship with external partners, businesses, and nongovernmental organizations (Marginson & Considine, 2000). Importantly, there is also a need to include both campus and city police in the governance process. There are few conversations about including police in the formal governance process of the institution, yet this is necessary within HSIs that predominantly enroll students of color who interact with police in ways that are often inequitable and unjust or outright violent and racist (Davis & Matias Dizon, 2020; Jenkins et al., 2021). An abolitionist approach to organizing will require transformed HSIs to reconsider the funding and utilization of police for nonviolent matters and instead defer to communal, trauma-informed, and antiracist practices (Davis, 2020; Kaba, 2021). Overall, macro-level governance must be reimagined to allow for equity, justice, and liberation to emerge in the strategic planning and decision-making processes and to advance the HSI identity, mission, and purpose.

Advancing Shared Governance for Servingness

Shared governance is the process that allows trustees or governing boards, administrators, and faculty (by way of senates) to manage institutions of higher education at each level of the organization, independently leading the organizations within their individual spheres and then collaboratively making decisions for the advancement of the entire institution (Eckel & Kezar, 2016). The board of trustees (or just "the board") is at the top of the organizational governance structure, made up of independent volunteers granted decision-making power, despite not being formal employees of the institution or involved in the day-to-day operations. They generally have five distinct tasks: (1) setting the institution's mission and strategy, (2) monitoring organizational and administrator performance, (3) selecting and evaluating the president of the institution, (4) safeguarding the institution's finances, and (5) advocating on behalf of the institution to the general public. The president (or chancellor) is the highest positional leader, charged with overseeing the institution's resources, managing key administrators on campus, coordinating the strategic direction of the institution, and serving as the institution's primary liaison with the external world (Eckel & Kezar, 2016).

Importantly, the president is hired, monitored, and advised by the board. As such, the board must hire a president that is truly committed to the institution's HSI designation and work collaboratively with the president to ensure that the institution has the strategic planning and resource allocation in place to elevate the institution's commitment to its racially, ethnically, and economically diverse students. Scott (2018) argues that boards must also be well versed in the history of the institution, yet HSI boards must be well versed in the contemporary history of the institution, including the emergence of the racial-ethnic-Indigenous populations within the institution and the process of becoming an HSI. Boards of trustees and presidents making decisions with and for transformed HSIs must enact an approach to organizing that acknowledges the harm that the institution has caused to people of color and actively work to address inequities in outcomes and experiences and create spaces and structures that are responsive to the needs of minoritized members of the organization.

HSI Governing Boards

There is an emergence of work around culturally sustaining governing boards that can inform the institution's movement toward servingness. As with every dimension of the transformed HSIs framework, culturally sustaining the governing board's decision-making, evaluation and assessment, and advocacy work should center the racial-ethnic-Indigenous identities of the students, families, and communities they serve. This includes a need for intentional conversations about race and social identities as well as long-standing systems of oppression that have led to inequities in outcomes and experiences. Rall et al. (2020) proposed four domains of culturally sustaining governing boards, including (1) equity knowledge, (2) motivation for equity, (3) value of equity, and (4) sociopolitical consciousness. Equity knowledge requires the use of disaggregated data to inform decision-making, which should include the efforts of institutional research, human resources, and diversity affairs offices. Equity motivation requires a deep commitment and drive for advancing equitable outcomes and experiences for all members of the institution, not just for the sake of "checking off a box." This means that as HSIs shift toward a mission, identity, and purpose grounded in principles of equity, justice, and liberation, governing boards too must shift their approach to decision-making that is grounded in their commitment to the HSI designation. The Association of Governing Boards (AGB, 2007) has made it clear that governing boards shall be held accountable for upholding the mission and identity of the institution. Yet HSIs often pursue the HSI designation and HSI funding without consulting the governing boards, with the most significant commitment to the HSI identity coming from grant implementers (Garcia, 2013a; Petrov & Garcia, 2021).

Rall et al. (2020) advance the idea that governing boards should express their value for equity by creating a statement that defines equity, lays out goals and assessment measures, and provides accountability measures. The board of trustees at Metropolitan State University of Denver, for example, established a Sustained Racial Justice Committee in order to engage in systemic antiracist work as a board (Coulter, 2020). The final dimension of a culturally sustaining governing board is that of sociopolitical consciousness, which requires the board to receive regular training around issues of equity and justice and specifically for the minoritized populations within the institutions that they serve (Rall et al., 2020). This aligns with AGB (2007), which states that governing boards should be accountable to the values and principles of higher education as a field. The field of higher education itself may not be changing fast enough when it comes to advancing equity, justice, and liberation, yet there are loud calls for an elevated focus on racial justice and antiracist education practices within higher education (Elliott & Jones, 2021; Gaston Gayles & Rockenbach, 2021). There is also a shifting policy context among staunch advocates of equity and social justice, including the American

Council on Education, the Education Trust, and the Institute for Higher Education Policy (Jaschik, 2021). Transformed HSIs should respond to this shift toward greater equity and justice conversations, particularly when it comes to governance, leadership, and decision-making.

Faculty Governance at Transformed HSIs

Within a shared governance model, faculty members are also part of the governing body and charged with overseeing the curricular structures and making major decisions by ways of faculty senates. Shared governance, however, has declined in recent years, with boards and administrators assuming most of the decision-making, policymaking, budgetary oversight, and overall power and control of the institution, leaving faculty on the margins (Kezar & Matias Dizon, 2020). While a traditional model of shared governance has historically been limited, as it only grants power to boards, presidents, and faculty, it has become even more restricted, with faculty senates often being at odds with administrators, having limited decision-making power, and having limited participation of full-time tenured faculty, excluding the largest populations of faculty (part-time, adjunct, nontenure stream, and faculty of color) (Eckel & Kezar, 2016). The trend away from shared governance is wrapped up in neoliberal ideals where colleges and universities value managerialism and academic capitalism with a focus on revenue-generating endeavors (Kezar & Matias Dizon, 2020). True democratic participation must be restored within a transformed HSI, with intentional efforts to include faculty that have been pushed to the margins (i.e., faculty of color and contingent faculty).

Villarreal Sosa et al. (2022) proposed a democratic, participatory faculty governance model for HSIs grounded in decolonial ideals. Using a testimonio approach, they first described their experiences within the faculty governance structures at one small private Catholic HSI. They outlined the lack of representation of women and people of color within faculty governance, much of it resulting from rank and tenure but also from longevity of representation of disciplines and colleges that are dominated by white men. They also described a deep-seated culture of white fragility wrapped up in an institutional ethos of "niceness" and relationship-centered decision-making. As a result, when women and people of color experienced microaggressions, they often felt compelled to remain quiet in the spirit of "collegiality" and/or to avoid being perceived as angry or hostile. The authors stated that even when women and faculty of color were appointed to positions within the faculty governance structure, they often left these positions because they would experience racial battle fatigue.

The authors also gave a specific example of a proposal from the Spanish department that was rejected by the formal faculty governance process, despite the fact that it centered Latinx students, which represented over 50% of the student population, and addressed equity issues, with much of the opposition grounded in neoliberalism and student enrollment issues in other language departments. Based on their detailed account with faculty governance, Villarreal Sosa et al. (2022) proposed five tenets for a decolonized faculty governance structure within HSIs: (1) equitable representation of faculty of color; (2) expanded representation to include staff and part-time/contingent faculty; (3) active dismantling of whiteness and racial microaggressions within the governance structures; (4) additional oversight of faculty governance by administrators charged with diversity, equity, and inclusion work as well as Title V and Title II HSI grant directors; and (5) the adoption of a critically reflexive process including equity checks and accountability. As one of few empirically grounded models of faculty governance within HSIs, this approach should be strongly considered by transformed HSIs. Moreover, the authors described specific reasons why women, femmes, and faculty of color should be compensated for the extra labor and work that they contribute within a transformed HSI, raising the question of rewards within the Transforming HSIs Framework.

Democratizing Governance to Enhance Servingness

The shared governance model has historically had very little involvement from students, staff, alumni, and other external partners

(Kezar & Matias Dizon, 2020). Even those who have traditionally been included in the shared governance process feel that there is a greater need to align the goals and mission of the institution and to create greater accountability for all members to advance the institution (AGB, 2016). Shared governance within a transformed HSI must reject the long-standing commitment to centralized reporting structures, bureaucratic hierarchies, and positional leadership and move toward a model that allows for decision-making with and for stakeholders across the institution (Garcia, 2018). Equal participatory power at every level of decision-making is the only way to restore education as a public good and truly achieve equity, justice, and liberatory outcomes.

Shared governance must involve students who work collaboratively with institutional educators, leaders, governing boards, and external partners to make decisions for becoming a transformed HSI. In 2016, after a surge of student activism on college campuses, minoritized students from 80 campuses across the country made a list of demands pertaining to equity and justice, with a majority calling for policy changes around issues of climate assessments, protocols for hate speech and bias incidents, affordability, student advocacy, faculty reviews, and administrator transparency (Chessman & Wayt, 2016). What their demands suggest is that governance decisions are often inequitable and ineffective for adequately serving students of color and must be changed. Yet these voices are not included in the traditional models of shared governance.

Within a transformed HSI, voices of students, staff, alumni, community members, and other external partners must be elevated. Those traditionally on the margins should be given opportunities to engage in the decision-making process. For example, when a campus engages in problem-solving conversations and/or those pertaining to new policy development, there should be a process of transformative discourse that fosters democratic participation from those outside of the normative bureaucratic decision-making circles (Kezar & Matias Dizon, 2020). These important conversations may be moved to staff council meetings, student organization meetings, or community open forums. Every member and external stakeholder should be given ample opportunity to provide feedback through formal and informal surveys, focus groups, or listening sessions. Committees are also an effective way to share decision-making power (Scott, 2018) and should be used to extend governance to students, staff, alumni, and community members.

Overall, governance within a transformed HSI ought to be innovative and forward-thinking, it must be inclusive of those often on the margins, and it must be guided by the principles of equity-mindedness and race-consciousness. Soft reform, characterized by efforts to include minoritized people in spaces that have been exclusionary, oppressive, and outright violent are not going to work; governance and leadership instead must be radically reformed to empower people of color and people with minoritized identities, to redistribute resources and power, and to reconcile and heal past injustices (de Oliveira Andreotti et al., 2015). The topic of governance within HSIs has not been extensively covered in research or transformed in practice. Moreover, a majority of the research focuses solely on administrators rather than on governing boards or faculty senates as formal shared governance structures, and students, staff, and external partners as informal governing bodies. Rethinking shared governance within a transformed HSI should be a priority in order to disrupt the ways that HSIs are continuing to govern, make decisions, develop policies, and allocate resources like historically white institutions.

Strategic Planning as a Dimension of Servingness

Governance and decision-making within the Transformed HSI Framework are directly connected to the strategic purpose of the institution (see chapter 2), with a need for intentional planning and strategizing for *becoming* an HSI that fulfills equitable educational and liberatory outcomes and validating experiences. As noted by Vargas and Ward (2020), increasing the racial-ethnic composition of the student population is a quicker process than gaining strategic buy-in from institutional leaders and fully embracing the HSI identity, mission, and purpose. In other words, meeting the enrollment criteria to become HSI eligible is the easy part; strategically planning for adequately serving Latinx, Black, Indigenous, Asian American, Pacific Islander, and Mixed-Race students is more challenging. In outlining California Lutheran University's process of becoming an HSI, Vargas and Ward (2020) noted various tensions within the governance structures. For example, institutional leaders and the board of regents supported the new enrollment policies and practices that would lead to greater enrollment of Latinx students but did not address broader institutional policies and practices for supporting these students, such as those related to faculty hiring and teaching. As institutions move toward HSI status, there must be strategic buy-in from trustees, presidents, and administrators and an intentional effort to review and develop policies and practices, make decisions, and allocate resources that will move the institution from Latinx-enrolling to Latinx-serving.

Launch an HSI Task Force

One important strategic decision that an institution can make is to launch an HSI task force. Cal Lutheran created an HSI task force, inclusive of faculty, administrators, and students that examined institutional policies that would support their efforts to embrace the HSI identity (Vargas & Ward, 2020). The task force also created a specific mission and vision for the institution's HSI identity and designed a Cal Lutheran HSI logo. The University of California, Santa Cruz (UCSC), similarly established a cross-functional HSI team of staff, faculty, and students, charged by administration to determine what it would mean for UCSC to become an HSI (Reguerín et al., 2020). The team developed a multiphased strategic roadmap inclusive of a self-study of the institution's progress toward enhancing academic outcomes (e.g., disaggregated retention rates, progress rates in STEM courses) and focus groups to better understand students' experiences with the climate and racial microaggressions. The HSI team used a data-driven approach to inform their decision-making and became increasingly focused on race and racial inequities in the process. In doing so, their strategy turned toward principles and practices for becoming a racially just HSI that centers innovation and transformation (Reguerín et al., 2020). An HSI task force inclusive of members from across the institution, including students, staff, faculty, administrators, and community members, is an important governance strategy for HSIs. Yet the task force must be supported by administrators and given a specific charge related to becoming an HSI.

Seek Counsel and Collaborations from External Partners

HSIs should seek counsel and support from organizations that are actively thinking about and working toward defining servingness in practice and policy, including the Hispanic Association of Colleges and Universities (HACU), *Excelencia* in Education, and the Alliance of HSI Educators (AHSIE). They should also engage with external partners and develop strategic collaborations that will support their enactment of the HSI identity, mission, and purpose. Cal Lutheran sought counsel from HACU, AHSIE, and the University of Southern California's Center for Urban Education. Moreover, they elevated strategic partnerships both within and external to the institution as a way to advance conversations about becoming a Latinx-serving HSI (Vargas & Ward, 2020). Specifically, they improved relationships with STEM partners, local community colleges, P–20 education networks in their county, and community-based STEM organizations, as a way to enhance the institution's capacity for applying for a STEM-specific HSI Title III, Part F grant (Ramirez & Rodriguez-Kiino, 2020). Similarly, UCSC developed strategic partnerships with their feeder institutions in order to apply for a Title V cooperative HSI grant (Reguerín et al., 2020).

Develop a Strategic Plan That Centers Servingness

Strategic planning is crucial for all postsecondary institutions, yet transformed HSIs must strategically plan for enacting an HSI identity, mission, and purpose. In examining the strategic plans of 19 public two- and four-year HSIs in Texas, Flores and Leal (2020) noted that only five had Latinx-serving strategic plans, meaning the plans mentioned the institution's HSI designation mentioned Latinx students, demonstrated an understanding of the surrounding community and geographic region, and noted the ways that the institution elevated Latinx ways of knowing. It is crucial for transformed HSIs to acknowledge their HSI status and to take steps to understand how to center Latinxs in their decision-making. Rodriguez et al. (2018) conducted a study with 39 administrators across seven community colleges in Texas, and although they did not indicate if the seven cases were HSIs, their focus on understanding how these institutions prioritized resources for Latino men offer important suggestions for HSIs seeking to prioritize Latinxs within their strategic planning processes.

Administrators noted that external influences, specifically state and federal priorities, informed and enhanced the way they made decisions for equity and justice (Rodriguez et al., 2018). These administrators said that state-level initiatives to decrease inequitable outcomes by race and gender as well as their pursuit of federal funds earmarked for HSIs allowed them to disrupt racial and gender inequities in their resource allocation and program planning (Rodriguez et al., 2018). In other words, HSIs have the opportunity to align their on-campus equity and justice initiatives with state and federal initiatives centering equity and justice.

The five institutions that Flores and Leal (2020) noted as having Latinx-serving strategic plans stressed their data-informed decision-making, drawing on community feedback, campus climate surveys, and faculty evaluations. Rodriguez et al. (2018) also found that administrators seeking to center Latinxs in their strategic planning pushed for disaggregated decision-making. Leaders within transformed HSIs must enhance the institutions' technological infrastructure to support data-driven decision-making that will improve the outcomes and experiences of students and transparent dissemination of information to all members of the organization (Canales & Chahin, 2019). Flores and Leal (2020) noted, however, that even when institutions used data-informed decision-making strategies, some lacked specific measures for assessing their progress toward serving-ness, which is essential for transformed HSIs. There are numerous "indicators of serving" that can be used to assess progress toward servingness, including academic and liberatory outcomes as well as validating and racialized experiences on campus (Garcia et al., 2019; Garcia, 2020b; see chapter 2).

Allocate Resources for Servingness

Effectively governing HSIs requires decision makers to allocate fund-ing to develop the intellectual, resource, and human capacity for meeting the needs of the minoritized students who attend HSIs (Ca-nales & Chahin, 2019). Rodriguez et al. (2018) found that administra-tors talked specifically about the need to maximize resources within a fiscal climate of budgetary limitations, shortfalls, and accountabil-ity, which included an increased focus on human resources. They rec-ognized that their greatest resources were actually their current employees and found ways to reward and incentivize them. These ad-ministrators also talked about the need to identify a champion for equity and justice initiatives while building a coalition of supporters for these efforts (Rodriguez et al., 2018). Canales and Chahin (2019) argued that enhancing human resources includes the development of a recruitment plan for hiring faculty and staff who are committed to the mission, purpose, and identity of the HSI. Moreover, resources must be allocated for training and developing the capacity of faculty and staff to serve minoritized students. Flores and Leal (2020) noted that the five HSIs with Latinx-focused strategic plans stressed the need to develop and train faculty to meet the needs of students and even allowed for flexible faculty workloads to meet this increased demand.

Like Cal Lutheran and UCSC, all five HSIs that had Latinx-serving strategic plans had Title V HSI grants (Flores & Leal, 2020), reinforc-ing the need for institutions to pursue federal funding in order to develop their HSI identity, mission, and purpose and overall ability to enact servingness. With the support of three federal HSI grants, UCSC redesigned its gateway math, writing, and STEM curricula, strengthened its faculty and staff's ability to advise and support students and increased support for bilingual families, to name a few (Cooper et al., 2020). Similarly, with the support of a federal HSI grant, Cal Lutheran launched an ALLIES in STEM program inclusive of summer bridge activities for incoming STEM students, mentoring for current STEM students, and a dedicated space for ALLIES in STEM students to study, connect, and collaborate (Vargas & Ward, 2020). Decision makers at transformed HSIs must support and encourage efforts to seek and get grants, especially federal grants designated for HSIs as developing institutions.

Plan for Accreditation

Another important governance process that HSI administrators must navigate is the accreditation process. Fernandez and Burnett (2020) interviewed 13 administrators at nine HSIs about accreditation and found that they displayed organizational resilience as an ordinary adaptive process, despite the fact that all MSIs, including HSIs, often come under public scrutiny as they are compared to historically white institutions using white normative measures of effectiveness. The unique mission of MSIs and the racially and economically diverse population within them are often disregarded in the accreditation process, which requires administrators to adapt in unique ways. Although the authors noted that the 13 administrators did not specifically address the construct of HSI in preparing for accreditation, they made suggestions that could help HSIs going through the process. Administrators suggested the use of internal software to update required accreditation documents annually rather than waiting until the review year. They also warned against maladaptive tendencies to neglect the accreditation process, such as staffing down and neglecting the accreditation process after a successful review. These administrators stressed that organizational leaders should create a collegial environment; develop trust, flexibility, and malleability in the data collection process; and foster a culture that views accreditation as an opportunity to positively change students' lives (Fernandez & Burnett, 2020).

Franco and Hernández (2018) also emphasized that the conversation about HSIs is often null and void in the accreditation process. Moreover, they argued that the metrics used to assess performance and quality are often one dimensional, normative, and ineffective for accounting for the specific context that HSIs operate in and the resource-deprived situation they often face despite serving historically minoritized students with high need. As HSIs prepare for accreditation, Franco and Hernández (2018) said that they must accurately account for the campus racial climate using frameworks such as the Diverse Learning Environments (Hurtado et al., 20120) or Culturally Engaging Campus Environments (Museus, 2014). This has also been labeled as the organizational culture for serving Latinxs, which includes an assessment of structures such as Latinx-centered programs and services, curriculum for serving Latinxs, and engagement with the Latinx community (Garcia, 2017). It is critical that administrators at HSIs pressure the macro-level structures, including accreditation boards, to adapt their normative measures of effectiveness to include more HSI- and Latinx-specific measures.

Key Takeaways about Governance in HSIs

What we can learn from these studies about formal governance at HSIs is that becoming an HSI must be intentional and requires buy-in from all formal governing bodies, including the board of trustees, the president, and administrators. Identifying an HSI task force or committee is an important way to extend governance to nonpositional leaders on campus, with faculty, students, alumni, and external partners being essential members of the HSI task force. Data-informed decision-making is also critical, with a specific need to disaggregate data by race/ethnicity in order to make decisions to empower, support, and educate Latinxs and other people of color within the institution. Leaders must also develop measurable indicators of serving that they will use to document progress (Garcia, et al., 2019; Garcia, 2020b). Importantly, leaders must cultivate their resource capacity for serving students, including their financial and human resources, including seeking out external grants to develop their structures for serving and providing extensive professional development and training to current organizational members on how to be race-conscious, equity-minded, antiracist educators. With so many distinct aspects to governance, there are many areas for HSIs to consider as they rethink and transform their formal governance structures.

Conceptualizing Leadership within a Transformed HSI

Although leadership is one aspect of governance, I conceptualize it distinctly from governance in the Transforming HSIs Framework. Governance is the formal process of making decisions, developing policies, allocating resources, and strategically planning for equity, justice, and liberation, while leadership includes the philosophies, ideologies, and practices of both positional and nonpositional leaders who work for change, both within and outside of the formal governance structures. Higher education leadership literature often conflates the concept of leadership with administrative decision-making and management, top-down authority, and individualized approaches to governing the institution (Kezar & Lester, 2011). Within a transformed HSI, leadership should be reconsidered and decoupled from the formal governance structures.

Positional leaders, including academic deans, deans of students, vice presidents, presidents, and trustees, have the positional power and duty to lead, manage, and govern the organization. Positional leaders at a transformed HSI should set strategic goals, make decisions, allocate resources, and develop policies to meet the desired HSI mission, identity, and purpose while simultaneously becoming more intentional about disrupting whiteness, redistributing resources for equity and justice, and empowering people of color within the institution. They must understand their own racial-ethnic-Indigenous identities and the racial-ethnic-Indigenous identities of the students and organizational members they seek to lead. They should also work toward developing an organization that centers the ways of knowing of students of color and other minoritized students. Positional leaders are essential, as they have administrative power and access to institutional decision-making structures that are vital to moving institutions toward embracing the HSI identity (Vargas & Ward, 2020). Positional leaders also have the power, resources, and status to act as institutional agents committed to uplifting and empowering Latinxs and other minoritized students (Stanton-Salazar, 2011).

Effective leadership within transformed HSIs, however, can and should include informal and nonpositional members such as faculty (those who are not a part of formal structures such as the faculty senate), student services staff, coordinators, administrative support, classified staff, students, alumni, and external partners who act as grassroots leaders within the institution, despite being outside the formal positional leadership structure. In essence, all members of the organization are policy implementers and should do that work through a race-conscious, equity-centered lens (Felix, 2021). All leaders at HSIs, regardless of position, must be committed to the mission, purpose, and identity of the HSI and focused on making changes within the infrastructure and beyond the institution in order to support and empower minoritized students and their families. Moreover, the goal of leadership within a transformed HSI is to *change the institution* with the goals of educating, validating, empowering, and centering minoritized students and the communities they come from. Of importance, grassroots leaders working for racial equity, social justice, and radical transformation are most effective when supported by formal leaders within the institution (Kezar & Eckel, 2002a, 2002b; Petrov & Garcia, 2021).

Rethinking Leadership in HSIs

In conceptualizing effective leadership at transformed HSIs, I draw on numerous theories of leadership, including institutional agency (Stanton-Salazar, 2011), grassroots leadership (Kezar & Lester, 2011), applied critical leadership (Santamaría & Santamaría, 2013), Latino educational leadership (Rodríguez et al., 2016), and decolonizing leadership practices at HSIs (Garcia & Natividad, 2018). Institutional agency is afforded to positional leaders with high status, resources, and power within an organization (Stanton-Salazar, 2011). Institutional agents, however, seek to uplift minoritized people and communities by using their position, privileges, and resources. They generally have social, cultural, and economic capital that they actively share with minoritized groups through either direct or indirect support. They also develop systems of support for minoritized groups and provide access to networks so that minoritized groups can access the resources they need to be successful.

Alternatively, grassroots leaders are individuals who do not have formal or positional authority and decision-making power, yet they seek to make change and challenge the status quo from the bottom up (Kezar & Lester, 2011). Grassroots leaders are often volunteers who build their own networks of change makers despite the lack of access to resources and incentives often afforded to positional leaders. Grassroots leadership is similar to social movement, as it is networked based and uses collective strategies to push for change, yet it happens at the local and community level with less attention than large-scale social movements. Grassroots leadership and activism also have similarities, as they often happen outside of formal channels and use noninstitutionalized practices to enact change. Kezar and Lester (2011), however, align their conceptualization of grassroots leadership with Debra Meyerson's definition of "tempered radicals," stressing that grassroots leaders within colleges and universities have to temper their strategies and tactics in order to remain employed, while activists may be willing to sacrifice their jobs for the cause. Grassroots leaders necessarily lead from within the institution while questioning the historical morals and ethics of the organization and seeking to challenge and change it from the ground up. Grassroots leaders are perfectly placed within the institution to become "system hackers" who work toward radical reform and beyond by using the institution's resources to address the violence and oppression produced by it (de Oliveira Andreotti et al., 2015).

Institutional agency and grassroots leadership are concepts that can and should be applied and utilized within transformed HSIs. But there must also be an effort to center the identity and experiences of Latinx, Black, Indigenous, Asian American, Pacific Islander, and Mixed-Race people. Applied critical leadership is conceptualized by and for people of color in leadership positions. As such, identity is an essential aspect of applied critical leadership, with Santamaría and Santamaría (2013) suggesting "educational leaders consider the social context of their educational communities and empower individual members of these communities based on the educational leaders' identities (i.e., subjectivity, biases, assumptions, race, class, gender, and traditions) as perceived through a CRT lens (p. 5). They call it a strengths-based approach to leading within educational settings that are becoming more diverse by race, ethnicity, class, and gender. Educational leaders who access applied critical leadership do so through the lenses of transformational leadership, critical pedagogy, and critical race theory. Critical leaders understand and acknowledge their own sociopolitical history and context as well as the sociopolitical history and context of their students, question how identity affects their ability to make decisions with and for minoritized groups, empower and center minoritized people, and seek to redistribute power within their educational settings. They also *choose change* as a way to proactively transform, adapt, and create new realities.

While applied critical leadership is an important guiding theory for HSI leaders, as it centers the identity of the leaders and the students, Rodríguez et al. (2016) went a step further to propose a Latino educational leadership model specifically for Latinx leaders who have leadership positions within K–12 schools and institutions of higher education that enroll predominantly Latinx students. Like Santamaría and Santamaría, they argue that Latinx leaders must recognize and address the dominant sociohistorical-political system that has historically oppressed Latinx students due to their positioning within society as racially, ethnically, linguistically, and economically minoritized individuals. They also stress that Latinx leaders must operate through an antideficit frame, which requires them to eliminate blaming the students for their struggles within the educational system and acknowledging that educational policies and practices have historically been developed based on racist pseudoscience and techniques that work for the dominant groups (i.e., white, middle- and upper-class students). In moving away from deficit thinking, Latinx leaders must come to value, appreciate, and center students' ways of knowing and community cultural wealth, which includes promoting their cultural, linguistic, familial, aspirational, and resistance capital.

Garcia and Natividad (2018) proposed specific processes and practices that leaders at HSIs should adhere to in order to effectively serve, support, and empower Latinxs, grounded in decolonial ideologies. They argued that leaders at HSIs must understand their own identities in relation to systems of oppression, noting that both privileged and minoritized identities are essential to enacting leadership practices grounded in equity and justice. This diverges from Santamaría and Santamaría and Rodríguez et al. who focused on the racialized identities of the leaders, while Garcia and Natividad stressed that white leaders in HSIs must also be intentional in leading for racial equity, social justice, and collective liberation. They stated that HSI leaders should read, study, and come to understand how to use critical theory (e.g., decolonial, critical race theory) in practice. Leading through the lens of critical theory will help leaders understand the dominant sociohistorical-political systems that Santamaría and Santamaría (2012) and Rodríguez et al. (2016) noted as an essential part of leading with and for people of color. Connected to processes of learning about self and larger social systems is the idea that leaders at HSIs should have critical conversations about systems of oppression that have historically oppressed minoritized students (Garcia & Natividad, 2018).

Garcia and Natividad (2018) also recommended that HSI leaders access and utilize disaggregated data in order to make data-informed decisions. Data-informed decision-making will allow HSI leaders to lead through an antideficit frame. Garcia and Natividad (2018) further stressed that consensus building must be part of the data-informed decision-making process, which includes the need to collaborate with leaders across the institution and community leaders outside of the institution. Finally, Garcia and Natividad (2018) emphasized that HSI leaders must act, as simply recognizing inequities and engaging in critical conversations about historical forms of oppression toward students within HSIs is insufficient. In other words, social action is a necessary part of leading for change within transformed HSIs. Together these five theories offer guidance on how both positional and grassroots leaders within transformed HSIs can and should lead. A number of articles and book chapters have highlighted HSI leaders as single case studies. In using leaders as the case, researchers have connected principles of institutional agency, applied critical leadership, Latino educational leadership, and grassroots leadership with the praxis utilized by these leaders.

Center Minoritized Identities in Leadership Processes

As noted by guiding theories of critical leadership, the centering of minoritized identities is essential when leading for change. This may include racial-ethnic-Indigenous identities, low-income identities, first generation identities, queer identities, Trans* identities, and more. Cortez (2015) described how five institutional leaders (two white, two Latina, and one Black) at one four-year HSI in Texas, University of Texas-Pan American, used their own funds of knowledge (the knowledge that people have based on their own personal and life experiences) to support, mentor, and connect with students while advocating for their needs and implementing change within the institution. Participants described their motivation for supporting students, which included their seeing themselves within the students. One administrator said, "I am them," while another stated, "I don't see them as solely a number. I look at them as if they were me just a few years ago" (Cortez, 2015, p. 140–141). Their personal experiences drove these leaders to work for change on their campuses, stressing the need for student-centered services and intensive academic and career advisement on campus. Both applied critical leadership and Latino educational leadership call attention to the need for educational leaders to draw on their own social identities as they lead with and for minoritized students.

Similarly, Valadez (2015) centered his identity in his own leadership practices at one four-year HSI, California State University, San Marcos (CSUSM). As a faculty member he was part of the formal governance structures of the institution, serving on multiple committees within the academic senate and ultimately being elected as the chair. In his role as chair, he launched World AIDS Day observance at CSUSM, which was both personal and political for him as a self-identified gay Latino man with AIDS. In developing this event, he worked directly with the LGBT community on campus, seeking their support and guidance in implementing the program. He also became keenly aware of the support structures on campus for LGBT students, making connections between the joint struggles and liberation that LGBT students and Latinx students at an HSI share. This also allowed him to make connections with and mentor LGBT students while also supporting their development and political advocacy on campus. Valadez's story shows the need for more leaders on campus with multiple minoritized identities, including LGBT leaders, who view educational advocacy as both personal and political and through the lenses of their own sociohistorical-political positioning.

Doran (2019b) described one instance of a Latinx president (President Romo) at an urban HSI in Texas (University of Texas at San Antonio) supporting student activists. Like Valadez and the leaders described by Cortez, President Romo saw himself in the students, with his leadership being shaped by his own experiences as an activist during the Civil Rights Movements of the 1960s. When eight UTSA students joined a pro–DREAM Act hunger strike, President Romo allowed the students to present the administration with their concerns, signed their online petition, showed his overall respect for their rights to protest, and elevated coconstructed knowledge with his students. Not only did he help them find productive ways to elevate their message, but he also learned about issues facing undocumented students from them. In many ways, this process influenced the establishment of a Dreamers Resource Center on campus (Doran, 2019b).

Share and Redistribute Resources and Capital

I call on leaders of transformed HSIs to redistribute resources to people of color for efforts that advance racial equity, social justice, and collective liberation. But this is hard to imagine, as it is not the norm in racialized organizations, with a majority of resources supporting the dominant white normative structures (Ray, 2019). Garcia and Ramirez (2018) documented how four leaders (three Latinas and one white man) at one four-year HSI in the Southwest served as institutional agents, using their own social capital and positional resources to support and empower students while also moving the institution toward better serving Latinxs. These four leaders served as resource agents, political advocates, networking coaches, lobbyists, and institutional brokers, all with the goal of disrupting long-standing oppressive structures hindering students within the institution from achieving their academic and liberatory goals. One full professor was known on campus for getting federal grants that support the implementation of programs to ones that have historically served low-income students of color in STEM (e.g., Maximizing Access to Research Careers [MARC]) while another was known for her advocacy within organizations like HACU, gaining access to resources to support the institution's movement toward becoming a fully functional HSI. In many ways their actions bring together concepts of institutional agency, applied critical leadership, and Latino educational leadership, with the core focus on the disruption of inequitable and unjust educational systems. Importantly, these four leaders were known for their longtime advocacy efforts with minoritized students, both at the institution and prior to coming there; in other words, they were ideologically committed to equity and justice prior to the institution becoming an HSI (Garcia & Ramirez, 2018).

Lead through Antideficit and Data-Driven Approaches

Throughout this chapter there is a recurring theme to disaggregate data and disrupt deficit thinking as part of the governance and leadership redesigning efforts, with much of this work driven by efforts to enact race-conscious and equity-minded approaches to leadership (e.g., Bensimon, 2007; Felix, 2021). Jones and Sáenz (2020) talked to 72 educators at three Hispanic-serving community colleges in Texas to learn more about how they are specifically serving Latino men. Several leadership actions arose, including the use of data-driven decision-making to address equity issues, not just by race and ethnicity but also by gender. More specifically, participants described the ways that administrators prioritized the success of Latino men, working with faculty and staff to ensure that they had the skills and resources necessary to serve them. Steady efforts on the part of institutional leaders to center Latino men eventually led to an overall paradigm shift on campus for supporting Latino men and created a culture of connectedness to the needs and experiences of these students. Although the focus of Jones and Sáenz's (2020) research was on ways that institutions prioritize Latino men, there is much to be learned from their efforts to uncover how administrators intentionally prioritize a minoritized group, including the paradigm shift that has to occur in order to become race-conscious and equity-minded.

White Men, Too, Must Lead for Equity, Justice, and Liberation

Throughout each of these cases, leaders placed the students' identities at the core of their own decision-making, taking into consideration the needs that students have based on their social identities and personal trajectories into higher education. Although these HSI leaders seemingly connect with students at HSIs because they have similar social identities and backgrounds, that is not always the case. Espinoza and Espinoza (2012) wrote a case study about a white middle-class male associate dean who felt obliged to support Latinx low-income first-generation students at his HSI. The case study highlights his own struggles to determine where the institution went wrong in supporting a seventh-year undergraduate student who was struggling to finish his degree. Rather than blaming the student, the associate dean recognized that the institution itself has failed the student and worked with other administrators to address some of the concerns he sees arising with the student, including the need for better advising to support students through the degree process, the need for greater family engagement, and the need for creating better awareness of mental health and counseling services on campus (Espinoza & Espinoza, 2012).

Garcia and Ramirez (2018) similarly talked about one white-identified institutional agent in their study whom other members on campus recognized as leading for equity and justice. Numerous participants stressed that the white male provost on campus often used his positional power to question inequitable outcomes and experiences of minoritized students on campus. As a high-status positional leader on campus, he regularly used his personal and positional resources and networks to support minoritized students (Garcia & Ramirez, 2018). These examples reinforce and support the idea that all leaders at HSIs, including white administrators, must work to disrupt historical inequities and oppressive structures on campus.

Key Takeaways on Leadership in HSIs

Some of the common themes in these studies that we can learn from include the idea of positional leaders seeing themselves within the student population, highlighting the need to hire more administrators of color from low-income backgrounds to lead HSIs where a majority of students are similarly low-income people of color. Yet we also see how important it is for people with dominant identities, including white, middle-class, and wealthy people to work for equity, justice, and collective liberation on campus. Another common theme is the way that these leaders utilized their own social and cultural capital to advocate for students and disrupt oppressive structures on campus. Jones and Sáenz (2020) also stressed the need for data-driven decision-making, thoughtful resource allocation, and long-term cultural change, while Valadez (2015) highlighted the need to leverage collaborations with external community partners and internal university partners in order to enhance resources and develop meaningful educational programming on campus.

Conclusion

Formal, normative governance and less formal, transformative leadership are vital to the revolution of HSIs toward a greater focus on racial equity, social justice, and collective liberation. Governance and leadership bring each of the organizational dimensions of the transformed HSI together, driving the mission, identity, and purpose and guiding the institution's efforts in centering minoritized students and voices in the curriculum, decision-making, and policy development. A majority of attention in HSI research has been given to administrators, with very little attention on governing boards, boards of trustees, faculty senates, and student senates as formal shared-governance structures. Moreover, students, families, staff, and community members have nearly been excluded from formal governance structures. Transformed HSIs must rethink traditional and normative approaches to shared governance while disrupting the whiteness and coloniality of power embedded within the structures, decisions, and policies of the institution. The focus on formal governance processes, however, is insufficient. I call on all the tempered radicals and grassroots leaders within the institution to stay focused on the goals of equity, social justice, and collective liberation. The efforts of these informal leaders cannot be understated in the transformed HSIs framework, as they are often the people who make substantial change on campus, mentor and empower students of color, and call for greater accountability among formal governing bodies. Not everyone will show up for the social movement and transformation, but committed leaders will make a difference that should not be underestimated.

6

Including External Partnerships
and Influences

ENGAGING WITH EXTERNAL PARTNERS, conceptualized here as alumni, donors, and local communities, is a necessary dimension of the Transforming HSIs Framework. These processes typically fall under the purview of institutional advancement, alumni affairs, development, and community engagement offices, yet the campus's status as an HSI is often overlooked in these departments, and conversations about equity and justice may not be salient within these spaces. Moreover, institutional advancement, development, and alumni engagement staff tend to be predominantly white and may lack the knowledge to adequately engage with potential donors, alumni, and communities of color (Drezner & Villarreal, 2015; Gasman & Bowman, 2013). Within the framework, external partners are critical contributors who can elevate and prioritize the institution's commitment to equity, justice, and liberation. I conceptualize partnerships as reciprocal relationships in which HSIs extend servingness to alumni, donors, and communities while simultaneously calling on these partners to engage in the process of defining and elevating what a liberatory and humanizing educational experience looks like for students of color and their families and for communities. Partners can and should become coconspirators in the movement toward creating liberatory spaces within and beyond the institution.

In the original conception of HSI as a political construct, there was no mention of the racial-ethnic-Indigenous composition of the alumni base, yet HSIs must recognize that the compositional diversity present at the undergraduate level is translating into increased racial-ethnic-Indigenous diversity at the alumni level. Alumni of transformed HSIs must become partners in servingness. There were also no conversations about donors and their necessary commitment to the HSI construct within the original description of HSI. As the campus enhances its commitment to these values as part of its HSI identity, mission, and strategic purpose, the donor base must also commit to these values and goals toward racial equity and social justice. At the community level, the advocates who fought for the HSI designation didn't talk about how HSIs could become essential partners in fighting for justice with local Latinx and low-income communities. Transformed HSIs should intentionally work with communities of color and low-income communities in order to understand their needs and ensure that the institution is working toward collective goals of racial justice and community empowerment.

In focusing on external partners, however, HSIs must interrogate their motivation to partner with alumni, donors, and communities. Transformed HSIs should access critical frameworks and utilize a social justice orientation, resisting the neoliberal impetus to work with partners as a way to develop and enhance revenues sources (Castañeda & Krupczynski, 2018). At the same time, some HSIs historically face a bleak financial reality, elevating the need to find ways to bring in more resources. Mulnix et al. (2002) note that strong institutional advancement activities at HSIs, including alumni relations, fundraising, and government relations are "instrumental in building healthy institutions and ensuring high graduation rates" for Latinxs at HSIs (p. 60). Although improving the ability of HSIs to raise funds and elevate opportunities for philanthropy are vital to the economic future of these institutions, transformed HSIs should embrace external partnerships as a way to better serve their external constituents. Within the Transforming HSIs Framework the primary goal of partnerships shall be to advance the institution's ability to adequately educate and serve students that attend HSIs while recognizing that strong external partnerships and advancement activities will ultimately enhance the institution's economic viability.

I call on transformed HSIs to recognize that institutions of higher education have historically ignored people and communities of color within institutional advancement efforts and work toward amending that (Drezner, 2013). As noted by Villanueva (2018), healing is at the core of decolonizing philanthropy and fundraising, which requires fundraisers to grieve and apologize for the pain caused to minoritized communities, to listen and relate to those excluded from our institutions, and to build new decision-making opportunities that center those formerly excluded. Cortés (2002) too stressed that Latinx people value confianza (trust) and the importance of la palabra (one's word) when engaging in philanthropy. As transformed HSIs work through grieving and building trusting relationships, they must invest in areas where their values and their partners' values lie and utilize funds to repair and heal minoritized communities (Villanueva, 2018).

Garcia (2016a) argues that "giving back to the community" is at the core of an HSI organizational identity, and with HSIs often being situated in predominantly Latinx communities, this extends to serving the Latinx community. Moreover, Garcia (2016a) notes that HSIs have a regional focus, with a majority of students being from local communities. As such, HSIs are a direct reflection of their communities and must enhance their commitment to communities as part of their efforts to become HSIs. Moving toward transformation requires HSIs to engage with external partners that believe in and support the institution's commitment to equity, justice, and liberation for students of color. Advancement, philanthropy, and community engagement activities must be multifaceted and intentional, with the institution's commitment to address racial inequities while advancing social justice and collective liberation at the core.

Empowering and Engaging Alumni of Color

Mulnix et al. (2002) surveyed 80 HSI presidents, who indicated that alumni relations were the least important institutional advancement activity on their campus. This might be because HSI presidents and decision makers are often concerned with issues such as addressing racial equity gaps in completion rates, ensuring quality and affordable education for students, and hiring and retaining faculty who can address the needs of students attending HSIs (de los Santos & Cuamea, 2010). Yet these same decision makers have noted that funding and financial constraints are the most pressing issues they are facing as they lead HSIs (de los Santos & Cuamea, 2010), with little recongnition of how institutional advancement activities may enhance their racial equity goals while also increasing the institution's economic viability. Transformed HSIs must embrace Latinx, Black, Indigenous, Asian American, and Pacific Islander alumni as important external partners, recognizing that not only are they the fastest-growing group of alumni but they are becoming wealthier and can offer greater monetary donations to their colleges and universities, especially if they had liberatory, validating, and empowering experiences as undergraduates, thus reinforcing the need to provide a transformative experience while they are undergraduate students (see chapter 4) (Cabrales, 2013; Gasman & Bowman, 2013). Engaging alumni of color, however, must be a priority for reasons other than financial. As the institution transforms, there should be a focus on cultivating an alumni base that is committed to the HSI mission, identity, and purpose.

In an effort to cultivate and engage the increasingly diverse alumni base at HSIs, there is a need to understand the engagement patterns of alumni of color. It has been documented that alumni of color often don't engage with their former colleges and universities, not because they don't want to but because these institutions simply don't ask (Gasman & Bowman, 2011, 2013). This is often based on false notions that focusing on alumni of color will provide little return on investment. Alumni of color also might not engage with colleges and universities because they don't trust them or because they had negative racialized experiences as undergraduates on campus (Drezner & Villarreal, 2015; Haywood, 2017b). Moreover, alumni of color may value noneconomic forms of capital and giving and may not fit into the normative ways of engaging as alumni (Cabrales, 2013). Cabrales (2011) found that Latinx alumni are typically engaged with their communities in various ways and often give at the intersection of their careers and community engagement. For example, they may become involved with the community as part of their jobs as lawyers, with a specific focus on advocacy with and for the Latinx community. They may raise money for scholarships, participate in local politics, provide mentoring and support to Latinxs planning to attend college, or develop conferences for Latinx youth, regardless of their alma mater's efforts.

With this in mind, Cabrales (2013) proposed the compadres model of giving, citing the system of coparenthood that is common in the Latinx community as a form of sponsorship where *madrinas* and *padrinos* (godparents) assist their extended family networks by sponsoring various aspects of cultural and often religious events for these families. Extending this idea, Latinx alumni can become compadres to colleges and universities, serving as *madrinas* and *padrinos* to both Latinx students on campus and the surrounding Latinx communities. In developing this type of compadre system that centers Latinx ways of giving, transformed HSIs should provide targeted giving opportunities that allow Latinx alumni to sponsor one cause that is meaningful to them, whether it be to support fundraising efforts for scholarships for Latinxs or undocumented students, to support Latinx student organizations, or to support efforts to develop a Latinx cultural center on campus. As is common in the compadre system, *madrinas* and *padrinos* should have the opportunity to sponsor one specific effort that they select.

Transformed HSIs must also make a concerted effort to understand the diversity within and among the Latinx alumni population (Cortés, 2002; Drezner & Villarreal, 2015), including their diverse ethnic and racial backgrounds, countries of origin, languages used, and regional differences, as these differences may affect an HSI's ability to engage them. There ought to be intentional efforts to collect data about alumni of color, as there are often insufficient data about these groups (Gasman & Bowman, 2013). Collecting data can help determine the intersectional needs within the Latinx alumni base and the differences in their desires to engage. Although Latinxs are likely to contribute to causes that center equity and social justice for Latinxs, there may be differences in the issues that they are committed to supporting. For example, Puerto Ricans in the Northeast may be more concerned about issues such urban revival, gentrification, and poverty, while Chicanxs in the Southwest may be committed to migrant worker rights, immigration reform, and bilingual education (Mora, 2014). Afro-Latinxs and Indigenous Latinxs might also have different commitments than white and mestizo Latinxs, as issues of race, racism, and the coloniality of power in the United States more directly affects them on a daily basis. Afro-Latinx alumni may have had negative experiences on campus as undergraduates, and specifically when it comes to the social exclusion and racial discrimination they often experience among other Latinx college students (Haywood, 2017b). Similarly, Indigenous Latinxs may have felt excluded from the curriculum or had negative experiences interacting with mestizo peers who lack an understanding of the Indigenous Latinx experience (Kovats Sánchez, 2018, 2021), making it important for the institution to take time to understand the diversity of experiences among Latinxs rather than treating them like a monolithic group.

Other things to consider are the implementation of alumni affinity groups for alumni of color (Cabrales, 2013; Gasman & Bowman, 2013). Alumni of color affinity groups can provide the opportunity to engage with alumni in ways that center their identities, culture, and values while also connecting them with other alumni of color. Through affinity groups, alumni of color can be motivated to participate in university events that elevate students of color, families, and communities; raise money for scholarships that support Latinx, Black, Indigenous, Asian Americans, and Pacific Islanders in need;

and/or give back in nonmonetary ways. Yet in taking note of the diversity within and among alumni of color, there may also be a need to develop affinity groups across intersectional identities such as LGBTQIA, people of color, undocumented and/or immigrant Latinxs, or gender-specific mujerista groups, noting that women and femmes need their own spaces of affirmation that are free of patriarchy and sexism. Transformed HSIs should consider hiring staff of color to work with these affinity groups, as the alumni staff at most campuses remains predominantly white (Gasman & Bowman, 2013). There are many ways to engage alumni of color, but the bottom line is that there must be an intentional effort to do so. Alumni engagement is an important way to enhance the institution's commitment to equity, justice, and liberation, which includes engaging alumni of color with multiple and intersectional identities.

Fundraising for Equity and Justice

Beyond empowering and engaging alumni with the goal of cultivating life-long givers in monetary and nonmonetary ways, transformed HSIs must also engage with nonalumni donors. Fundraising and philanthropy shall become as important as changing the compositional diversity of educators and decision makers at the institution (see chapter 3), transforming the infrastructure (see chapter 4), and redefining the governance and leadership processes (see chapter 5) and should assist with these processes. Yet Mulnix et al. (2002) found that only 65% of the 80 HSI presidents surveyed said that they have program officers who interact with private foundations. A similar percentage of HSI presidents in the same survey (62%) also indicated that they hired outside consultants to assist with fundraising activities (Mulnix et al., 2002), suggesting that they might not have the internal capacity to raise additional funds for the institution. Approximately 58% also stated that their fundraising efforts were not very effective or only somewhat effective. There is a clear need for HSIs to focus more directly on their fundraising and philanthropic activities.

Transformed HSIs should engage with donors as partners toward the goal of becoming racially just and equitable institutions working for joint liberation and empowerment for Latinx, Black, Indigenous, Asian American, and Pacific Islander people. Transformed HSIs must also engage with donors of color, disrupting false or deficit notions about people of color not being able or willing to become monetary donors. Committing to fundraising and philanthropy that aligns with the transformed mission, identity, and strategic purpose of HSIs should be done through a decolonial lens, focusing on wealth acquisition for the sake of healing, connecting, relating, and belonging (Villanueva, 2018). Wealth within nonprofit organizations in the settler colonial state has historically been used to divide, control, and exploit (Villanueva, 2018). Similarly, wealth has been used in this way within the neoliberal university, which is guided by the fundamentals of privatization, commodification, and self-interest, and often at odds with justice and liberation of minoritized groups (Giroux, 2014).

Cultivating and engaging donors committed to healing, connecting, relating, and belonging will require an understanding of the engagement patterns of donors of color. Gasman and Bowman (2013) noted that Latinxs often give to educational efforts and often with the goal of addressing barriers to Latinx involvement in education or to address inequities in educational outcomes. Latinxs also support churches, elders, emergency assistance efforts, and the arts at greater rates than some other communities of color, while Cortés (2002) argued that Latinxs also engage in philanthropy as a form of service, obligation, and giving back. Royce and Rodriguez (1999) similarly found that *servicio* (service), *obligación* (obligation) and giving back were at the root of the Latinx worldview, including both the spiritual and material worlds. Service may be in the form of *tiempo* (time), *talento* (talent), or *tesoro* (treasure), as Latinxs are often taught by their families to give in small ways, whether it be donating a toy to the church's toy drive or inviting low-income members of the community to dinner.

Royce and Rodriguez (1999) found that *personalismo* (personalism), *confianza* (trust), *la importancia de la palabra* (the importance of one's word), *el valor de la persona* (the intrinsic worth of each person) are fundamental values at the center of Latinx giving and philanthropy. *Personalismo* (personalism) is key to engaging Latinxs, as they prefer personal, intimate, one-on-one relationship building and often make connections through personal networks. For Latinxs, the *who* is as important as the cause in philanthropic activities and can't be understated as HSIs consider the best ways to engage Latinxs in giving opportunities. This reinforces the idea of hiring more staff of color to work directly with people color. *Confianza* extends from *personalismo*, as Latinxs must trust the philanthropic organizations that they work with. Using networks to build trust and hiring Latinx-identified institutional advancement and development staff members is crucial, yet Royce and Rodriguez (1999) found that Latinxs are critical of people, especially of other Latinxs who they think have "sold out" to a larger organization that is beyond their community. Building trust and *confianza*, therefore must be at the center of all philanthropic work. Institutional advancement and development staff members at transformed HSIs should strive to work within the borderlands, connecting education and the Latinx community in strategic ways that might be messy, meaning donor engagement may be outside the normative ways that institutions have done philanthropic work.

Like alumni engagement, donor engagement requires a deeper understanding of the diversity among and within the Latinx umbrella, including countries of origin, immigration background and generational status in the United States, preferred languages, religious preferences, regional differences, and historical experiences with discrimination in the United States and specifically within educational systems, as it may affect trust and confidence in colleges and universities. A focus on acknowledging and healing historical harm for the sake of elevating relationships and connections necessitates an understanding of how diverse groups within the Latinx umbrella and at the intersections of oppression have historically been harmed by the US educational system. For example, Mexican Americans in the Southwest may have a historical memory of being discriminated against based on clothing, hygiene, or their use of the

Spanish language in the classroom (González, 2008; MacDonald, 2004), while Puerto Ricans in the Northeast may have memories of forced assimilation, erasure, and Americanization with the imposition of English in all schooling on the island, which was met with great resistance by Puerto Rican parents (Martínez-Roldán & Quiñones, 2016). Even if Latinxs are likely to give in order to support efforts to ameliorate educational inequities, they may be drawn to efforts that are more aligned with their own experiences with discrimination and injustices. As noted by Royce and Rodriguez (1999), giving patterns also range by religious affiliations, with very different patterns of giving between Catholic and Evangelic Latinxs. Understanding the Latinx community beyond a reified monolith is vital to engaging them in meaningful ways.

There are numerous ways to engage donors committed to the transformed mission, identity, and purpose of HSIs. Acosta (2010) argues that there must be an elevated connection between the personal Latinx identity and the HSI identity, as Latinxs are more likely to give to an institution that reflects their own personal and cultural values, a concept known as organizational identification. As such, various targeted communication systems should be used to engage donors in a process of seeing themselves reflected in the institution. For example, targeted newsletters that cite statistics about Latinx, Black, Indigenous, Asian American, and Pacific Islander students entering and graduating from the institution or that provide personal stories about students of color or alumni of color might be an effective way to elevate identification with the institution (Cabrales, 2013). Targeted communication may also provide information about the institution's efforts to become an HSI, noting how the institution is conducting research with and for Latinxs as part of its HSI identity and how it is becoming a resource to the Latinx alumni, families, and communities it serves (Acosta, 2010). This is important, as donors motivated by social justice need to know the direct connection between their gifts and the impact on the people who receive the benefit of the gift, rather than focusing on the institution (Drezner & Huehls, 2015). As with alumni engagement, donor engagement and philanthropy must be an intentional effort at transformed HSIs. Philanthropy is an important way to enhance the institution's mission, identity, and purpose while working toward healing and relationship building with the Latinx community and other communities of color.

Community Engagement and Collective Liberation

The triad of external partnerships in the transformed HSIs framework includes local communities that HSIs serve, especially communities of color and low-income communities. With a large percentage of students at HSIs identifying as students of color and/or low income, and with the general patterns showing that Latinxs in particular are likely to attend college close to home, HSIs tend to be situated within contexts that have high populations of people of color and may be closer to low-income communities (Cuellar, 2019; Espinosa et al., 2019). As such, engagement with the community is an extension of servingness with a focus on communities and families. Transformed HSIs must commit to working with communities of color and low-income communities to address issues such as poverty, homelessness, joblessness, lack of access to health care, and inadequate water and food sources, as these are issues that students and families are dealing with. There must also be a recognition of local and transnational contexts, as needs are specific to regions and identities (Castañeda & Krupczynski, 2018). Importantly, community-engaged activities can and should be part of the federal HSI grant efforts (Garcia, 2016a, 2017; Ramirez & Rodriguez-Kiino, 2020). Grant writers and principle investigators should conceptualize community engagement as a way to achieve the liberatory purpose of the institution and convince the federal government to fund these types of efforts as part of capacity building.

Research suggests that community engagement is one dimension of an HSI's organizational identity (Garcia, 2017) and can be used as an indicator of serving (Garcia et al., 2019). In her study, Garcia (2016a) found that at one public four-year HSI, faculty had been awarded federal HSI grants to enhance the campus's engagement with the community, including working with predominantly Latinx schools to develop nutrition and physical activity programs and developing Spanish lactation consultation programs to support nursing Latina mothers. One student in the study who was hired to provide nutrition education to the local Spanish-speaking Latinx community said that the experience had elevated her commitment to the community. Other participants stated that the campus had a long-standing commitment to creating partnerships with the local community, including school districts, that were simply enhanced by HSI federal grants. Similarly, Ramirez and Rodriguez-Kiino (2020) highlighted how California Lutheran University, a private four-year HSI, used its Title III, Part F STEM Articulation grant to create and implement STEM-focused community engagement, which included the development of statewide agreements and memoranda with local high school districts, California community colleges, the Ventura County Office of Education, and local STEM networks to support various initiatives, including the development of an equity committee conference. They also provided experiential learning opportunities for Latinx students who served as "STEM stewards" for Latinx and low-income high school students in the community, with the goal of fostering a STEM identity and college-going culture and developing trust in the institution.

Community engagement within transformed HSIs must center empowerment and self-determination, rather than saviorism, with multiple dimensions to consider. Franco et al. (2020) proposed the Latinx-Informed Framework for Community Engagement to help HSIs engage with Latinx communities in ways that are grounded in community empowerment rather than focusing primarily on the benefits to the institution. The framework includes three core elements, including a Latinx-informed purpose, a reciprocal process, and asset-enhancing outcomes. A Latinx-informed purpose is one that centers the needs of Latinxs both within the institution and in the community, noting that the diversity within the Latinx population necessitates purposeful, race- and identity-conscious multidirectional conversations with institutional members and community members.

The reciprocal process goes beyond the normative focus on mutual benefit and reciprocity and instead focuses on building solidarity, trust, unity, communalism, integrity, and accountability. As with the philanthropic process, there must be an acknowledgment of past harms and injustices to communities caused by the institution before moving toward healing, trust-building, and long-term relational engagement. Asset-enhancing outcomes include mutually beneficial, meaningful, and race- and identity-conscious outcomes around equity, justice, and liberation for the community and the institutional partners. With the framework, the focus is on enhancing servingness for all partners, both through short-term and long-term engagement.

Community engagement within transformed HSIs must also draw on critical frameworks that disrupt historical university-centered approaches and instead focus on community cultural wealth and funds of knowledge present within Latinx, Black, Indigenous, Asian American, and Pacific Islander communities (Castañeda & Krupczynski, 2018). A Latinx community-academic praxis repositions the focus of knowledge creation from the university to the communities of color and low-income communities that the university works with. Community engagement becomes more than simply addressing inequities and historic forms of oppression faced by people of color at the intersections of race, class, sex, gender, immigration status, religion, spirituality, and ability and instead elevates the knowledge creation that happens within these communities. Members of communities of color and low-income communities must become central actors in the creation of community-based partnerships, pedagogical solutions, and knowledge creation that are grounded in social justice, antiracism, and collective liberation (Castañeda & Krupczynski, 2018).

Community engagement work at transformed HSIs should be intersectional, placing the needs of people of color at the center while recognizing the diversity within these groups. Working with communities of color and low-income communities should center the goals of empowerment, self-determination, and an overall fight for the fulfillment of basic needs such as livable wages, food, housing, health care, and education (Kendall, 2020). Importantly, transformed HSIs must follow community leaders, allowing them to name their struggles and goals for social justice and liberation. Latinx and Black Trans* women and femmes in the community, for example, may be struggling with violence and discrimination, fighting for reproductive rights, equal pay, and health care, and/or addressing the needs of sex workers. In New York City, for example, where there is the largest concentration of Afro-Indigenous Garífuna outside of Honduras, organizations like the Garífuna Solidarity Network advocate for Garífuna women and children seeking asylum (Saldaña-Portillo, 2017), while in California, there are over 100,000 Indigenous Mexicans with grassroots advocacy organizations emerging across the state to address their needs (Kovats Sánchez, 2018). Community engagement may also include work with populations that have been denied access to college, such as formerly incarcerated people who often face oppression at the intersections of race, class, and gender and who may face extreme challenges in trying to enter college (Abeyta, 2020). Intentional community engagement that focuses on racial equity, social justice, and collective liberation can have many important outcomes for transformed HSIs. For example, it may become an important driver of change of the compositional diversity of members (see chapter 3) with efforts to work with communities formerly excluded from the institution and often at the margins of higher education. Overall, community engagement at transformed HSIs must be grounded in long-term trust building and intentional efforts to center the knowledge and cultural wealth of the partners and communities involved in the engagement.

Conceptualizing External Influences within a Transformed HSI

In our original conception of external influences on servingness, Garcia et al. (2019) did not distinguish between external *partners* and external *influences*. Here I conceptualize engagement with external influences separately from external partners, as I see them as distinctly different. External partners (alumni, donors, communities) in a transformed HSI will become collaborators in the institution's efforts to enact an HSI mission, identity, and purpose. Alternatively, external influences, understood here to include federal and state governments, private foundations, policy intermediaries, professional associations, accreditation boards, and the media, are entities that institutions must respond to and engage with, but they may not rise to the level of partners.

State and federal governments set policies, regulations, and guidelines that institutions must abide by, but they don't necessarily interact with institutions in ways that are collaborative. The federal government offers competitive grant funding to HSIs, but they don't become collaborative partners in servingness upon awarding grants. Private foundations, too, offer competitive funding to institutions of higher education that align with their goals, missions, and values, but they don't necessarily commit to partnering with institutions in order to implement funded projects. Policy intermediaries and professional associations lobby legislators, advocate on Capitol Hill for HSIs, students of color, and low-income (Pell Grant) students, and develop reports and policy briefs that highlight inequities across the educational pipeline, yet they too lack a commitment to partner with individual HSIs. Accreditation bodies influence all institutions of higher education, potentially affecting their ability to access federal financial aid, yet there is no conversation about servingness or partnerships among these organizations and HSIs. Relationships with the media are also essential, yet the media do not necessarily partner with HSIs in servingness.

Transformed HSIs will necessarily learn to manage relationships with external influences, recognizing that they may hinder or enhance the institution's ability to enact a mission, identity, and purpose grounded in equity, justice, and liberation. As institutionalized organizations, HSIs often make decisions that are symbolically legitimated within the organizational field of higher education, and they adopt behaviors that conform with normative expectations of the environment (Suddaby, 2010), which are arguably white normative (Garcia, 2019). HSIs, like all colleges and universities, also conform to the rules and myths of the external environment, often adopting policies and practices that are driven by the laws, policies, and decisions set by local-, state-, and national-level influences (DiMaggio & Powell, 1983; Meyer & Rowan, 1977). In their effort to legitimate themselves as effective institutions, HSIs often respond to behaviors and norms that the field has of white institutions without acknowledging that their Latinx, Black, Indigenous, Asian American, and Pacific Islander students, families, and partners have different needs that require the field to adapt and respond to. Transformed HSIs must work with the ecosystem of external influences in order to offer practical solutions and advance coalition building toward policy change that centers Latinxs, people of color, and low-income constituents and the HSI mission, identity, and purpose.

Federal Government: Funding Equity and Justice?

The federal government plays an essential role in servingness, as policies, guidelines, executive orders, and funding may all enhance or hinder an institution's ability to effectively advance equity, justice, and liberation. While the federal government has shaped higher education in significant ways, from the passing of the Morrill Acts of 1862 and 1890 that contributed to the development of public institutions to the landmark GI Bill that expanded educational opportunities to veterans, especially to the Higher Education Act (HEA), which legitimized HSIs and other MSIs, the federal government's role in higher education continues to evolve. A core function of the federal government is to supply direct aid to students in the form of financial aid (Mumper et al., 2016). This commitment is historical, with the HEA of 1965 and Title IV specifically providing funding to low-income students by way of Pell Grants and middle- and high-income students by way of Guaranteed Student Loan Programs, as well as a variety of other federally supported programs such as the Federal Work-Study Program, the Perkins Loan Program, and other opportunity programs that have evolved over the years (Mumper et al., 2016). Since enrolling a significant portion of low-incomes students (over 50%) is a part of the HSI designation, federal financial aid and support is vital to transformed HSIs, with over 50% of all Latinx students receiving Pell Grants and an even greater number of Black (62%) and Native American (54%) students receiving aid (*Excelencia* in Education, 2017).

The federal government also provides indirect aid in the form of tax deductions and credits, which are constantly evolving in response to the economy and other influences such as the global COVID-19 pandemic. Moreover, institutions of higher education receive funding from the federal government through acts such as the Coronavirus Aid, Relief, and Economic Security Act and the Coronavirus Response and Relief Supplemental Appropriations Act of 2021 (US Dept of the Treasury, n.d.). Institutions of higher education also respond to and abide by federal regulations such as Title IX of the Education Amendments of 1972, the Americans with Disabilities Act of 1990, the Crime Awareness and Campus Security Act of 1990 (the Clery Act), and Deferred Action for Childhood Arrivals (DACA, to name a few. Compliance can enhance or hinder a transformed HSI's ability to act for social justice and collective liberation, especially in consideration of the needs of students of color at the intersections of identity. Latinx and Black Trans* students, for example, were threatened by decisions made by former secretary Betsy DeVos to discontinue investigation of anti-Trans* complaints made, further reinforcing the lack of protection offered to Trans* students by Title IX (Mirza & Bewkes, 2019). Transformed HSIs must remain steady in their legislative lobbying in order to secure funding and support for students of color and low-income students at the intersections of identity.

The federal government has also historically provided funding to institutions by way of research and development grants, with requests for proposals (RFPs) often guided by the most pressing issues facing the United States as a country, from national security to global health crises (Mumper et al., 2016). Specific to HSIs, these grants are capacity-building grants, with federal agencies playing a crucial role in funding HSIs through the competitive grant process. Grant seeking allows HSIs to increase their capacity for meeting the basic needs of students and educating them in innovative ways. In applying for these grants, institutions engage in a process of defining servingness and attaching meaning to the HSI identity (Garcia, 2016a; Garcia et al., 2019). HSIs must honor those who fought vehemently for the HSI federal designation while enhancing their ability to effectively serve minoritized students through grant seeking (Garcia et al., 2019). Political advocates achieved great victory upon gaining a distinct HSI designation in 1995 and a funding source in 1998 under Title V, Part A, specific to undergraduate education, and Title V, Part B, specific to graduate education in 2008. Yet these programs and others (e.g., Title III, Part F HSI STEM program; National Science Foundation HSI Program) have never had a focus on racial equity, social justice, or collective liberation. The freedom dream I lay out in this book is my own conceptualization of what HSIs can be (spaces of liberation and justice); this book is a call to federal agencies to reconsider the RFP process for HSI grant programs and to center racial equity, social justice, and collective liberation in the goals and objectives of these programs.

In thinking about how organizations influence and respond to external forces, transformed HSIs should foster their ability to apply for federal grants by hiring grant and sponsored programs professionals to monitor, track, and apply for federal grants earmarked for HSIs. Mulnix et al. (2002) found that enrollment management and public relations were ranked higher in importance than fundraising and sponsored programs by the 80 HSI presidents they surveyed. This suggests that HSI presidents are more reliant on tuition as a source of revenue than funding from government and private source despite the fact that the high percentage of low-income students who attend HSIs may present challenges to increasing tuition as a form of revenue generation (Nellum & Valle, 2015). Mulnix et al. (2002) also found that 70% of the 80 presidents surveyed indicated that they have a sponsored program office that applies for federal grants and 70% said that they have staff who regularly monitor the *Federal Register* or other federal funding websites.

Sponsored program offices must regularly monitor federal HSI grant opportunities and interact with federal agencies that support HSIs. They should regularly inform the campus community of grant opportunities earmarked for HSIs and call on campus constituents to develop transdisciplinary teams to apply for and implement HSI grants that are grounded in equity, justice, and liberation. Some agencies offer a line of funding for HSIs that have never received federal funds, and a majority of federal agencies offer collaborative grants, allowing HSIs that may not have the capacity to write and seek grants to collaborate with HSIs that have the research and grant-seeking infrastructure necessary to secure federal grants. It is vital for transformed HSIs to not only seek federal grants as part of their efforts to enhance servingness but also to lobby and advocate to legislators on Capitol Hill for an increased focus on racial equity and social justice.

State Government: Helping or Hindering Equity and Justice?

State governments also play a vital role in supporting institutions, with state-level governance, funding, and regulations playing an instrumental role in how transformed HSIs enact their mission, identity, and purpose. Some state-level policies that might help or hinder institutional efforts to advance racial equity and social justice include affirmative action policies, state-level DREAM Acts and in-state tuition for undocumented students, performance- or outcomes-based funding, guided pathways policies and grants, free tuition for college programs, and ethnic studies requirements. Although none of these policies are specific to HSIs, institutions must respond to them. The historical trend in state-level higher education has included a tremendous amount of autonomy and variation in organizing and decision-making (McGuinness, 2016b). Since 2015, which was the latest wave of change in state-level higher education, there have been six primary functions including state-level planning; state finance policy (e.g., budgeting and resource allocation); use of data and information to monitor progress, regulation, administration or service agency functions; and system and institutional governance (McGuinness, 2016a). Importantly, states have become increasingly focused on issues such as affordability and completion, which align with the HSI mission identity and purpose to serve economically minoritized students. There is also an increasing focus on racial equity at the state level (e.g., Felix, 2021; Felix & Fernandez Castro, 2018; Felix & Trinidad, 2020), which is essential for transformed HSIs as they focus on advancing racial justice for Latinx, Black, Indigenous, Asian American, Pacific Islander, and Mixed-Race students. State legislators, and particularly those that have a high percentage of HSIs, must think about servingness, making decisions that are centered on educational justice for students of color who have historically been at the margins of education. Transformed HSIs should also manage those relationships, lobbying and advocating for an increased focus on racial equity and liberatory outcomes at the state level.

States primarily finance colleges and universities through direct subsidies (McGuinness, 2016b). State finance policies, however, vary by state and change regularly as institutions adapt to economic crises, public education agenda reform, and deregulation of fiscal policies, among other issues (McGuinness, 2016a). Importantly, state governments, as organizational entities, are subject to mimetic functioning that is typical in a highly institutionalized field (DiMaggio & Powell, 1983). As such, state higher education governing bodies often adopt policies and practices that other states implement, particularly as the results of the adopted practices show signs of effectiveness. Performance-based funding (PBF), which links appropriations to specifically identified outcomes such as earned credit hours, graduation rates, and increased racial diversity, is one of those policies that has been adopted by 41 states as of fiscal year 2020 (Ortagus et al., 2020).

PBF arose as a part of the accountability movement, with states publicly committing to providing quality public education. Some of the intended outcomes include an institutional response to improving academic and student support (Ortagus et al., 2020), which is an essential dimension of the transformed HSI framework, yet Jones et al. (2017) found that PBF has a number of unintended consequences, particularly for MSIs, which tend to be underresourced and disadvantaged when it comes to elevating institutional capacity for servingness. Studies have found that some institutions have limited the enrollment of students of color, who historically had lower persistence and completion rates than white students, in order to increase these performance measures in a PBF model (Ortagus et al., 2020). Jones et al. (2017) argue that as a race-neutral policy, PBF will continue to have unintended consequences for students of color and the institutions that they enroll in, including MSIs. They argue that states must consider the historical context that institutions operate in (e.g., desegregation laws), the historical need of racially and economically minoritized students in the institution, and the available institutional resources. Transformed HSIs must understand how state funding models such as PBF affect their ability to enact an HSI mission, identity, and purpose and increase their interaction with state legislators in order to advocate for equitable policies for HSIs as a whole.

States also provide direct aid to students, yet there is variation by state. With such a high number of low-income students enrolling in HSIs, working with state policy makers is important, with transformed HSIs needing to advocate for greater financial aid and tuition support for students. There is currently a state-level movement to adopt free college tuition programs (Campaign for Free College Tuition, 2019), which could have profound effects on the number of students enrolling in HSIs. Each state has taken an individual approach to making college affordable for its residents, with many focusing on increasing access by offering free tuition to the state's community colleges. With 46% of all HSIs being Hispanic-serving community colleges (HSCCs), these institutions are likely to receive the benefits of free in-state tuition and could see an increase in enrollment of students of color and low-income students.

Other statewide policies such as in-state tuition for DREAMers are also essential to supporting undocumented students who enroll in

HSIs. As of early 2021, 17 states and the District of Columbia offered in-state tuition for undocumented students, many of whom have a high number of HSIs, including California, Texas, Florida, New Mexico, and New York (National Conference of State Legislatures, 2021). At least 11 states also offer some form of financial assistance to undocumented students (National Conference of State Legislatures, 2021). The guided pathways movement at community colleges across the United States, which often includes institutional grants to support the implementation of a holistic program that supports students from entry through completion. The move to implement guided pathways could have a significant impact on the way HSCCs serve students. Yet HSCCs must avoid implementing policies such as guided pathways through a race-neutral lens, as a narrative that relies on *all* students succeeding is insufficient in addressing the specific needs and challenges that face students of color with intersecting minoritized identities (Bensimon, 2017). In responding to and implementing state-level mandates, transformed HSIs must couple race to these policies and redistribute resources to ensure the racially minoritized students are adequately served by a policy that was originally race-neutral.

Overall, state-level policies that align with the mission and overall identity and purpose of transformed HSIs will be better suited for supporting the institutions' efforts to transform. Practitioners at HSIs should actively engage with and influence state legislators in order to enhance the institutions' focus on racial equity, social justice, and collective liberation. In particular, institutions must remain vigilant about policies and mandates that could hinder their ability to enroll and serve students of color.

Private Foundations: Funding for Social Justice and Community Engagement

While a majority of competitive funding for HSIs comes through the federal government via agencies that provide earmarked funds for HSIs, private foundations are an important external influence on all institutions of higher education, as they offer competitive funding for innovative ideas that have the ability to change society. Empirically, less is known about how private foundations are influencing the work of HSIs. Moreover, income from private giving and endowments are almost nonexistent at a majority of two- and four-year public HSIs (Nellum & Valle, 2015). Engaging with private foundations is an important area of growth for transformed HSIs to consider.

It is critical for transformed HSIs to engage with private foundations that espouse the same values of advancing equity and justice for people of color as a societal value. As documented by The Foundation Center (2009) in its report *Social Justice Grantmaking II: Highlights*, there is growth in the commitment to social justice philanthropy, which is defined as "the granting of philanthropic contributions to nonprofit organizations based in the United States and other countries that work for structural change in order to increase the opportunity of those who are the least well off politically, economically, and socially" (p. 10). The W. K. Kellogg Foundation (2012) also noted the rise in identity-based philanthropy, which it defines as "a growing movement to democratize philanthropy from the grassroots up by activating and organizing its practice in marginalized communities, particularly communities of color" (p. 2). Of note, the W. K. Kellogg Foundation (2012) centers race, ethnicity, gender, and sexual orientation in its definition of identity-based philanthropy and add that there is also a growth in identity-based funds, which "work by pooling together solicited donations and contributions from community donors and then redistributing those funds (through grants) to individuals or organizations doing work in that community to promote social change" (p. 3). As identity-based funding often goes directly to the racial, ethnic, and Indigenous communities it is intended to support, there is a greater emphasis for transformed HSIs to develop mutually beneficial and reciprocal partnerships centered on advancing equity and justice for students, families, and communities, *not the institution.*

In interviewing 18 social justice funders and eight advocates/activists, The Foundation Center (2009) found that there is a desire to fund ideas that are grounded in social justice and that bridge the needs of identity-based groups by race, class, language, and region. This aligns with the model of transformed HSIs, which centers the intersectional experiences of students, families, and communities, with an increasing need to develop more projects that elevate these intersectionalities at HSIs. There is also a desire to fund ideas that allow for capacity building and strategic partnerships that connect community-based organizations, think tanks, and grassroots organizations. The report noted, however, that grassroots organizations often receive less philanthropic funding than larger think tanks and national policy groups, yet community-based organizing is one of the most effective levers of change. Aligning with the need to develop better community partnerships, transformed HSIs should access support for this type of work by engaging with private funders committed to funding social justice projects and developing the next generation of social justice leaders. Transdisciplinary efforts should also be embraced, as private foundations committed to social justice work fund projects about economic development, human rights and civil liberties, housing and shelter, and human services at the highest rate (The Foundation Center, 2009), which cuts across numerous disciplines on campus, from economics and law to social work and gender and women's studies.

Transformed HSIs must rethink the normative and traditional ways that they have done development and philanthropy work. Instead, they must center racial justice, equity, and empowerment for people of color while engaging private foundations that also support these efforts. There are a growing number of foundations that are committed to socially just philanthropy and some that have done it historically. The Ford Foundation, W. K. Kellogg Foundation, David and Lucile Packard Foundation, Bill and Melinda Gates Foundation, William T. Grant Foundation, and Spencer Foundation, to name a few, are leaders in identity-based and social justice funding and are committed to racial justice, educational equity, access to health care, environmental justice, reproductive rights, and training future scientists of color, among others. Beyond these national foundations, transformed HSIs should also engage with local foundations, as they are likely to be committed to the local communities of color and low-income communities in more regionally specific ways, which will allow HSIs to adequately address the needs of the region.

Policy Intermediaries: Influencing Servingness

Transformed HSIs should also engage with policy intermediaries, which include numerous entities that shape education policy, agendas, priorities, and decisions. This includes professional associations, think tanks, policy consultants, advocacy organizations, and the media. These groups build coalitions to address the most pressing issues facing higher education, they provide solutions to policy makers and legislators, and they activate constituents to advance policy change. The groups serve as intermediaries between colleges and universities (often engaging directly with presidents, chancellors, and governing boards), state and federal governments, and private foundations, with the goal of shaping policy. For HSIs, less is known about how these intermediaries are influencing servingness.

Some policy advocates have been shaping the HSI agenda since the founding of HSIs. The Hispanic Association of Colleges and Universities (HACU), for example, advocated for the HSI designation even before its official founding in 1986. HACU carried on the legacy of the Hispanic Higher Education Coalition, which fought vehemently for the HSI designation, yet HACU had an advantage as it effectively engaged the leaders of the HSIs it was advocating for while also perfecting its ability to lobby legislators in Washington, DC (Valdez, 2015). HACU continues this legacy today, advocating for Latinx students and HSIs on Capitol Hill, and supporting HSI leaders through the Annual National Capital Forum on Hispanic Higher Education, the HACU Annual Conference, and the HACU Latino Higher Education Leadership Institute. HACU also continues its governmental relations and advocacy work and offers the HACU National Internship Program, which is intended to develop future Latinx leaders in government. *Excelencia* in Education is also a key policy intermediary, founded in

2004 by Sarita Brown and Deborah Santiago to accelerate Latinx student success in higher education by focusing on data-driven solutions that link research, practice, and policy. *Excelencia* in Education is known for its detailed policy reports and infographics that show trends in Latinx educational access and attainment. The organization recognizes evidence-based best practices for serving Latinxs, both through its Examples of *Excelencia* initiative and its Seal of *Excelencia*, which gives HSIs something to strive for. The professional associations create a mimicry effect seen within institutionalized fields in which organizations strive to do what similar legitimized organizations do (DiMaggio & Powell, 1983), which is important for a field that is still evolving. As the HSI field emerges, these professional organizations are shaping what it means to effectively serve students of color and low-income students.

The Alliance of HSI Educators is a professional association that specifically supports HSIs and the practitioners within them. Membership provides access to a network of professionals who share best practices and collaborate toward servingness. The organization also works with federal agencies and HACU to provide grant writing and project management workshops to help HSIs become successful at securing and managing these essential funds and hosts an annual best practices conference. The American Association of Hispanics in Higher Education (AAHHE) also advocates for Latinxs in higher education, focusing broadly on Latinxs but adding HSI to the conversation over the years as important spaces for educating Latinxs. AAHHE's fellowship programs are specifically designed to support doctoral students and early career faculty to successfully complete their degrees and get tenure, which will ultimately help elevate the number of Latinxs entering faculty positions at HSIs, which is an urgent matter. AAHHE also supports the professional development of future administrators and policy makers who study and understand the educational issues facing the Latinx community. Importantly, AAHHE celebrates the academic accomplishments of Latinxs through a series of awards, which is important for a population of scholars that is not always recognized by mainstream professional organizations. In 2020, *Becoming Hispanic-Serving Institutions: Opportunities for Colleges and Universities* (Johns Hopkins University Press; Garcia, 2019) was recognized by AAHHE as the book of year, with all conference attendees receiving the book, thus elevating the HSI knowledge production and dissemination. There are also state-level HSI consortia emerging, such as the Southern California Consortium of HSIs, that are committed to Latinx student success by collaborating and leveraging individual institutional strengths. For all these professional associations, the networking and training opportunities are fundamental elements offered to member institutions as they enhance their understanding of becoming HSIs that are committed to racial equity, social justice, and collective liberation.

Other policy intermediaries that include a focus on diversity and equity in their education agenda also advocate for HSIs in various ways, working to influence servingness by shaping policy. The American Council on Education, an organization that mobilizes the higher education community in order to shape policy and foster innovative practice, has published several reports about MSIs that provide evidence of the various ways that HSIs are equitably graduating students (Espinosa et al., 2017) and providing upward mobility to their graduates (Espinosa et al., 2018). These reports are important to the development of policy because they are written through an asset-based lens that frames HSIs as important contributors to the overall higher education landscape, and particularly with regard to educating Latinx, Black, Indigenous, Asian American, and Pacific Islander students. The Education Trust, an organization that seeks to close gaps in educational outcomes and achievement for students of color, similarly has produced a series of reports that frame HSIs as effective institutions in closing the six-year graduation gap for Latinxs (Nichols, 2017). The Education Trust has also launched special initiatives such as OASIS (Optimizing Academic Success and Institutional Strategy), which developed a network of HSIs and HBCUs to collaboratively work toward implementing high-impact practices that work for minoritized students in MSIs (Cabrales, 2016). These are just two examples of the numerous policy intermediaries that write reports and develop policy briefs that highlight inequities across educational pathways as a way to leverage legislatives conversations about racial equity and that actively work with institutional leaders to elevate a focus on diversity, equity, and justice in higher education.

There are many examples of the ways that the ecosystem of policy makers and policy intermediaries influence institutions of higher education. Many of these entities are invisible to most, with less attention given to their power and influence. Transformed HSIs must come to understand how these external influences operate and shape higher education and actively learn to manage and collaborate with them in order to advance the transformed HSI mission, identity, and purpose. This will take a long-term commitment, yet institutions of higher education have been doing this for centuries. I call on transformed HSIs to be intentional in their efforts to manage external influences with the goal of racial equity and social justice for students of color, families, alumni, and communities at the center. The external influences can and should elevate the external partnerships and vice versa.

Conclusion

External partners and external influences are mostly overlooked in HSI research, practice, and policy. The conversation about becoming HSIs tends to focus on changing the racial-ethnic-Indigenous composition of the faculty, training faculty to do better, and developing curricular and cocurricular structures that center minoritized students and their histories and social contexts. The transformed HSIs framework takes an organizational approach, elevating every dimension needed to drive real change that is grounded in racial equity, social justice, collective liberation, and overall healing for people harmed by educational systems. Alumni, donors, community members, and the institutional advancement and alumni engagement offices that work with these groups have mostly been ignored in all HSI conversations. I call on transformed HSIs to engage these partners as essential collaborators in servingness and to consider these partnerships as mutually beneficial. In other words, transformed HSIs should also commit to serving alumni, donors, and communities in ways that are transformative and liberatory. Simultaneously, transformed HSIs must consider the most appropriate ways to manage and engage with external influences, from state and federal governments to private funders and media. These forces are shaping servingness, whether intentionally or not, yet their goals and priorities may not align with the mission, identity, and strategic purpose of transformed HSIs. The power of working with external partners and influences should not be underestimated when it comes to transforming HSIs. The Transforming HSIs Framework will require members internal to the organization and partners external to the organization to fulfill the freedom dream, to transform higher education, to implement pedagogies of the oppressed, to decolonize the institution, to disrupt and decouple whiteness, and to challenge racialized institutions to create a new approach to liberatory education at the postsecondary level. I call on all the freedom-dreaming educators to enact this framework grounded in their own approaches to radical liberation, critical love, collective healing, and social justice.

REFERENCES

Abeyta, M. (2020). Formerly incarcerated Latino men in California community colleges. *Journal of Applied Research in the Community College, 27*(2), 51–62.

Abrica, E. J., García-Louis, C., & Gallaway, C. D. J. (2020). Antiblackness in the Hispanic-serving community college (HSCC) context: Black male collegiate experiences through the lens of settler colonial logics. *Race Ethnicity and Education, 23*(1), 55–73. https://doi.org/10.1080/13613324.2019.1631781

Abrica, E. J., & Rivas, M. (2017). Chicanas in IR: Advocacy for Latinx students from institutional research contexts in the community college. *Association for Mexican American Educators Journal, 11*(2), 43–64. http://dx.doi.org/10.24974/amae.11.2.349

Acevedo-Gil, N. (2017). College *conocimiento:* Toward an interdisciplinary college choice framework for Latinx students. *Race Ethnicity and Education, 20*(6), 829–850.

Acevedo-Gil, N., Santos, R. E., Alonso, L., & Solorzano, D. G. (2015). Latinas/os in community college developmental education: Increasing moments of academic and interpersonal validation. *Journal of Hispanic Higher Education, 14*(2), 101–127. https://doi.org/10.1177/1538192715572893

Acosta, S. Y. (2010). *Corazón a corazón: Examining the philanthropic motivations, priorities, and relational connectedness of Mexican American, Spanish American, and other Latino/Hispano university alumni/alumnae to a Hispanic Serving Institution* [Unpublished dissertation]. New Mexico State University.

ACPA: College Student Educators International. (2008). *The student learning imperative: Implications for student affairs.* https://archive.myacpa.org/sites/default/files/ACPA%27s%20Student%20Learning%20Imperative.pdf

Adams State University. (2018). *2018 Unidos Equity Leadership Institute.* https://www.adams.edu/titlev/equity-retreat/

Aguilar-Hernández, J. M., Benavides López, C., & Gutierrez Keeton, R. (2021). Resisting the "death of diversity": A historical analysis of the formation of the César E. Chávez Center for Higher Education at Cal Poly Pomona, 1990–1995. *Latino Studies, 19*, 27–46. https://doi.org/10.1057/s41276-021-00284-w

Aguilar-Smith, S. (2021). Seeking to serve or $erve? Hispanic-Serving Institutions' race-evasive pursuit of racialized funding. *AERA Open, 7*(1), 1–15. https://doi.org/10.1177/23328584211057097

Aguirre, A., Jr., & Martinez, R. (2002). Leadership practices and diversity in higher education: Transitional and transformational frameworks. *Journal of Leadership Studies, 8*, 53–62.

Ahmed, S. (2012). *On being included: Racism and diversity in institutional life.* Duke University Press.

Akbar, A. A. (2020). An abolitionist horizon for (police) reform. *California Law Review, 108*(6), 1781–1846. https://doi.org/10.15779/Z38M32NB2K

Albert, S., & Whetten, D. A. (1985). Organizational identity. In L. L. Cummings & B. M. Staw (Eds.), *Research in organizational behavior* (Vol. 7, pp. 263–295). JAI Press.

Alcantar, C. M., & Hernandez, E. (2020). "Here the professors are your guide, tus guías": Latina/o student validating experiences with faculty at a Hispanic-Serving community college. *Journal of Hispanic Higher Education, 19*(1), 3–18. https://doi.org/10.1177/1538192718766234

Alcantar, C. M., Rincón, B. E., & Espinoza, K. J. (2020). In a state of becoming: How institutions communicate Asian American and Pacific Islander- and Latinx-servingness through campus artifacts. *Association of Mexican American Educators Journal, 14*(3), 104–119. https://doi.org/10.24974/amae.14.3.405

Andrade, L. M., & Lundberg, C. A. (2018). The function to serve: A social-justice-oriented investigation of community college mission statements. *Journal of Hispanic Higher Education, 17*(1), 61–75. https://doi.org/10.1177/1538192716653503

Anzaldúa, G. (2012). *Borderlands/La Frontera: The new mestiza* (3rd ed.). Aunt Lute Books.

Association of American Colleges and Universities [AAC&U]. (2005). *Liberal education outcomes: A preliminary report on student achievement in college.* https://www.aacu.org/sites/default/files/files/LEAP/LEAP_Report_2005.pdf

Association of Governing Boards of Universities and Colleges [AGB]. (2007). AGB statement on board accountability [Statement].

Association of Governing Boards of Universities and Colleges [AGB]. (2010). Association of Governing Boards of Universities and Colleges statement on board responsibility for institutional governance [Statement]. https://agb.org/wp-content/uploads/2019/01/statement_2010_institutional_governance.pdf

Association of Governing Boards of Universities and Colleges [AGB]. (2016). *Shared governance: Is OK good enough?* https://www.agb.org/sites/default/files/survey_2016_shared_governance.pdf

Astin, A. W. (1984). Student involvement: A developmental theory for higher education. *Journal of College Student Development, 25*, 297–308.

Astin, A. W. (1993). *What matters in college? Four critical years revisited.* Jossey-Bass.

Austin, I., & Jones, G. A. (2016). *Governance of higher education: Global perspectives, theories, and practices.* Routledge.

Baca, I., Hinojosa, Y. I., & Wolff Murphy, S. (2019). *Bordered writers: Latinx identities and literacy practices at Hispanic-Serving Institutions*. State University of New York Press.

B. A. L. (2019). The hidden costs of serving our community: Women faculty of color, racist sexism, and false security in a Hispanic-Serving Institution. *Feminist Teacher, 27*(2-3), 176-195.

Bale, J., & Knopp, S. (2012). *Education and capitalism: Struggles for learning and liberation*. Haymarket Books.

Banks, J. A. (2010). Approaches to multicultural curricular reform. In J. A. Banks & C. A. M. Banks (Eds.), *Multicultural education: Issues and perspectives* (7th ed., pp. 233-258). Wiley.

Banning, J. H., & Bartels, S. (1997). A taxonomy: Campus physical artifacts as communicators of campus multiculturalism. *NASPA Journal, 35*(1), 29-37. https://doi.org/10.2202/1949-6605.1032

Banning, J. H., Middleton, V., & Deniston, T. L. (2008). Using photographs to assess equity climate: A taxonomy. *Multicultural Perspectives, 10*(1), 41-46. https://doi.org/10.1080/15210960701869611

Barnett, N. C., Freeman, Jr., S., & Freeman, M. L. (2016). Higher education as a field of study at Minority Serving Institutions. *The Western Journal of Black Studies, 40*(3), 3-19.

Barr, M. J., & McClellan, G. S. (2018). *Budgets and financial management in higher education* (3rd ed.). Jossey-Bass.

Bensimon, E. M. (2007). The underestimated significance of practitioner knowledge in the scholarship on student success. *The Review of Higher Education, 30*(4), 441-469. https://doi.org/10.1353/rhe.2007.0032

Bensimon, E. M. (2012). The equity scorecard: Theory of change. In E. M. Bensimon and L. Malcom (Eds.), *Confronting equity issues on campus: Implementing the equity scorecard in theory and practice* (pp. 17-44). Stylus.

Bensimon, E. M. (2017). *Making American higher education just*. Center for Urban Education. https://cue.usc.edu/files/2017/06/Bensimon_Making-American -Higher-Education-Just_AERA-SJ-Award-Lecture.pdf

Berne, P., & Sins Invalid. (n.d.). *10 principles of disability justice*. https://static1 .squarespace.com/static/5bed3674f8370ad8c02efd9a/t/5f1f0783916d8a179c 46126d/1595869064521/10_Principles_of_DJ-2ndEd.pdf

Bhattacharya, N., Sánchez Ordaz, A., Mosqueda, E., & Cooper, C. R. (2020). Redesigning the gateway college algebra course with inclusive and assets-based pedagogy: Rethinking "servingness" at a Hispanic Serving Institution. In G. A. Garcia (Ed.), *Hispanic Serving Institutions (HSIs) in practice: Defining "servingness" at HSIs* (pp. 97-116). Information Age Publishing.

Boland, W. C. (2018). The Higher Education Act and Minority Serving Institutions: Towards a typology of Title III and V funded programs. *Education Sciences, 8*(33). https://doi.org/10.3390/educsci8010033

Cabrales, J. A. (2011). *Conceptualizing Latina/o philanthropy in higher education: A study of Latina/o undergraduate alumni from a predominantly white Jesuit institution* [Unpublished dissertation]. Iowa State University.

Cabrales, J. A. (2013). An approach to engaging Latina/o alumni in giving initiatives: Madrinas y Padrinos. In N. D. Drezner (Ed.), *Expanding the donor base in higher education: Engaging non-traditional donors* (pp. 26–39). Routledge.

Cabrales, J. A. (2016). *Eleven higher education institutions unite to improve graduation rates*. The Education Trust. https://edtrust.org/the-equity-line/eleven -higher-education-institutions-unite-to-improve-graduation-rates/

Cabrera, N. L. (2019). *White guys on campus: Racism, white immunity, and the myth of "post-racial" higher education*. Rutgers University Press.

Cabrera, N. L., Franklin, J. D., & Watson, J. S. (2017). *Whiteness in higher education: The invisible missing link in diversity and racial analyses*. Wiley.

Calderón, D., & Urrieta, Jr., L. (2019). Studying in relation: Critical Latinx Indigeneities and education. *Equity & Excellence in Education, 52*(2–3), 219–238. https://doi.org/10.1080/10665684.2019.1672591

Camacho Parra, N. R. (2012). Afro-Venezuelan cimarronas: Desde adentro. In M. M. Vega, M. Alba, & Y. Modestin (Eds.), *Women warriors of the Afro-Latina diaspora* (pp. 1–16). Arte Público Press.

Campaign for College Opportunity (2020). *Left out: California's higher education governing boards do not reflect the racial and gender diversity of California and its student body*. https://files.constantcontact.com/64b4a2b1101/2b25a7cd-eff8 -40d7-bbaa-896105d4485d.pdf

Campaign for Free College Tuition (2019). *Making public colleges tuition free: A briefing book for state leaders*. https://www.freecollegenow.org/briefing _book

Canales, J., & Chahin, T. J. (2019). Effective leadership at a Hispanic-Serving Institution: Critical attributes and principles. In R. T. Palmer, D. Preston, & A. Assalone (Eds.), *Examining effective practices at Minority-Serving Institutions: Beyond deficit framing of leadership* (pp. 113–140). Palgrave Macmillan.

Castañeda, M., & Krupczynski, J. (2018). Introduction: Toward a Latinx community-academic praxis of civic engagement. In M. Castañeda & J. Krupczynski (Eds.), *Civic engagement in diverse Latinx communities: Learning from social justice partnerships in action* (pp. 1–17). Peter Lang.

Castillo-Montoya, M. (2019). Professors' pedagogical strategies for teaching through diversity. *The Review of Higher Education, 42*(Supplemental), 199–226. https://doi.org/10.1353/rhe.2019.0050

Castillo-Montoya, M., & Ives, J. (2020). A liberating education: Integrating funds of knowledge and disciplinary knowledge to create tools for students' lives. In K. C. Culver & T. L. Trolian (Eds.), *New Directions for Teaching and Learning* (no. 164, pp. 39–48). Wiley.

Cataño, Y., & González, A. (2021). Examining *servingness* at California community college Hispanic-Serving Institutions (HSIs) for LGBTQ+ Latinx students. *Journal of the Alliance for Hispanic Serving Institution Educators, 1*(1), 55–72.

Cervantes, M. A., & Saldaña, L. P. (2015). Hip hop and *nueva canción* as decolonial pedagogies of epistemic justice. *Decolonization: Indigeneity, Education, & Society, 4*(1), 84–108.

Chessman, H., & Wayt, L. (2016). What are students demanding? *Higher Education Today: A Blog by ACE (American Council on Education).* https://www.higheredtoday.org/2016/01/13/what-are-students-demanding/

Ching, C. D. (2019). Supporting Latinx students in Hispanic-Serving Institutions: An exploration of faculty perceptions and actions. *Journal of Latinos and Education.* Online first. https://doi.org/10.1080/15348431.2019.1612398

Cohen, A. M., & Brawer, F. B. (2008). *The American community college.* Jossey-Bass.

Cole, E. R., & Harper, S. R. (2017). Race and rhetoric: An analysis of college presidents' statements on campus racial incidents. *Journal of Diversity in Higher Education, 10*(4), 318–333. https://doi.org/10.1037/dhe00000044

Comeaux, E., Grummert, S. E., & Cruz, N. (2021). Strategies of resistance among racially minoritized students at a Hispanic-Serving Institution: A critical race theory perspective. *The Journal of Higher Education, 92*(3), 465–498. https://doi.org/10.1080/00221546.2020.1851569

Commodore, F. (2018). The tie that binds: Trusteeship, values, and the decision-making process at AME-affiliated HBCUs. *The Journal of Higher Education, 89*(4), 397–421. https://doi.org/10.1080/00221546.2017.1396949

Conchas, G. Q., & Acevedo, N. (2020). *The Chicana/o/x dream: Hope, resistance, and educational success.* Harvard Education Press

Contreras, F. E. (2017). Latino faculty in Hispanic-Serving Institutions: Where is the diversity? *Association of Mexican American Educators Journal, 11*(3), 223–250. https://doi.org/10.24974/amae.11.3.368

Contreras, F. E., Malcom, L. E., & Bensimon, E. M. (2008). Hispanic-Serving Institutions: Closeted identity and the production of equitable outcomes for Latina/o students. In M. Gasman, B. Baez, & C. S. T. Turner (Eds.), *Understanding Minority-Serving Institutions* (pp. 71–90). State University of New York Press.

Contreras Aguirre, H. C., Gonzalez, E., & Banda, R. M. (2020). Latina college students' experiences in STEM at Hispanic-Serving Institutions: Framed within Latino critical race theory. *International Journal of Qualitative Studies in Education.* https://doi.org/10.1080/09518398.2020.1751894

Cooper, C. R., Reguerín, P. G., Herzon, C., Sánchez Ordaz, A., Gonzalez, E., & Rocha-Ruiz, M. (2020). Unifying equity practice, research, and policies at a Hispanic Serving Institution for systemic servingness. In G. A. Garcia (Ed.), *Hispanic Serving Institutions (HSIs) in practice: Defining "servingness" at HSIs* (pp. 173–191). Information Age Publishing.

Corcoran, L., & Wilkinson, C. (2019). Translingualism and ALP: A rhetorical model for bordered Latinx writers. In I. Baca, Y. I. Hinojosa, & S. Wolff Murphy (Eds.), *Bordered writers: Latinx identities and literacy practices at Hispanic-Serving Institutions* (pp. 19–36). State University of New York Press.

Cortés, M. (2002). Questions about Hispanics and fundraising. *New Directions for Philanthropic Fundraising, 37,* 45–54.

Cortez, L. J. (2015). Enacting leadership at Hispanic-Serving Institutions. In A.-M. Núñez, S. Hurtado, & E. Calderón Galdeano (Eds.), *Hispanic-Serving Institutions: Advancing research and transformative practice* (pp. 136–152). Routledge.

Coulter, L. (2020, September 10). Sustained racial justice committee moves forward: Members commit themselves to serve as agents of change and advance racial-justice efforts. https://webapp.msudenver.edu/smc/ebird /temp.msudenver.edu/early-bird/2020/9/10-committee.html

Covarubbias, R. (2021). What we bring with us: Investing in Latinx students means investing in families. *Policy Insights from the Behavioral and Brain Sciences, 8*(1), 3–10. https://doi.org/10.1177/2372732220983855

Covarubbias, R., Vazquez, A., Moreno, R., Estrada, J., Valle, I., & Zuñiga, K. (2020). Engaging families to foster holistic success of low-income, Latinx first-generation students at a Hispanic Serving Institution. In G. A. Garcia (Ed.), *Hispanic Serving Institutions (HSIs) in practice: Defining "servingness" at HSIs* (pp. 313–336). Information Age Publishing.

Cuellar, M. (2014). The impact of Hispanic-Serving Institutions (HSIs), emerging HSIs, and non-HSIs on Latina/o academic self-concept. *The Review of Higher Education, 37*(4), 499–530. https://doi.org/10.1353/rhe.2014.0032

Cuellar, M. (2015). Latina/o student characteristics and outcomes at four-year Hispanic-Serving Institutions (HSIs), emerging HSIs, and non-HSIs. In A.-M. Núñez, S. Hurtado, & E. Calderón Galdeano (Eds.), *Hispanic-Serving Institutions: Advancing research and transformative practices* (pp. 101–120). Routledge.

Cuellar, M. (2019). Creating Hispanic-Serving Institutions (HSIs) and emerging HSIs: Latina/o college choice at 4-year institutions. *American Journal of Education, 125*(2), 231–258.

Cuellar, M., & Johnson-Ahorlu, R. N. (2016). Examining the complexity of the campus racial climate at a Hispanic serving community college. *Community College Review, 44*(2), 135–152. https://doi.org/10.1177/0091552116632584

Cuellar, M., & Johnson-Ahorlu, R. N. (2020). Racialized experiences off and on campus: Contextualizing Latina/o students' perceptions of climate at an emerging Hispanic-Serving Institution (HSI). *Urban Education.* https://doi.org /10.1177/0042085920927772

Cuellar, M., Segundo, V., & Muñoz, Y. (2017). Assessing empowerment at HSIs: An adapted inputs-environments-outcomes model. *Association of Mexican American Educators Journal, 11*(3), 84–108. http://dx.doi.org/10.24974/amae.11.3 .362

Dale, J., & Hyslop-Margison, E. J. (2010). *Paulo Freire: Teaching for freedom and transformation: The philosophical influences of the work of Paulo Freire.* Springer.

Dancy, T. E., Edwards, K. T., & Davis, J. E. (2018). Historically white universities and plantation politics: Anti-Blackness and higher education in the Black Lives Matter era. *Urban Education, 53*(2), 176–195.

Davila, V. M., & Montelongo, R. (2020). Considering digital technology and innovative learning spaces as "structures for serving" at Hispanic Serving

Institutions. In G. A. Garcia (Ed.), *Hispanic Serving Institutions (HSIs) in practice: Defining "servingness" at HSIs* (pp. 117–134). Information Age Publishing.

Davis, S., & Harris, J. D. (2015). But we didn't mean it like that: A critical race analysis of campus responses to racial incidents. *Journal of Critical Scholarship on Higher Education and Student Affairs, 2*(1), 62–78.

Davis III, C. H. F. (2020, July). Op-ed: If Black lives matter to colleges, they'll divest from campus policing. *Los Angeles Times.* https://www.latimes.com /opinion/story/2020-07-09/campus-police-divestment-racism

Davis III, C. H. F., & Matias Dizon, J. P. (2020). *More colleges should divest from the institution of policing.* Inside Higher Ed. https://www.insidehighered.com /views/2020/06/02/heels-george-floyd-killing-colleges-have-moral -imperative-not-work-local-police

Degges-White, S. (2013). *College student mental health counseling: A developmental approach.* Springer.

Delgado, S. J., Collazo Reyes, J. J., Gómez Dopazo, S. I., Rodríguez Díaz, E. A., & Torres Arroyo, K. M. (2019). Hispanic ESL science majors need more practice using English for scientific purposes. *Journal of Hispanic Higher Education.* Online first. https://doi.org/10.1177/1538192719852025

Delgado Bernal, D. (2001). Learning and living pedagogies of the home: The mestiza consciousness of Chicana students. *International Journal of Qualitative Studies in Education, 14*(5), 623–639. https://doi.org/10.1080 /09518390110059838

de los Ríos, C. V. (2013). A curriculum of the borderlands: High school Chicana/o-Latina/o Studies as *sitios y lengua. Urban Review, 45,* 58–73. https://doi.org/10.1007/s11256-012-0224-3

de los Ríos, C. V. (2019). "Los músicos": Mexican corridos, the aural border, and the evocative musical renderings of transnational youth. *Harvard Education Review, 89*(2), 177–200.

de los Santos, A. G. J., & Cuamea, K. M. (2010). Challenges facing Hispanic-Serving Institutions in the first decade of the 21st century. *Journal of Latinos and Education, 9*(2), 90–107.

de Oliveira Andreotti, V., Stein, S., Ahenakew, C., & Hunt, D. (2015). Mapping interpretations of decolonization in the context of higher education. *Decolonization: Indigeneity, Education & Society, 4*(1), 21–40.

Desai, S. R., & Abeita, A. (2017). Institutional microaggressions at a Hispanic Serving Institution: A Diné (Navajo) woman utilizing Tribal Critical Race Theory through student activism. *Equity & Excellence in Education, 50*(3), 275–289. https://doi.org/10.1080/10665684.2017.1336498

Diemer, M. A., Rapa, L. J., Park, C. J., & Perry, J. C. (2017). Development and validation of the critical consciousness scale. *Youth & Society, 49*(4), 461–483. https://doi.org/10.1177/0044118X14538289

DiMaggio, P. J., & Powell, W. W. (1983). The iron cage revisited: Institutional isomorphism and collective rationality in organizational fields. *American Sociological Review, 48*(2), 147–160.

Doran, E. (2017). An empowerment framework for Latinx students in developmental education. *Association of Mexican American Educators Journal, 11*(2), 133–154. http://dx.doi.org/10/24974/amae.11.2.353

Doran, E. (2019a). Developmental instructors in the contact zone: Perspectives from Hispanic-serving community colleges. In I. Baca, Y. I. Hinojosa, & S. Wolff Murphy (Eds.), *Bordered writers: Latinx identities and literacy practices at Hispanic-Serving Institutions* (pp. 37–51). State University of New York Press.

Doran, E. (2019b). "This was different, and I wanted to learn": A president's response to a student hunger strike at a Hispanic-Serving University. In R. T. Palmer, D. Preston, & A. Assalone (Eds.), *Examining effective practices at Minority-Serving Institutions: Beyond deficit framing of leadership* (pp. 141–160). Palgrave Macmillan.

Doran, E. (in press). Toward a new understanding of Hispanic-Serving community colleges. *Community College Review.*

Drezner, N. D. (2013). Introduction. In N. D. Drezner (Ed.), *Expanding the donor base in higher education: Engaging non-traditional donors* (pp. 26–39). Routledge.

Drezner, N. D., & Huehls, F. (2015). *Fundraising and institutional advancement: Theory, practice, and new paradigms.* Routledge.

Drezner, N. D., & Villarreal, R. C. (2015). Engaging the Latino community: Enhancing Hispanic-Serving Institutions' Latino donor base. In J. P. Mendez, I. F. A. Bonner, J. Méndez-Negrete, & R. T. Palmer (Eds.), *Hispanic-Serving Institutions in American higher education: Their origin, and present and future challenges* (pp. 178–193). Stylus.

Duran, A., & Núñez, A.-M. (2020). Food and housing insecurity for Latinx/a/o college students: Advancing an intersectional research agenda. *Journal of Hispanic Higher Education.* Online first. https://doi.org/10.1177/1538192720963579

Eckel, P. D., & Kezar, A. (2016). The intersecting authority of boards, presidents, and faculty: Toward shared leadership. In M. N. Bastedo, P. G. Altbach, & P. J. Gumport (Eds.), *American higher education in the 21st century: Social, political, and economic challenges* (4th ed., pp. 155–187). Johns Hopkins University Press.

Edwards, K. E. (2006). Aspiring social justice ally identity development: A conceptual model. *NASPA Journal, 43*(4), 39–60.

Ek, L. D., Quijada Cerecer, P. D., Alanís, I., & Rodríguez, M. A. (2010). "I don't belong here": Chicanas/Latinas at a Hispanic Serving Institution creating community through muxerista mentoring. *Equity & Excellence in Education, 43*(4), 539–553. https://doi.org/10.1080/10665684.2010.510069

Elliott, K. C., & Jones, T. (2021, May). *Beyond dollars and cents.* Inside Higher Ed. https://www.insidehighered.com/views/2021/05/19/any-measure-value-higher-ed-must-take-account-advancement-social-justice-opinion

ESCALA Educational Services (2022). *ESCALA's 2022 Courses.* http://www.escalaeducation.com/

España, C., & Herrera, L. Y. (2020). *En comunidad: Lessons for centering the voices and experiences of bilingual Latinx students.* Heinemann.

Espinosa, L. L., Crandall, J. R., & Tukibayeva, M. (2014). *Rankings, institutional behavior, and college and university choice: Framing the national dialogue on Obama's ratings plan.* American Council on Education.

Espinosa, L. L., Kelchen, R., & Taylor, M. (2018). *Minority Serving Institutions as Engines of Upward Mobility.* American Council on Education.

Espinosa, L. L., Turk, J. M., & Taylor, M. (2017). *Pulling back the curtain: Enrollment and outcomes at Minority Serving Institutions.* American Council on Education.

Espinosa, L. L., Turk, J. M., Taylor, M., & Chessman, H. M. (2019). *Race and ethnicity in higher education: A status report.* American Council on Education.

Espinoza, P. P., & Espinoza, C. C. (2012). Supporting the 7th-year undergraduate: Responsive leadership at a Hispanic-Serving Institution. *Journal of Cases in Educational Leadership, 15*(1), 32–50. https://doi.org/10.1177/1555458912440738

Evans, N. J., Broido, E. M., Brown, K. R., & Wilke, A. K. (2017). *Disability in higher education: A social justice approach.* Jossey-Bass.

Excelencia in Education (2017). *Latinos in higher education and Pell grants.* https://www.edexcelencia.org/media/141

Excelencia in Education. (2020). *25 years of Hispanic-Serving Institutions (HSIs): A glance on progress.* https://www.edexcelencia.org/Excelencia-25-Yrs-HSIs-Glance-On-Progress

Excelencia in Education. (2021a). *Emerging Hispanic-Serving Institutions (HSIs): 2019–20.* https://www.edexcelencia.org/research/publications/emerging-hispanic-serving-institutions-ehsis-2019-2020

Excelencia in Education. (2021b). *Hispanic-Serving Institutions (HSIs): 2019–20.* https://www.edexcelencia.org/research/publications/hispanic-serving-institutions-hsis-2019-2020

Excelencia in Education (2021c), *Hispanic-Serving Institutions with graduate programs (gHSIs), 2019–20: Fast facts.* https://www.edexcelencia.org/research/infographics/hispanic-serving-institutions-graduate-programs-ghsis-2019-20-fast-facts

Felix, E. R. (2021). For Latinx, by Latinx: Race-conscious leadership in policy implementation. *Education Policy Analysis Archives, 29*(30). https://doi.org/10.14507/epaa.29.5439

Felix, E. R., & Fernandez Castro, M. F. (2018). Planning as strategy for improving Black and Latinx student equity: Lessons from nine California community colleges. *Education Policy Analysis Archives, 26*(56). https://dx.doi.org/10.14507/epaa.26.3223

Felix, E. R., & Trinidad, A. (2020). The decentralization of race: Tracing the dilution of racial equity in educational policy. *International Journal of Qualitative Studies in Education, 33*(4), 465–490. https://doi.org/10.1080/09518398.2019.1681538

Fernandez, F., & Burnett, C. A. (2020). Considering the need for organizational resilience at Hispanic Serving Institutions: A study of how administrators navigate institutional accreditation in Southern states. *International Journal of Qualitative Studies in Education.* https://doi.org/10.1080/09518398.2020.1751895

Figueroa-Vásquez, Y. C. (2020). *Decolonizing diasporas: Radical mappings of Afro-Atlantic literature*. Northwestern University Press.

Flores, A., & Leal, D. R. (2020). Beyond enrollment and graduation: Examining strategic plans from Hispanic-Serving Institutions in Texas. *Journal of Latinos and Education*. https://doi.org/10.1080/15348431.2020.1791121

Fosnacht, K., & Nailos, J. N. (2016). Impact of the environment: How does attending a Hispanic-Serving Institution influence the engagement of baccalaureate-seeking Latina/o students? *Journal of Hispanic Higher Education, 15*(3), 187–204. https://doi.org/10.1177/1538192715597739

Foundation Center (2009). *Social justice grantmaking II, highlights*. https://foundationcenter.org/gainknowledge/research/pdf/socialjustice2009_highlights.pdf

Franco, M. A., & Hernández, S. (2018). Assessing the capacity of Hispanic Serving Institutions to serve Latinx students: Moving beyond compositional diversity. In D. Zerquera, I. Hernández, & J. G. Berumen (Eds.), *New Directions for Institutional Research: Special Issue: Assessment and social justice: Pushing through paradox* (pp. 57–71). Wiley.

Franco, M. A., Lozano, G. I., & Subbian, V. (2020). HSIs and community partners: A framework for strengthening servingness through engagement. In G. A. Garcia (Ed.), *Hispanic Serving Institutions (HSIs) in practice: Defining "serving-ness" at HSIs* (pp. 151–172). Information Age Publishing.

Freeman, M. L. (2015). HEALing higher education: An innovative approach to preparing HSI leaders. In M. L. Freeman & M. Martinez (Eds.), *New Directions for Higher Education: Special Issue: College completion for Latino/a students: Institutional and system approaches* (pp. 7–18). Wiley.

Freire, P. (2018). *Pedagogy of the Oppressed* (50th anniversary ed.). Bloomsbury. (Original work published 1970)

Garcia, G. A. (2013a). *Challenging the manufactured identity of Hispanic Serving Institutions: Co-constructing an organizational identity* [Unpublished dissertation]. University of California, Los Angeles.

Garcia, G. A. (2013b). Does the percentage of Latinas/os affect graduation rates at four-year Hispanic Serving Institutions (HSIs), emerging HSIs, and non-HSIs? *Journal of Hispanic Higher Education, 12*, 256–268. https://doi.org/10.1177/1538192712467203

Garcia, G. A. (2015). Using organizational theory to study Hispanic-Serving Institutions (HSIs): An imperative research agenda. In A.-M. Núñez, S. Hurtado, & E. Calderón Galdeano (Eds.), *Hispanic-Serving Institutions: Advancing research and transformative practices* (pp. 82–98). Routledge.

Garcia, G. A. (2016a). Complicating a Latina/o-serving Identity at a Hispanic Serving Institution. *The Review of Higher Education, 40*(1), 117–143. https://doi.org/10.1353/rhe.2016.0040

Garcia, G. A. (2016b). Exploring student affairs professionals' experiences with the campus racial climate at a Hispanic Serving Institution (HSI). *Journal of Diversity in Higher Education, 9*(1), 20–33. https://doi.org/10.1037/a0039199

Garcia, G. A. (2017). Defined by outcomes or culture? Constructing an organizational identity for Hispanic-Serving Institutions. *American Educational
Research Journal, 54*(1S), 111S–134S. https://doi.org/10.3102/0002831216669779

Garcia, G. A. (2018). Decolonizing Hispanic-Serving Institutions: A framework
for organizing. *Journal of Hispanic Higher Education, 17*(2), 132–147. https://doi
.org/10.1177/1538192717734289

Garcia, G. A. (2019). *Becoming Hispanic-Serving Institutions: Opportunities for
Colleges and Universities.* Johns Hopkins University Press.

Garcia, G. A. (2020a). Defining social justice curriculum in postsecondary
education. *HigherEdJobs.* https://bit.ly/33xZ8xs

Garcia, G. A. (2020b). Is liberation a viable outcome for students who attend
college? *HigherEdJobs.* https://bit.ly/3qHmAB1

Garcia, G. A. (2021). A love letter to HSI grant seekers/implementers and the
federal agencies that fund them: Defining servingness in research, practice,
& policy. *Journal of the Alliance for Hispanic Serving Institution Educators, 1*(1),
1–14.

Garcia, G. A., & Cuellar, M. (2018). Exploring curricular and cocurricular effects
on civic engagement at emerging Hispanic-Serving Institutions. *Teachers
College Record, 120*(4), 1–36.

Garcia, G. A., DeCostanza, Jr., J., & Romo, J. (2021). Theorizing a Catholic
Hispanic-Serving Institution (C-HSI) identity through Latinx theological
lenses of lo cotidiano and traditioning. *Journal of Catholic Education, 24*(2),
20–42. https://files.eric.ed.gov/fulltext/EJ1330470.pdf

Garcia, G. A., & Dwyer, B. (2018). Exploring college students' identification with
an organizational identity for serving Latina/o students at a Hispanic Serving
Institution (HSI) and emerging HSI. *American Journal of Education, 124*(2)
191–215. https://doi.org/10.1086/695609

Garcia, G. A., & Guzman-Alvarez, A. (2021). Descriptive analysis of graduate
enrollment trends at Hispanic Serving Institutions (HSIs): 2005–2015. *Journal
of Hispanic Higher Education, 20*(2), 196–212. https://doi.org/10.1177
/1538192719835681

Garcia, G. A., & Koren, E. R. (2020). Connecting research, practice, and policy to
define "servingness" at Hispanic Serving Institutions. In G. A. Garcia
(Ed.), *Hispanic Serving Institutions (HSIs) in practice: Defining "servingness" at
HSIs* (pp. 1–20). Information Age Publishing.

Garcia, G. A., Koren, E. R., & Cuellar, M. G. (2020). Assessing color-neutral racial
attitudes of faculty at Hispanic-Serving Institutions (HSIs). *AERA Open, 6*(3),
1–14. https://doi.org/10.1177/2332858420944906

Garcia, G. A., & Natividad, N. D. (2018). Decolonizing leadership practices:
Towards equity and justice at Hispanic-Serving Institutions (HSIs) and
emerging HSIs (eHSIs). *Journal of Transformative Leadership and Policy Studies,
7*(2), 25–39. https://doi.org/10.36851/jtlps.v7i2.505

Garcia, G. A., Núñez, A.-M., & Sansone, V. A. (2019). Toward a multidimensional
conceptual framework for understanding "servingness" in Hispanic-Serving

Institutions (HSIs): A synthesis of the research. *Review of Educational Research, 89*(5), 745–784. https://doi.org/10.3102/0034654319864591

Garcia, G. A., & Okhidoi, O. (2015). Culturally relevant practices that "serve" students at a Hispanic Serving Institution. *Innovative Higher Education, 40*(4), 345–357. https://doi.org/10.1007/s10755-015-9318-7

Garcia, G. A., Patrón, O. E., Ramirez, J. J., & Hudson, L. T. (2018). Identity salience for Latino male collegians at Hispanic Serving Institutions (HSIs), emerging HSIs, and non-HSIs. *Journal of Hispanic Higher Education, 17*(3), 171–186. https://doi.org/10.1177/1538192716661907

Garcia, G. A., & Ramirez, J. J. (2018). Institutional agency at a Hispanic Serving institution (HSI): Using social capital to empower students. *Urban Education, 53*(3), 355–381. https://doi.org/10.1177/0042085915623341

Garcia, G. A., Ramirez, J. J., & Patrón, O. E. (2020). Rethinking Weidman's models of socialization for Latinxs along the postsecondary educational pipeline. In J. C. Weidman & L. DeAngelo (Eds.), *Socialization in higher education and early career: Theory, research, and practice* (pp. 55–72). Springer.

Garcia, G. A., & Zaragoza, M. (2020). Students' perceptions of diversity at two Hispanic-Serving Institutions through pictures: A focus on structures for serving. *Association of Mexican American Educators Journal, 14*(3), 10–29. https://doi.org/10.24974/amae.14.3.388

Gasman, M., & Bowman, N. (2011). Cultivating and soliciting donors of color. *Advancing Philanthropy*, 23–28.

Gasman, M., & Bowman, N. (2013). *Engaging diverse college alumni: The essential guide to fundraising.* Routledge.

Gaston Gayles, J., & Rockenbach, A. N. (2021, May). *The transformative power of student voices in the midst of racial injustice.* Inside Higher Ed. https://www.insidehighered.com/views/2021/05/17/engaging-students-about-racial-injustice

Ginsberg, A., Gasman, M., & Samayoa, A. C. (2018). "It's in your heart": How the California Mini-Corps program and Hispanic Serving Institutions are transforming migrant student education. *The Teacher Educator, 53*(3), 244–262. https://doi.org/10.1080/08878730.2018.1441349

Giroux, H. (2014). *Neoliberalism's War on Higher Education.* Haymarket Books.

Gonzales, L. D. (2015). The horizon of possibilities: How HSI faculty can reshape the production and legitimization of knowledge within academia. In A.-M. Núñez, S. Hurtado, & E. Calderón Galdeano (Eds.), *Hispanic-Serving Institutions: Advancing research and transformative practices* (pp. 121–135). Routledge.

Gonzales, L. D., Murakami, E., & Núñez, A.-M. (2015). Latina faculty in the labyrinth: Constructing and contesting legitimacy in Hispanic Serving Institutions. *Educational Foundations, 27*(1-2), 65–89.

González, A. D. J., & Cataño, Y. (2020). Queering community college HSIs: An environmental scan of current programs and services for Latinx students. *Journal of Applied Research in the Community College, 27*(1), 74–88.

Gonzalez, E., Ortega, G., Molina, M., & Lizalde, G. (2020). What does it mean to be a Hispanic-Serving Institution? Listening to the Latina/o/x voices of students. *International Journal of Qualitative Studies in Education*. https://doi.org/10.1080/09518398.2020.1751896

González, G. G. (2008). Segregation and the education of Mexican children, 1900-1940. In J. F. Moreno (Ed.), *The elusive quest for equality: 150 years of Chicano/Chicana education* (pp. 53-76). Harvard Educational Review.

Griffin-Fennel, F. D., & Lerner, J. E. (2020). Professional development for faculty and staff at a Hispanic Serving Institution: A prerequisite to serving minoritized students. In G. A. Garcia (Ed.), *Hispanic Serving Institutions (HSIs) in practice: Defining "servingness" at HSIs* (pp. 61-77). Information Age Publishing.

Guardia, J. R., & Evans, N. J. (2008). Factors influencing the ethnic identity development of Latino fraternity members at a Hispanic Serving Institution. *Journal of College Student Development, 49*(3), 163-181. https://doi.org/10.1353/csd.0.0011

Gusa, D. L. (2010). White institutional presence: The impact of Whiteness on campus climate. *Harvard Educational Review, 80*(4), 464-489.

Gutiérrez, R. (2002). Enabling the practice of mathematics teachers in context: Toward a new equity research agenda. *Mathematical Thinking and Learning, 4*(2-3), 145-187.

Gutiérrez, R. (2013). The sociopolitical turn in mathematics education. *Journal for Research in Mathematics Education, 44*(1), 37-68.

Gutstein, E. (2006). *Reading and writing the world with mathematics: Toward a pedagogy for social justice*. Routledge.

Harper, S. R., & Quaye, S. J. (2008). *Student engagement in higher education: Theoretical perspectives and practical approaches for diverse populations*. Routledge.

Haywood, J. M. (2017a). Anti-Black Latino racism in an era of Trumpismo. *International Journal of Qualitative Studies in Education, 30*(10), 957-964. https://doi.org/10.1080/09518398.2017.1312613

Haywood, J. M. (2017b). "Latino spaces have always been the most violent": Afro-Latino collegians' perceptions of colorism and Latino intragroup marginalization. *International Journal of Qualitative Studies in Education, 30*(8), 759-782. https://doi.org/10.1080/09518398.2017.1350298

Hinton, K. E. (2012). *A practical guide to strategic planning in higher education*. Society for College and University Planning.

Hispanic Association of Colleges and Universities [HACU]. (2020). *2019 HACU Legislative Agenda*. https://www.hacu.net/images/hacu/2019%20HACU%20Legislative%20Agenda.pdf

hooks, b. (2001). *All about love: New visions*. William Morrow.

Hurtado, S., Alvarez, C. L., Guillermo-Wann, C., Cuellar, M., & Arellano, L. (2012). A model for diverse learning environments: The scholarship on creating and assessing conditions for student success. In J. C. Smart & M. B.

Paulsen (Eds.), *Higher education: Handbook for theory and research* (pp. 41-122). Springer.

Hurtado, S., & Ruiz Alvarado, A. (2015). Realizing the potential of Hispanic-Serving Institutions: Multiple dimensions of organizational transformation. In A.-M. Núñez, S. Hurtado, & E. Calderón Galdeano (Eds.), *Hispanic-Serving Institutions: Advancing research and transformative practices* (pp. 25-46). Routledge.

Jankowski, N., & Provezis, S. (2014). Neoliberal ideologies, governmentality and the academy: An examination of accountability through assessment and transparency. *Educational Philosophy and Theory, 46*(5), 475-487. http://dx.doi.org/10.1080/00131857.2012.721736

Jaschik, S. (2021, May). Redefining *"value"* in higher education. Inside Higher Ed. https://www.insidehighered.com/news/2021/05/12/gates-foundation-attempts-redefine-value-higher-education

Jefferson, A., Gutierrez, C., & Silverstein, L. (2018). Liberatory public education: A framework for centering community and democracy in public education. *The Urban Review, 50*, 735-756. https://doi.org/10.1007/s11256-018-0467-8

Jenkins, D. A., Tichavakunda, A. A., & Coles, J. A. (2021). The second ID: Critical race counterstories of campus police interactions with Black men at historically white institutions. *Race Ethnicity and Education, 24*(2), 149-166.

Jenkins, T. S. (2010). Viewing cultural practice through a lens of innovation and intentionality: Strategies for student personnel administrators in culture centers. In L. D. Patton (Ed.), *Culture centers in higher education: Perspectives on identity, theory, and practice* (pp. 137-156). Stylus.

Jimenez Hernandez, N. V. (2020). Yes, you *are* my business! Examining the effects of intrusive advising at a Hispanic-serving community college. In G. A. Garcia (Ed.), *Hispanic Serving Institutions (HSIs) in practice: Defining "serving-ness" at HSIs* (pp. 213-229). Information Age Publishing.

Johnston-Guerrero, M. P. (2016). Embracing the messiness: Critical and diverse perspectives on racial and ethnic identity development. In E. S. Abes (Ed.), *New Directions for Student Services: Special Issue: Critical perspectives on student development theory* (pp. 43-55). Wiley.

Jones, S. (2019). Subversion or cooptation? Tactics for engaging in diversity work in a race-adverse climate. *Journal of Educational Leadership and Policy Studies: Special issue #2 on educational leadership and social justice, 3*(2).

Jones, T., Jones, S., Elliot, K. C., Russell Owens, L., Assalone, A. E., & Gándara, D. (2017). *Outcomes based funding and race in higher education: Can equity be bought?* Palgrave Macmillan.

Jones, V., & Sáenz, V. (2020). Enacting a Latino male-serving organizational identity: The role of HSI community colleges. *Community College Journal of Research and Practice.* https://doi.org/10.1080/10668926.2020.1741475

Kaba, M. (2021). *We do this 'til we free us: Abolitionist organizing and transforming justice.* Haymarket Books.

Keeton, R. G. (2002). *Reframing identities for justice: Honoring multiple identities* [Unpublished dissertation]. Claremont Graduate University.

Keeton, R. G., López, C. B., & Aguilar-Hernández, J. M. (2021). "It shaped who I am": Reframing identities for justice through student activism. *Association of Mexican American Educators Journal, 15*(1), 1–28. https://doi.org/10.24974/amae.15.1.414

Kelley, R. D. G. (2002). *Freedom dreams: The Black radical imagination.* Beacon Press.

Kelly, B. T., Gaston Gayles, J., & Williams C. D. (2017). Recruitment without retention: A critical case of Black faculty unrest. *The Journal of Negro Education, 86*(3), 305–317.

Kendall, M. (2020). *Hood feminism: Notes from the women that a movement forgot.* Viking.

Kezar, A. (2006). Rethinking public higher education governing boards performance: Results of a national study of governing boards in the United States. *The Journal of Higher Education, 77*(6), 968–1008.

Kezar, A., & Eckel, P. (2002a). Examining the institutional transformation process: The importance of sensemaking, interrelated strategies, and balance. *Research in Higher Education, 43*(3), 295–328.

Kezar, A., & Eckel, P. D. (2002b). The effect of institutional culture on change strategies in higher education: Universal principles or culturally responsive concepts? *The Journal of Higher Education, 73*(4), 435–460. https://doi.org/10.1353/jhe.2002.0038

Kezar, A., & Matias Dizon, J. P. (2020). Renewing and revitalizing shared governance: A social justice and equity framework. In A. Kezar & J. Posselt (Eds.), *Higher education administration for social justice and equity: Critical perspectives for leadership* (pp. 21–42). Routledge.

Kezar, A. J., & Lester, J. (2009). *Organizing higher education for collaboration: A guide for campus leaders.* Jossey-Bass.

Kezar, A. J., & Lester, J. (2011). *Enhancing campus capacity for leadership: An examination of grassroots leaders in higher education.* Stanford University Press.

Kirklighter, C., Cárdenas, D., & Wolff Murphy, S. (2007). *Teaching writing with Latina/o students: Lessons learned at Hispanic-Serving Institutions.* State University of New York Press.

Kokka, K. (2019). Healing-informed social justice mathematics: Promoting students' sociopolitical consciousness and well-being in mathematics class. *Urban Education, 54*(9), 1179–1209. https://doi.org/10.1177/0042085918806947

Koren, E. R., Garcia, G. A., & Cuellar, M. (in development). Assessing faculty knowledge and skills for teaching minoritized students at Hispanic-Serving Institutions (HSIs).

Kovats Sánchez, G. (2018). Reaffirming Indigenous identity: Understanding experiences of stigmatization and marginalization among Mexican Indigenous college students. *Journal of Latinos and Education, 19*(1), 31–44. https://doi.org/10.1080/15348431.2018.1447484

Kovats Sánchez, G. (2021). "If we don't do it, nobody is going to talk about it": Indigenous students disrupting Latinidad at Hispanic-Serving Institutions. *AERA Open, 7*(1), 1–13. https://doi.org/10.1177/23328584211059194

Kuh, G. D. (2009). What student affairs professionals need to know about student engagement. *Journal of College Student Development, 50*(6), 683–706. https://doi.org/10.1353/csd.0.0099

la paperson (2017). *A third university is possible.* University of Minnesota Press.

Laden, B. V. (2001). Hispanic-Serving Institutions: Myths and realities. *Peabody Journal of Education, 76,* 73–92.

Laden, B. V. (2004). Hispanic-Serving Institutions: What are they? Where are they? *Community College Journal of Research and Practice, 28,* 181–198.

Ladson-Billings, G. (1995a). But that's just good teaching! The case for culturally relevant pedagogy. *Theory into Practice, 34*(3), 159–165.

Ladson-Billings, G. (1995b). Toward a theory of culturally relevant pedagogy. *American Educational Research Journal, 32*(3), 465–491.

Ledesma, M. C., & Burciaga, R. (2015). Faculty governance at Hispanic-Serving Institutions through the lens of critical race theory. In J. P. Mendez, I. F. A. Bonner, J. Méndz-Negrete, & R. T. Palmer (Eds.), *Hispanic-Serving Institutions in American higher education: Their origin, and present and future challenges* (pp. 40–57). Stylus.

Leija, M. G., Lara, G. P., Aponte-Safe, G., & Kambara, H. (2020). Reflections on teacher education practices of first-year tenure-track professors at an HSI. In J. M. Schall, P. A. McHatton, & E. L. Sáenz (Eds.), *Teacher education at Hispanic-Serving Institutions: Exploring identity, practice, and culture* (pp. 21–36). Routledge.

Liera, R. (2020). Equity advocates using equity-mindedness to interrupt faculty hiring's racial structure. *Teachers College Record, 122*(9), 1–42.

Liera, R., & Ching, C. (2020). Reconceptualizing "merit" and "fit:" An equity-minded approach to hiring. In A. Kezar & J. Posselt (Eds.), *Higher education administration for social justice and equity: Critical perspectives for leadership* (pp. 111–131). Routledge.

Lipkin, S. (2009). With 'restorative justice,' colleges strive to educate student offenders. *Education Digest, 75*(2), 36–38.

Love, B. L. (2019). *We want to do more than survive: Abolitionist teaching and the pursuit of educational freedom.* Beacon Press.

MacDonald, V. M. (2004). *Latino education in the United States: A narrated history from 1513–2000.* Palgrave Macmillan.

Malcom-Piqueux, L., & Bensimon, E. M. (2015). Design principles for equity and excellence at Hispanic-Serving Institutions. *PERSPECTIVAS: Issues in Higher Education Policy and Practice,* (4), 1–16.

Malcom-Piqueux, L., & Lee, Jr., J. M. (2011). *Hispanic-Serving Institutions: Contributions and challenges* [Policy brief]. https://files.eric.ed.gov/fulltext/ED562686.pdf

Maldonado, C. (2019). "Where your ethnic kids go": How counselors as first responders legitimate proper course placements for community college students. *Community College Journal of Research and Practice, 43*(4), 280–294. https://doi.org/10.1080/10668926.2018.1463303

Marginson, S., & Considine, M. (2000). *The enterprise university: Power, governance and reinvention in Australia.* Cambridge University Press.

Marin, P. (2019). Is "business as usual" enough to be Hispanic-Serving? Becoming a Hispanic-Serving Research Institution. *Journal of Hispanic Higher Education, 18*(2), 165–181. https://doi.org/10.1177/1538192719832250

Marin, P., & Pereschica, P. (2017). Becoming an Hispanic-Serving Research Institution: Involving graduate students in organizational change. *Association of Mexican American Educators Journal, 11*(3), 154–177. https://doi.org/10.24974/amae.11.3.365

Martinez, E. (2020). Trading inequities: Hispanic-serving community colleges and baccalaureate degree programs. In E. E. Doran (Ed.), *New Directions for Community Colleges: Special Issue: Emerging issues for Latinx students* (pp. 59–68). Wiley. https://doi.org/10.1002/cc.20387

Martinez, M. A., Chang, A., & Welton, A. D. (2017). Assistant professors of color confront the inequitable terrain of academia: A community cultural wealth perspective. *Race Ethnicity and Education, 20*(5), 696–710. https://doi.org/10.1080/13613324.2016.1150826

Martínez-Roldán, C. M., & Quiñones, S. (2016). Resisting erasure and developing networks of solidarity: Testimonios of two Puerto Rican scholars in the academy. *Journal of Language, Identity & Education, 15*(3), 151–164.

Masters, B. G., Beltran, E., & Rodriguez-Kiino, D. (2020). Academic mindset development at a Hispanic-Serving Institution: Using non-academic outcomes as indicators of "serving" STEM students. In G. A. Garcia (Ed.), *Hispanic Serving Institutions (HSIs) in practice: Defining "servingness" at HSIs* (pp. 231–252). Information Age Publishing.

McGee, E. O., & Stovall, D. (2015). Reimagining critical race theory in education: Mental health, healing, and the pathway to liberatory praxis. *Educational Theory, 65*(5), 491–511.

McGuinness, Jr., A. C. (2016a). *State policy leadership for the future: History of state coordination and governance and alternatives for the future.* Education Commission of the States. https://www.alaska.edu/bor/files/Task_Force/Education-Commission-of-the-States-_-State-Policy-Leadership-for-the-Future-051616_McGuinness.pdf

McGuinness, Jr., A. C. (2016b). The states and higher education. In M. N. Bastedo, P. G. Altbach, & P. J. Gumport (Eds.), *American higher education in the 21st century: Social, political, and economic challenges* (4th ed., pp. 238–280). Johns Hopkins University Press.

Means, D. R., Hudson, T. D., & Tish, E. (2019). A snapshot of college access and inequity: Using photography to illuminate the pathways to higher education for underserved youth. *High School Journal, 102*(2), 139–158.

Meyer, J. W., & Rowan, B. (1977). Institutionalized organizations: Formal structure as myth and ceremony. *American Journal of Sociology, 83*(2), 340–363.

Mirza, S. A., & Bewkes, F. J. (2019). *Secretary DeVos is failing to protect the civil rights of LGBTQ students.* Center for American Progress. https://www

.americanprogress.org/issues/lgbtq-rights/reports/2019/07/29/472636
/secretary-devos-failing-protect-civil-rights-lgbtq-students/

Moll, L. C., Amanti, C., Neff, D., & González, N. (1992). Funds of knowledge for teaching: Using qualitative approach to connect homes and classrooms. *Theory into Practice, 31*(2), 132–141.

Moll, L. C., Soto-Santiago, S. L., & Schwartz, L. (2013). Funds of knowledge in changing communities. In K. Hall, T. Cremin, B. Comber, & L. Moll (Eds.), *International handbook of research on children's literacy, learning, and culture* (pp. 172–183). Wiley-Blackwell.

Mora, G. C. (2014). *Making Hispanics: How activists, bureaucrats, and media constructed a new American.* University of Chicago Press.

Mora, J., & Rios-Aguilar, C. (2017). Aligning practice with pedagogy: Funds of knowledge for community college teaching. In. J. Marquez Kiyama & C. Rios-Aguilar (Eds.), *Funds of knowledge in higher education: Honoring students' cultural experiences and resources as strengths* (pp. 145–159). Taylor & Francis

Mulnix, M. W., Bowden, R. G., & López, E. E. (2002). A brief examination of institutional advancement activities at Hispanic Serving Institutions. *Journal of Hispanic Higher Education, 1*(2), 174–190.

Mulnix, M. W., Bowden, R. G., & López, E. E. (2004). Institutional advancement activities at select Hispanic-serving Institutions: The politics of raising funds. *International Journal of Educational Advancement, 5,* 60–75.

Mumper, M., Gladieux, L. E., King, J. E., & Corrigan, M. E. (2016). The federal government and higher education. In M. N. Bastedo, P. G. Altbach, & P. J. Gumport (Eds.), *American higher education in the 21st century: Social, political, and economic challenges* (4th ed., pp. 212–237). Johns Hopkins University Press.

Muñoz, S. M., Basile, V., Gonzalez, J., Birmingham, D., Aragon, A., Jennings, L., Gloeckner, G. (2017). (Counter)narratives and complexities: Critical perspectives from a university cluster hire focused on diversity, equity, and inclusion. *Journal of Critical Thought and Praxis, 6*(2), 1–21.

Murakami, E. T., & Núñez, A.-M. (2014). Latina faculty transcending barriers: Peer mentoring in a Hispanic-Serving Institution. *Mentoring & Tutoring: Partnership in Learning, 22*(4), 284–301. http://dx.doi.org/10.1080/13611267.2014.945739

Murakami-Ramalho, E., Nuñez, A.-M., & Cuero, K. K. (2010). Latin@ advocacy in the hyphen: Faculty identity and commitment in a Hispanic-Serving Institution. *International Journal of Qualitative Studies in Education, 23,* 699–717. https://doi.org/10.1080/09518391003641924

Museus, S. D. (2014). The culturally engaging campus environments (CECE) model: A new theory of college success among racially diverse student populations. In M. B. Paulsen (Ed.), *Higher education: Handbook of theory and research* (Vol. 29, pp. 190–227). Springer.

Museus, S. D., Ledesma, M. C., & Parker, T. L. (2015). *Racism and racial equity in higher education.* Jossey-Bass.

Museus, S. D., & Lepeau, L. A. (2020). Navigating neoliberal organizational cultures: Implications for higher education leaders advancing social justice agendas. In A. Kezar & J. Posselt (Eds.), *Higher education administration for social justice and equity: Critical perspectives for leadership* (pp. 209–224). Routledge.

Nasir, N. S. (2012). *Racialized identities: Race and achievement among African American youth.* Stanford University Press.

National Conference of State Legislatures (2021). *Tuition benefits for immigrants.* https://www.ncsl.org/research/immigration/tuition-benefits-for -immigrants.aspx

National Survey of Student Engagement [NSSE]. (2007). *Experiences that matter: Enhancing student learning and success.* Indiana University Center for Postsecondary Research. https://files.eric.ed.gov/fulltext/ED512620.pdf

Nellum, C. J., & Valle, C. (2015). *Government investment in public Hispanic-Serving Institutions.* American Council on Education. https://www.acenet.edu /Documents/Persistent-Funding-Inequities.pdf

Nelson Laird, T. F., Bridges, B. K., Morelon-Quainoo, C. L., Williams, J. M., & Salinas Holmes, M. (2007). African American and Hispanic student engagement at minority serving and predominantly white institutions. *Journal of College Student Development, 48*, 39–56. https://doi.org/10.1353/csd.2007.0005

Nichols, A. H. (2017). *A look at Latino student success: Identifying top- and bottom-performing institutions.* The Education Trust. https://edtrust.org/resource /look-latino-student-success

Núñez, A.-M. (2014). Employing multilevel intersectionality in educational research: Latino identities, contexts, and college access. *Educational Researcher, 43*(2), 85–92.

Núñez, A.-M., & Bowers, A. J. (2011). Exploring what leads high school students to enroll in Hispanic-Serving Institutions: A multilevel analysis. *American Educational Research Journal, 48*(6), 1286–1313. https://doi.org/10.3102 /0002831211408061

Núñez, A.-M, Crisp, G., & Elizondo, D. (2015). Hispanic-serving community colleges and their role in Hispanic transfer. In A.-M. Nuñez, S. Hurtado, E. Calderón Galdeano (Eds.), *Hispanic-Serving Institutions: Advancing research and transformative practice* (pp. 47–64). Routledge.

Núñez, A.-M., Crisp, G., & Elizondo, D. (2016). Mapping Hispanic-Serving Institutions: A typology of institutional diversity. *The Journal of Higher Education, 87*(1), 55–83. https://doi.org/10.1353/jhe.2016.0001

Núñez, A.-M., & Elizondo, D. (2012). *Hispanic-Serving Institutions in the U.S. mainland and Puerto Rico: Organizational characteristics, institutional financial context, and graduation outcomes* [White Paper]. Hispanic Association of Colleges and Universities.

Núñez, A.-M, Murakami Ramalho, E., & Cuero, K. K. (2010). Pedagogy for equity: Teaching in a Hispanic-Serving Institution. *Innovative Higher Education, 35*, 177–190. https://doi.org/10.1007/s10755-010-9139-7

Núñez, A.-M, Sparks, P. J., & Hernández, E. A. (2011). Latino access to community colleges and Hispanic-Serving Institutions: A national study. *Journal of Hispanic Higher Education, 10*(1), 18–40. https://doi.org/10.1177/1538192710391801

Olivas, M. (1982). Indian, Chicano, and Puerto Rican colleges: Status and issues. *Bilingual Review, 9*(1), 36–58.

Onorato, S., & Musoba, G. D. (2015). La líder: Developing a leadership identity as a Hispanic woman at a Hispanic-Serving Institution. *Journal of College Student Development, 56*(1), 15–31. https://doi.org/10.1353/csd.2015.0003

Ortagus, J. C., Kelchen, R., Rosinger, K., & Voorhees, N. (2020). Performance-based funding in American higher education: A synthesis of the intended and unintended consequences. *Educational Evaluation and Policy Analysis, 42*(4), 520–550. https://doi.org/10.3102/0162373720953128

Ortega, N., Nellum, C., Frye, J., Kamimura, A., & Vidal-Rodriguez, A. (2015). Examining the financial resilience of Hispanic-Serving Institutions. In A.-M. Núñez, S. Hurtado, E. Calderón Galdeano (Eds.), *Hispanic-Serving Institutions: Advancing research and transformative practice* (pp. 155–176). Routledge.

Osher, D., Cantor, P., Berg, J., Steyer, L., & Rose, T. (2019). Drivers of human development: How relationships and context shape learning and development. *Applied Developmental Science, 24*(1), 6–36. https://doi.org/10.1080/10888691.2017.1398650

Patton, L. D. (2010). A call to action: Historical and contemporary reflections on the relevance of campus culture centers in higher education. In L. D. Patton (Ed.), *Culture centers in higher education: Perspectives on identity, theory, and practice* (pp. xiii–xvii). Stylus.

Patton, L. D. (2016). Disrupting postsecondary prose: Toward a critical race theory of higher education. *Urban Education, 51*(3), 315–342.

Paredes, A. D., Estrada, C., Venturanza, R. J., & Teranishi, R. T. (2021). *La lucha sigue: The University of California's role as a Hispanic-Serving Research Institution system*. The Institute for Immigration, Globalization, and Education. https://www.ucop.edu/hsi-initiative/_files/report-la-lucha-sigue.pdf

Petrov, L. A., & Garcia, G. A. (2021). Becoming a racially just Hispanic-Serving Institution (HSI): Leveraging HSI grants for organizational identity change. *Journal of Diversity in Higher Education, 14*(4), 463–467. http://dx.doi.org/10.1037/dhe0000356

Pour-Khorshid, F. (2018). Cultivating sacred spaces: A racial affinity group approach to support critical educators of color. *Teaching Education, 29*(4), 318–329. https://doi.org/10.1080/10476210.2018.1512092

Posselt, J., Hernandez, T., & Villarreal, C. (2020). Choose wisely: Making decisions with and for equity in higher education. In A. Kezar & J. Posselt (Eds.), *Higher education administration for social justice and equity: Critical perspectives for leadership* (pp. 43–66). Routledge.

Rall, R., Morgan, D., & Commodore, F. (2020). Toward culturally sustaining governance in higher education: Best practices of theory, research, and practice. *Journal of Education Human Resources, 38*(1), 139–164. https//doi.org/10 .3138/jehr.2019-0006

Ramirez, L., & Rodriguez-Kiino, D. (2020). Creating community engaged partnerships to foster trust with STEM and Hispanic Serving Institutions. In G. A. Garcia (Ed.), *Hispanic Serving Institutions (HSIs) in practice: Defining "servingness" at HSIs* (pp. 135–150). Information Age Publishing.

Rapa, L. J., Bolding, C. W., & Jamil, F. M. (2020). Development and initial validation of the short critical consciousness scale (CCS-S). *Journal of Applied Developmental Psychology, 70*. https://doi.org/10.1016/j.appdev.2020.101164

Ray, V. (2019). A theory of racialized organizations. *American Sociological Review, 84*(1), 26–53. https://doi.org/10.1177/0003122418822335

Reguerín, P. G., Poblete, J., Cooper, C. R., Sánchez Ordaz, A., & Moreno, R. (2020). Becoming a racially just Hispanic Serving Institution (HSI). In G. A. Garcia (Ed.), *Hispanic Serving Institutions (HSIs) in practice: Defining "servingness" at HSIs* (pp. 41–59). Information Age Publishing.

Rendon, L. I. (1994). Validating culturally diverse students: Toward a new model of learning and student development. *Innovative Higher Education, 19*(1), 33–51.

Rios-Aguilar, C., & Marquez Kiyama, J. (2017). A complimentary framework: Funds of knowledge and the forms of capital. In. J. Marquez Kiyama & C. Rios-Aguilar (Eds.), *Funds of knowledge in higher education: Honoring students' cultural experiences and resources as strengths* (pp. 7–24). Taylor & Francis.

Roberts, S. A., & Lucas, K. L. (2020). A Title V center as a counterspace for underrepresented minority and first-generation college students. *Journal of Hispanic Higher Education*. Online first. https://doi.org/10.1177/1538192720951307

Rodríguez, C., Martinez, M. A., & Valle, F. (2016). Latino educational leadership across the pipeline: For Latino communities and Latina/o leaders. *Journal of Hispanic Higher Education, 15*(2), 136–153.

Rodriguez, P. J., & Gonzales, R. M. (2020). Mentorship and cultural belonging for first generation and transfer students at an HSI in South Texas. In G. A. Garcia (Ed.), *Hispanic Serving Institutions (HSIs) in practice: Defining "servingness" at HSIs* (pp. 295–312). Information Age Publishing.

Rodriguez, S. L., Garbee, K. T., Miller, R. A., & Saenz, V. B. (2018). How community colleges in Texas prioritize resources for Latino men. *Community College Journal of Research and Practice, 42*(4), 229–244. http://dx.doi.org/10.1080 /10668926.2017.1281179

Royce, A. P., & Rodriguez, R. (1999). From personal charity to organized giving: Hispanic institutions and values of stewardship and philanthropy. *New Direction for Philanthropic Fundraising, 24*, 9–29.

Rerucha, M. Q. (2021). *Beyond the surface of restorative practices: Building a culture of equity, connection, and healing.* Dave Burgess Consulting.

Sáenz, V. B., Ponjuán, L., & Figueroa, J. L. (2016). Current trends and the future outlooks on the pervasive gender gap in educational attainment for Latino males. In V. B. Sáenz, L. Ponjuan, & J. L. Figueroa (Eds.), *Ensuring the success of Latino males in higher education: A national imperative* (pp. 3–20). Stylus.

Salazar, M. D. C. (2013). A humanizing pedagogy: Reinventing the principles and practice of education as a journey toward liberation. *Review of Research in Education, 37*(1), 121–148. https://doi.org/10.3102/0091732X12464032

Saldaña-Portillo, M. J. (2017). Critical Latinx Indigeneities: A paradigm drift. *Latino Studies, 15*, 138–155. https://doi.org/10.1057/s41276-017-0059-x

Salinas, C. (2020). The complexity of the "x" in *Latinx*: How Latinx/a/o students relate to, identify with, and understand the term *Latinx. Journal of Hispanic Higher Education, 19*(2), 149–168. https://doi.org/10.1177/1538192719900382

Salinas, C., & Lozano, A. S. (2019). Mapping and recontextualizing the evolution of the term *Latinx*: An environmental scanning in higher education. *Journal of Latino and Education, 18*(4), 302–315. https://doi.org/10.1080/15348431.2017 .1390464

Sanchez, M. E. (2019). Perceptions of campus climate and experiences of racial microaggressions for Latinos at Hispanic-Serving Institutions. *Journal of Hispanic Higher Education, 18*(3), 240–253. https://doi.org/10.1177/1538192717739351

Sánchez Ordaz, A., Reguerín, P. G., & Sánchez, S. E. (2020). Using interactive theater to strengthen holistic advising at a Hispanic Serving Institution. In G. A. Garcia (Ed.), *Hispanic Serving Institutions (HSIs) in practice: Defining "servingness" at HSIs* (pp. 79–95). Information Age Publishing.

Santamaría, L. J., & Santamaría, A. P. (2012). *Applied critical leadership in education: Choosing change.* Routledge.

Santiago, D. A. (2006). *Inventing Hispanic-Serving Institutions (HSIs): The basics.* Excelencia in Education.

Santiago, D. A. (2012). Public policy and Hispanic-Serving Institutions: From invention to accountability. *Journal of Latinos and Education, 11*(3), 163–167. https://doi.org/10.1080/15348431.2012.686367

Santiago, D. A., Taylor, M., & Calderón Galdeano, E. (2016). *From capacity to success: HSIs, Title V, and Latino students.* Excelencia in Education. http://www .edexcelencia.org/research/capacity

Santos, J. L., & Acevedo-Gil, N. (2013). A report card of Latina/o leadership in California's public universities: A trend analysis of faculty, students, and executives in the CSU and UC systems. *Journal of Hispanic Higher Education, 12*(2), 174–200. https://doi.org/10.1177/1538192712470844

Schall, J. M., McHatton, P. A., & Sáenz, E. L. (Eds.). (2021). *Teacher education at Hispanic-Serving Institutions: Exploring identity, practice, and culture.* Routledge.

Scott, R. A. (2018). *How university boards work: A guide for trustees, officers, and leaders in higher education.* Johns Hopkins University Press.

Sensoy, Ö., & DiAngelo, R. (2012). *Is everyone really equal? An introduction to key concepts in social justice education.* Teachers College Press.

Sensoy, Ö., & DiAngelo, R. (2017). *Is everyone really equal? An introduction to key concepts in social justice education* (2nd ed.). Teachers College Press.

Serrano, U. (2020). 'Finding home': Campus racial microclimates and academic homeplaces at a Hispanic-Serving Institution. *Race Ethnicity and Education.* https://doi.org/10.1080/13613324.2020.1718086

Sleeter, C. E. (2011). *The academic and social value of ethnic studies: A research review.* National Education Association.

Smith, W. A., Allen, W. R., & Danley, L. L. (2007). "Assume the position . . . you fit the description": Psychosocial experiences and racial battle fatigue among African American male college students. *American Behavioral Scientist, 51*(4), 551–578. https://doi.org/10.1177/0002764207307742

Squire, D., Nicolazzo, Z., & Perez, R. J. (2019). Institutional response as non-performative: What university communications (don't) say about movements toward justice. *The Review of Higher Education, 42*(Supplemental), 109–133. https://doi.org/10.1353/rhe.2019.0047

Stanton-Salazar, R. D. (2011). A social capital framework for the study of institutional agents and their role in the empowerment of low-status students and youth. *Youth & Society, 43*(3), 1066–1109.

Stein, S. (2021). What can decolonial and abolitionist critiques teach the field of higher education? *The Review of Higher Education, 44*(3), 387–414. https://doi.org/10.1353/rhe.2021.000

Suddaby, R. (2010). Challenges for institutional theory. *Journal of Management Inquiry, 19*(1), 14–20. https://doi.org/10.1177/1056492609347564

Summers, C., Mueller, V., Pechak, C., & Sias, J. J. (2018). Incorporating Spanish language instruction into health sciences programs in a Hispanic-Serving Institution. *Journal of Hispanic Higher Education, 17*(3), 187–201. https://doi.org/10.1177/1538192717699047

Takacs, D. (2003). How does your positionality bias your epistemology? *Thought & Action, 27,* 27–38. http://repository.uchastings.edu/faculty_scholarship/1264

Taylor, Z. W., & Burnett, C. A. (2019). Hispanic-Serving Institutions and web accessibility: Digital equity for Hispanic students with disabilities in the 21st century. *Journal of Hispanic Higher Education.* Online first. https://doi.org/10.1177/1538192719883966

Thomas, A. J., Barrie, R., Brunner, J., Clawson, A., Hewitt, A., Jeremie-Brink, G., & Rowe Johnson, M. (2014). Assessing critical consciousness in youth and young adults. *Journal of Research on Adolescence, 24*(3), 485–496. https://doi.org.10.1111/jora.12132

Tijerina Revilla, A., & Santillana, J. M. (2014). Jotería identity and consciousness. *Aztlán: A Journal of Chicano Studies, 39*(1), 167–179.

Tinto, V. (1993). *Leaving college: Rethinking the causes and cures of student attrition research.* University of Chicago Press.

Torres, V., & Hernández, E. (2007). The influence of ethnic identity on self-authorship: A longitudinal study of Latino/a college students. *Journal of College Student Development, 48*(5), 558–573. https://doi.org/10.1353/csd.2007.0057

Torres, V., Hernández, E., & Martinez, S. (2019). *Understanding the Latinx experience: Developmental and contextual influences.* Stylus.

Tuck, E., & Yang, K. W. (2012). Decolonization is not a metaphor. *Decolonization: Indigeneity, Education, & Society, 1*(1), 1–40.

Tugend, A. (2018, June). How serious are you about diversity hiring? *Chronicle of Higher Education*. https://www-chronicle-com.pitt.idm.oclc.org/article/how-serious-are-you-about-diversity-hiring/

Turk, J. Soler, M. C., Chessman, H., & Gonzalez, Á. (2020, December). *College and university presidents respond to COVID-19: 2020 fall term survey, part II.* American Council on Education. https://www.acenet.edu/Research-Insights/Pages/Senior-Leaders/College-and-University-Presidents-Respond-to-COVID-19-2020-Fall-Term-Part-Two.aspx

Urban Universities for Health (2015). *Faculty cluster hiring: For diversity and institutional climate.* https://www.aplu.org/library/faculty-cluster-hiring-for-diversity-and-institutional-climate/file

US Department of Education. (2022). *Developing Hispanic-Serving Institutions program—Title V.* https://www2.ed.gov/programs/idueshsi/index.html

US Department of the Treasury. (n.d.). *Covid-19 economic relief.* https://home.treasury.gov/policy-issues/cares

Valadez, G. (2015). World AIDS Day: A case study of how one Hispanic-Serving Institution's inclusive practices supported Lesbian, Gay, Bisexual, and Transgender students. In J. P. Mendez, I. F. A. Bonner, J. Méndez-Negrete, & R. T. Palmer (Eds.), *Hispanic-Serving Institutions in American higher education: Their origin, and present and future challenges* (pp. 154–177). Stylus.

Valdez, P. L. (2015). An overview of Hispanic-Serving Institutions' legislation: Legislation policy formation between 1979 and 1992. In J. P. Mendez, I. F. A. Bonner, J. Méndez-Negrete, & R. T. Palmer (Eds.), *Hispanic-Serving Institutions in American higher education: Their origin, and present and future challenges* (pp. 5–29). Stylus.

Vargas, N. (2018). Racial expropriation in higher education: Are whiter Hispanic Serving Institutions more likely to receive minority serving institution funds? *Socius: Sociological Research for a Dynamic World, 4*, 1–12. https://doi.org/10.1177%2F2378023118794077

Vargas, N., & Villa-Palomino, J. (2018). Racing to serve or race-ing for money? Hispanic-Serving Institutions and the colorblind allocation of racialized federal funding. *Sociology of Race and Ethnicity.* Online first. https://doi.org/10.1177/2332649218769409

Vargas, N., Villa-Palomino, J., & Davis, E. (2019). Latinx faculty representation and resource allocation at Hispanic Serving Institutions. *Race Ethnicity and Education, 23*(1), 39–54. https://doi.org/10.1080/13613324.2019.1679749

Vargas, P., & Ward, M. (2020). Building an HSI brand: A case study of California Lutheran University. In G. A. Garcia (Ed.), *Hispanic Serving Institutions (HSIs) in practice: Defining "servingness" at HSIs* (pp. 21–39). Information Age Publishing.

Venegas, E. M., Estrada, V. L., Schall, J. M., & De Leon, L. (2020). Language and literacy practices of bilingual education preservice teachers at a Hispanic-Serving College of Education. In J. M. Schall, P. A., McHatton, & E. L. Sáenz (Eds.), *Teacher education at Hispanic-Serving Institutions: Exploring identity, practice, and culture* (pp. 88–106). Routledge.

Venegas, E. M., Koonce, J. B., Lancaster, L., Bazan, J., & Garza, A. (2021). Diversifying the 'HSI bubble': Black and Asian women faculty at Hispanic-Serving Institutions. *Race Ethnicity and Education*. https://doi.org/10.1080/13613324.2021.1924139

Villanueva, E. (2018). *Decolonizing wealth: Indigenous wisdom to heal divides and restore balance*. Berrett-Koehler Publishers.

Villarreal Sosa, L., Garcia, G. A., & Bucher, J. (2022). Decolonizing faculty governance in Hispanic-Serving Institutions. *Journal of Hispanic Higher Education*. Online first.

W. K. Kellogg Foundation (2012). *Cultures of giving: Energizing and expanding philanthropy by and for communities of color*. www.wkkf.org

Watts, R. J., Diemer, M. A., & Voight, A. M. (2011). Critical consciousness: Current status and future directions. In C. A. Flanagan & B. D. Christens (Eds.), *New Directions for Child and Adolescent Development: Special Issue: Youth civic development: Work at the cutting edge* (pp. 43–57). Wiley.

Wessling, T. (2015, January 27). Mission vs. vision: What's the difference? *Carrier Management*.

Wilder, C. S. (2013). *Ebony and ivy: Race, slavery, and the troubled history of America's universities*. Bloomsbury.

Winn, M. T. (2018). *Justice on both sides: Transforming education through restorative justice*. Harvard Education Press.

Wright, B. (1988). "For the children of the infidels?" American Indian education in the colonial colleges. *American Indian Culture and Research Journal*, 12(3), 1–14.

Wright, B. (1991). The "untameable savage spirit:" American Indians in colonial colleges. *The Review of Higher Education*, 14(4), 429–452.

Yosso, T. J. (2005). Whose culture has capital? A critical race theory discussion of community cultural wealth. *Race Ethnicity and Education*, 8(1), 69–91.

Zald, M. N., Morrill, C., & Rao, H. (2005). The impact of social movements on organizations: Environment and responses. In G. F. Davis, D. McAdam, W. R. Scott, & M. N Zald (Eds.), *Social movements and organization theory* (pp. 253–279). Cambridge University Press.

Zambrana, R. E., Allen, A., Higginbotham, E., Mitchell, J., Pérez, D. J., Villarruel, A. (2020). *Equity and inclusion: Effective practices and responsive strategies: A guidebook for college and university leaders*. Consortium on Race, Gender, and Ethnicity, University of Maryland. http://crge.umd.edu/2020/07/09/equity-and-inclusion-effective-practices-and-responsive-strategies-a-guidebook-for-college-and-university-leaders/

Zaragoza, M., & Garcia, G. A. (2022, April). Latina faculty at a Hispanic-Serving Institution: Critical counterstories about servingness [Conference presentation]. American Educational Research Association annual meeting, San Diego, CA, United States.

Zerquera, D. D., Ballysingh, T. A., & Templeton, E. (2017). A critical look at perspectives of access and mission at high Latinx-enrolling urban universities. *Association of Mexican American Educators Journal*, 11(3), 199–222. http://dx.doi.org/10.24974/amae.11.3.367

INDEX

Metropolitan State University of Denver, 123

Mexican Americans, 8, 16, 63, 153. *See also* Chicanx

Mexican corridos, 96

microaffirmations, 84, 108

microaggressions, 34, 53, 55, 83–84, 107; institutional, 57; women of color and, 125

migrant workers, 33, 50

Minority-Serving Institutions (MSIs), 4; grant seeking and, 4; inequitable distribution of resources to, 22–23; mission of, 132; persistence and retention within, 4, 103, 165

Morrill Acts of 1862 and 1890, 160

multiply minoritized people of color, 29, 40–41, 46, 48, 95; education of, 63, 106, 109, 140; knowledge and skills for serving, 83, 95, 108

Muslim students, 3, 71, 86, 106

muxerista mentoring, 81

National Science Foundation's Improving Undergraduate STEM Education: HSI Program, 91

Native American students, 8, 56–57, 73, 114, 161

neurodivergent students, 3, 32, 63, 86, 106; accessibility and, 115

nonacademic outcomes, 47

non-Latinx women of color, 80

Olivas, Michael, 13

organizational approach, 18

organizational change, 14, 27

organizational identity theory, 40–41

paperson, la, 14

parenting students, 3, 33, 65

pathway programs, 78

Pell Grants, 49, 160–61

performance-based funding (PBF), 164–65

Perkins Loan Program, 160

personalismo, 152–53. *See also confianza*

philanthropy, 146, 152–54, 168; decolonizing, 147, 152

praxis, 31

private foundations, 32, 159, 166–69

private HSIs, 66

professional development, 83, 93, 108, 118, 134, 170

pseudo-allyship, 17

Puerto Rico, 16, 99, 154

queer faculty, 81

queer Hispanic-Serving Institution (Q-HSI), 44–45

queer students, 33, 63, 86, 106, 139–40

race-consciousness, 24–25, 31–32, 49, 70, 127; outcomes, 157; training, 73, 83–85, 95. *See also* transformed HSIs

race-neutral approaches, 19, 76, 88, 95, 118; disrupting, 29

racial affinity groups, 81, 151

racial battle fatigue, 125

racial equity, 7, 18, 50, 52, 59

racial-ethnic-Indigenous groups, 19, 21, 114, 116; alumni from, 146–49; criminalization of, 21; diversity and, 65; faculty members of, 64, 70, 77, 172; historical experiences of, 85; identities of, 58, 90; omission of, 63; student organizations and, 104–5

racialization, 18; racialized events, 20; racialized HSI missions, 36; racialized organizations, 20, 64, 107

racialized ethnic identities, 7, 32, 103, 134. *See also* Latinx students: racialized experiences of

racism, 21, 24, 56–57, 72, 79; faculty experiences with, 80. *See also* systemic racism

Ray, Victor, 15

redistribution of resources, 25–26, 30, 60–61, 75, 115; grants and, 167; power and, 127, 134, 141

relationship building, 111, 125; with communities, 155; external partners and, 120, 129, 145, 147, 158–59, 164, 173; faculty and students and, 94, 98–99, 153

reproductive rights, 52, 158, 168

restorative justice, 17, 110, 111

Rojas, Victor, 12

SACNAS, 11–12, 104

scholarships, 149–50

Turtle Island, 14
Typology of HSI Organizational Identities, 40

undergraduate student enrollment, 1; Latinx students and, 1–3, 21, 27, 36, 41–42, 64–66, 128; students of color and, 65–66, 165
undocumented students, 6, 8, 27, 32, 63, 70, 104–5, 107; experience of, 140; in-state tuition for, 163, 165–66
University of California, Santa Cruz (UCSC), 70, 83–84, 108, 128–29, 131
University of California system, 19, 49
University of Maryland, 12
University of Southern California's Center for Urban Education, 129
University of Texas at El Paso, 53
University of Texas at San Antonio, 102
University of Texas–Pan American, 139

University of Wisconsin–Madison, 77
upward mobility, 48–50, 171
US Department of Education, 47, 87
US imperialism, 7, 91

validation theory, 58
veteran students, 33, 106
vocational jobs, 43. *See also* Career and Technical Education

whiteness, 13, 15, 19–20, 35; decredentialing of, 25, 28, 61, 115; institutional, 25; policies to disrupt, 25, 62, 93, 134, 144; white fragility, 125; white normative measures of excellence, 73–74, 100, 118, 132; white normative expectations, 159; within HSIs, 23, 72, 84, 113
white racialized identity, 40
white supremacy, 18, 31, 33, 91, 100
W. K. Kellogg Foundation, 52, 83, 167–68
workforce development, 39, 48, 50